Private Ownership

The Problems of Philosophy:
Their Past and Present

General Editor: Ted Honderich
Professor of Philosophy
University College
London

Each book in this series brings into clear view and deals with a great, persistent or significant problem of philosophy. The first part of each book presents the history of the problem. The second part, of an analytical kind, develops and defends the author's preferred solution.

Private Ownership

James O. Grunebaum

Routledge & Kegan Paul
London and New York

First published in 1987 by
Routledge & Kegan Paul Ltd

11 New Fetter Lane, London EC4P 4EE

Published in the USA by
Routledge & Kegan Paul Inc.
in association with Methuen Inc.
29 West 35th Street, New York, NY 10001

Set in Times
by Input Typesetting Ltd, London
and printed in Great Britain
by Billings & Sons Ltd, Worcester

Library of Congress Cataloging in Publication Data

Grunebaum, James O.
Private ownership.
(Problems of philosophy)
Bibliography: p.
Includes index.
1. Property. 2. Property—Moral and ethical aspects.
I. Title. II. Series: Problems of philosophy
(Routledge & Kegan Paul)
HB711.G75   1987   330'.17   86–13092

British Library CIP Data also available

ISBN 0–7102–0706–9

*To Helen and Edward
and to Penny and Jason*

Every man has naturally a right to everything he needs;
but the positive act which makes him proprietor of one
thing excludes him from everything else.

J. J. Rousseau,
The Social Contract, Bk I, Ch. IX

Contents

Contents

Acknowledgments

There are many people I wish to thank and many degrees of gratitude I owe. First, I wish to thank the editors of the *Pacific Philosophical Quarterly* and the *American Philosophical Quarterly* for permission to use material I originally published in their journals. Second, thanks are owed to the State University College at Buffalo for supporting a sabbatical leave during the 1981–1982 academic year in which a preliminary draft of this book was completed. Many colleagues have discussed this material with me. John Abbarno, Alex Ratkowski, Fred Witthans, and Peter Hare made helpful suggestions during lengthy conversations while my thoughts were in development. Norman Bowie's careful and comprehensive comments on an earlier draft helped me improve several weak sections. To Lansing Pollock I am in debt not only for his insights and proofreading but also for decades of a truly philosophical friendship of thought, criticism, and inquiry. My wife Penelope Prentice, a writer, is responsible for any of my pretenses of style. She is also responsible for teaching me how two careers within a family are better than one. Marilyn Coyne, my secretary, performed many heroic tasks typing the manuscript not the least of which was the uncountable trips down the hall to have me read my handwriting. Finally, I wish to give special appreciation to Warner Wick who provided encouragement when I needed it most. I am saddened that his recent death prevents him from receiving it.

J.O.G.

CHAPTER I

The Concept of Ownership

A. Introduction

Private ownership is the main protagonist of this book. Also in
the cast are communal ownership, corporate ownership, feudal
ownership, ownership in common law and Roman law, and a new
form of ownership: autonomous ownership. The plot of the book
is to resolve the issue of moral justification. Which of the many
possible forms of ownership is morally justifiable? Is there one
form of ownership which is morally justifiable in all circumstances
and conditions or does the form of ownership which is morally
justifiable vary with or depend upon such factors as e.g., economic
development and efficiency? Before those questions can best be
addressed there are two preliminaries to be settled. The first is
logical and definitional. It must be known what ownership in
general is and what logical properties distinguish one specific form
of ownership from another form. In other words, it must be
possible to know what, for example, private ownership and
communal ownership have in common insofar as they are forms
of ownership and it must be possible to know the characteristics
by which they differ insofar as they are different specific forms.
The second preliminary concerns the method of moral justification. By what sorts of arguments is a form of ownership to
be morally justified? Many philosophers have argued that first
appropriation justifies private ownership, for example, but there
are other methods of justification which must be also considered.

The action of the plot will be carried on by means of an
historical survey which examines various attempts at justifying
some specific form of ownership. Private ownership is not the
only form of ownership for which philosophers have provided
justifications. Beginning with Plato, other forms have competed

with private ownership and the issue is far from being resolved today where clashing ideologies about the justifiable form of ownership create hostilities between great nation states. No protagonist is yet intellectually victorious. Contemporary thought still remains unsettled upon the issue. The historical survey does not, therefore, decide the issue and resolve the plot although the survey does sharpen the issues and focus more clearly upon the areas of disagreement making it possible in the last part of the book to offer a new form of ownership, autonomous ownership, which is morally justifiable within a schema of justification.

As a preview of the conclusion, it can be said that autonomous ownership resembles private ownership in some ways and in other ways it resembles communal ownership. Autonomous ownership resembles private ownership in the rules regarding self and labor. Autonomy requires that each individual have the right to direct his own labor and the right to the income from his labor. The alternative, to regard the self and labor as being owned wholly or in part by other members of society, violates individual autonomy. The autonomous ownership rules for land and resources resemble communal ownership in that each individual must have the right to participate in decisions about how land and resources are used as well as the right to a share of the income produced by land and resource utilization. Thus neither private ownership nor communal ownership is morally justifiable although each of them contains elements which are ultimately part of a morally justifiable form of ownership.

Chapters II through V comprise the historical survey. Philosophers are grouped together according to the method by which they attempt to provide a moral justification of ownership. Chapter II discusses the Natural Perfectionists, Plato, Aristotle, and Aquinas, who try to justify forms of ownership as means to human perfection and virtue. While they use the same method, they do not agree about which form best promotes virtue and perfection. Chapter III discusses the First Appropriationists, Locke, Rousseau, Kant, and Nozick. They all believe that private ownership is justified by an act of appropriation of what is unowned in a state of nature. In Chapter IV, Hobbes, Hume, and Rawls are discussed under the title of Conventionalists. These philosophers believe that some form of ownership is needed in all societies, but the specific form adopted for each of them is to a great extent a matter of social or political convention. The last of the historical survey, Chapter V, focuses on the extensive criticism of private ownership by Karl Marx and Robert Owen.

The historical survey does not proceed entirely chronologically. Both Chapters III and IV contain discussions of contemporary philosophers. Also, Hobbes, who is discussed in Chapter IV, predates Locke and the others who are discussed in Chapter III. A strictly chronological approach, whatever its merits, would have caused too much duplication and lengthening of the exposition. Also by grouping the philosophers according to their method of justification instead of by time period, the issues relevant to moral justification can be kept in better focus and contrast.

Chapters I, VI, and VII are original contributions to the solution of the problem of ownership. Chapters VI and VII defend autonomous ownership as the one form of ownership which is morally justifiable within a plausible schema of justification. A schema of justification is required, so that the conditions for a sound, conclusive justification can be developed even though there is now no agreed upon moral principle which is accepted by all rational persons. Autonomous ownership is derived from a moral principle, the principle of autonomy which prescribes each person's equal right to decide for himself what his own good is, how to pursue it, and the well-being necessary to be autonomous. Autonomous ownership prohibits communal ownership of self and labor as well as prohibiting private ownership of land and resources. Chapter I examines the concept of ownership in general and explains the necessary logical structure of all forms of ownership. The logical structure of ownership permits the historical survey to be carried out with a new and deeper understanding of what ownership is so that the survey has a fresh perspective which does not simply rehash and summarize previous discussions. This new understanding of ownership warrants radically different views about what can and what cannot be intellectually used as methods for justifying specific forms of ownership.

A brief word about the word 'property.' 'Ownership' and 'property' are sometimes used interchangeably and sometimes they are not. The word 'property' is banished from these pages and left to the metaphysicians for several reasons. First, and principally, the word 'property' seems to connote something in the thing or object rather than the idea that ownership is a relation between persons with respect to things. Ownership is a set of relations constituted by rights and duties among persons. There is nothing in the object owned which marks it off as mine, yours, or ours. Second, the word 'property' is too often used to refer only to land or what is called real property. 'Ownership' has a much broader connotation. Also, but this is not frequent among philosophers, 'property' is sometimes misused as a synonym for private ownership so that people only have property in what they privately own. Any chance of even such an unlikely misunderstanding still must be avoided. Thus the word 'property' is not to be found within this book except in direct quotations.

B. Definition of ownership

Ownership in general is a right constituted relationship, or set of relationships, between persons with respect to things.[1] This definition of ownership is not a recent conception but one that goes back at least to Hobbes, is found in Locke, and is explicitly used by Marx.[2] In *The German Ideology*, Marx defines ownership as "the relations of individuals to one another with reference to the material, instrument and product of labor."[3] Locke's clearest definition of ownership in the *Second Treatise* does not occur in Chapter V, "Of Property," but later on where he says:

> ". . . for I have truly no property in that, which another can by right take from me, against my consent."[4]

While Marx's definition is more general than Locke's, encompassing relations other than rights, Marx does recognize that the relation of individuals to one another is typically one of rights backed by the coercive power of the state. Locke's definition creates webs of rights and duties which focus about what is owned. Thus to own something involves rights of owners and creates in others duties not to take from or interfere with an owner's use of what he owns. Ownership may also involve duties on the part of owners, e.g., to care for and preserve their land for the members of their family who will inherit it. For now, the rights of owners will be emphasized. What duties owners have and to whom they are owed will be discussed later.

Things which are capable of being owned, henceforth 'ownables,' can be considered the object of the ownership relation; the persons who are capable of owning things can be considered the subject of the relation, and the rights and duties can be considered the content of the relation. A specific form of ownership is a unique particularization of the subject, object, and content of the relation from among the many possible ones. Specific forms of ownership such as private or communal ownership differ from each other because of differences in the subject of the relation, the object of the relation, or the content of the relation. Variation is possible within the subject of the ownership relation, e.g., some specific forms of ownership exclude married women from the subject of the relation, i.e., married women cannot be owners (although they might be owned), while other specific forms permit married women to own things. The domain of possible ownables also may vary from one specific form to another. In some specific forms, Roman Law, for example, coastal lands lying between the high and low tide lines may be unownable while in other specific forms, in parts of Canada, for example, those lands may be owned by those who own the adjacent lands. Another better known example is the difference in ownership of water running through the banks of a stream. The content of the ownership relation may vary from specific form to specific form. The rights and duties exercised over land in the feudal form of ownership differ from the rights and duties exercised in the private form of ownership.

Within any single specific form there is little reason to suppose that the content of the relation is exactly the same for all kinds or categories of ownables. In English common law, for example, ownership of a freehold estate included the right to cut standing timber while owning a lease for years excluded this right. The rules which govern the transfer of ownables may also vary within a specific form from kind of ownable to kind of ownable. Again in common law, chattel could be conveyed by means of an oral contract while land could not. It is not clear how much complexity in the content of the relation within one specific form of ownership is either possible or desirable. Too much variation might make the rules too difficult to learn or to administer; but insofar as there are relevant differences in the characteristics of kinds of ownables, it is reasonable to assume that variation in the content of the relation is desirable even within one specific form.

The rules which prescribe the rights and duties that constitute the ownership relation may be either moral or legal or both. In most large modern industrialized nations the rights and duties are both legal and moral; but this is not a conceptual requirement of ownership. In some societies the rules could merely be moral, i.e., in H. L. A. Hart's terms, the rights and duties could be part of a system of rules which contain only primary without any secondary rules.[5]

Whether the rules are legal or moral, owning something implies that the owner has rights over what he owns which non-owners lack. That Black, who may be an artificial person comprised of many co-owners, owns Greentree, a parcel of land, implies that Black has rights over Greentree which others do not have and that the others have duties to respect whatever those rights are. The rights which Black may exercise over Greentree depend upon the specific form of ownership that applies in Black's society. In a form of ownership which resembles the private ownership form, Black would be entitled to exercise all the so-called rights of innocent use which would include the rights to build a dwelling upon the land, sell the land, and bequeath the land to whomever he pleases. In other specific forms of ownership, Black might exercise a less inclusive range of rights over Greentree. Black might not have the right to sell the land since Black's children, or the children of the co-owners, have a right to inherit Greentree.

In order for a specific form of ownership to exist in a society, the rules which define or constitute the relation must be acknowledged by the members of the society. This is the truth of Hobbes' claim that there is no ownership, no mine and thine, in a state of nature. Unless the members of a society acknowledge the same set of ownership rules, ownership will make no sense at all. Suppose that Grey and Blue live in the same society but each acknowledges a different specific form of ownership. If, according to the specific form of ownership acknowledged by Grey he owns Greentree, then Blue and all others have a duty to respect Grey's rights over Greentree. But if the specific form of ownership acknowledged by Blue would imply that Greentree is his, then Blue would have rights over Greentree and others, including Grey, would have duties not to interfere with Blue's rights over Greentree. Obviously, if there were no single acknowledged specific form, Greentree would be owned by both Blue and Grey to the exclusion of the other or, which amounts to the same, each would both own and not own Greentree. Ownership makes no sense at all in this instance because everyone could own everything and no one could own anything. Ownership in a society must be based upon a specific form which the members acknowledge.

Acknowledging a specific form of ownership does not, however, imply that one endorses the specific form or believes that the specific form is morally justified. Both Blue and Grey could acknowledge that a specific form of ownership exists for their society and still disagree about its moral justifiability, Grey believing it is morally justifiable and Blue believing it is a plot of the ruling class designed to deprive him of wealth. Blue is not logically inconsistent in believing that a specific form of ownership exists for the society in which he lives and also that the specific form is immoral and ought to be changed. Nor is it necessary that literally everyone in the society acknowledge the same specific form. A small reactionary dissident group might believe that another specific form, one from the past, is still applicable. This need cause no conceptual problems. The conditions for the existence of a specific form of ownership in any society are not different from the condition for the existence of other social institutions such as a society's morality or its legal system. Not everyone need agree, although most of the members must. And, while there may be borderline cases, there must also be clear instances where there is little question whatsoever. In complex specific forms of ownership which are part of a legal system that includes rules for changing laws and rules for adjudicating disputes both about fact and law, there may be disagreements over some aspects of its specific form of ownership. One class of examples concerns new or novel kinds of possible ownables. A specific form of ownership might be confronted with the question whether or not new species of life created by DNA manipulation can be owned (patented) and their manufacture (breeding) licensed. While both sides of the issue could reasonably be argued, such disagreements, by themselves, so long as they are not too frequent or too fundamental, need not cast doubts about the existence of the specific form of ownership in the society.

Many different specific forms of ownership have actually been practiced. Many other specific forms are logically possible. Some specific forms which may seem plausible cannot fulfill the necessary logical structure of all forms of ownership, as shall be shown in the next section. Whether a specific form of ownership has actually existed or is only logically possible but unpracticed need not be an important consideration in the moral justification of a specific form. The mere fact that some society has a specific form of ownership is irrelevant to the justifiability of the form just as the fact that some societies have actually practiced totalitarian government is irrelevant to its justification. Naturally the consequences of practicing a specific form of ownership are relevant to its moral justifiability either from the perspective of a utilitarian justification in which the well-being of those affected is considered, or from the perspective of a deontological justification in which the rights of those affected are paramount. But, there is a difficulty in discerning the consequences of practicing a specific form of ownership. Specific forms only have tendencies to produce certain consequences "all else being equal." In actuality all else is rarely equal and consequences which are elicited in support of conclusions about the practice of a specific form of ownership may be, and sometimes are, explainable by social forces which have little relevance to the society's specific form of ownership. For example, it is claimed that private ownership of the means of production causes increasing concentrations of wealth in the hands of a few. While this may seem plausible it is in fact difficult to prove because countervailing forces such as labor unions, progressive income tax measures, and capitalization by issuing common stock, among other forces, have exerted pressures in the opposite direction. Actual statistics about wealth distribution may, by themselves, be irrelevant to proving or disproving the claim. This does not mean that moral justification is impossible. What is implied is that any justification which depends upon predictions about what the consequences will be of practicing a specific form must also discuss other social forces which may affect its tendencies.

Before considering the various roles which different forms of ownership play in society it is important to clarify the idea of private ownership which is, at the same time, the most discussed and the least understood form of ownership. In many ways private ownership is the primary antagonist of this book as well as its protagonist. Thus it is important to be as precise as possible about the idea of private ownership.

There is no real consensus about which rules define private ownership. Many different sets of rules are used which resemble each other in a variety of ways. One definition is that private ownership is "the exclusive right of a person over a thing." "And it is a majestic right a right so vast in scope that no other comes remotely close to it. It is indeed so total, so absolute that it alone of all rights survives death."[6] The core idea seems to derive from what John Locke characterized as the right to use what is privately owned as one pleases without asking for anyone else's consent and within the limits of the natural law proscription against harming others. If Locke's characterization that there are no limitations upon private owners' use of what they own is strictly interpreted, then forms of ownership which permit taxation of what is owned, zoning ordinances which restrict the purposes to which land or dwelling may be put, building codes, environmental protection standards, and limitations upon bequests or testaments are all incompatible with private ownership. They all limit what owners may do with what they own. The constitutional right of eminent domain by which a community can force an owner to sell his land to the community illustrates how these social rules limit owners' use of what they own. If Locke's characterization is strictly interpreted, then private ownership does not exist where any limitation other than natural law restricts rights of owners. Locke may not have intended such a strict interpretation, but a less strict interpretation leads to vagueness in the concept.

It is best to define private ownership as strictly interpreted. Other forms of ownership which resemble private ownership can then be defined by comparison with and contrast to the strictly interpreted form. Private ownership can be defined by specifying the subject, object, and content of the ownership relation. The subject of the relation is persons generally. Private ownership places no limits upon who may be owners. Owners may be single individuals or groups of individuals. Of course if persons are themselves owned, as slaves, children, or wives, then they cannot be owners. The object of the relation in a system of private ownership is any possible ownable, i.e., anything at all, including persons in some cases. Some forms of ownership may limit the domain of objects which may be privately owned, e.g., by excluding persons or by excluding lands and resources from the object of the relation. In that case, the form of ownership would not be private although some parts of it would resemble private ownership at least in content.

It is the content of the private ownership relation which best defines it in contrast to other forms. The content of the private ownership relation consists in vestiture of the right to use ownables in any way whatsoever limited only by the moral law. Private owners have the right to use and manage what they own as they please.[7] Use and management include not only physical control

9

of and alterations to what is owned but also the conditions in which others may use what is owned, e.g., when others may enter upon privately owned land. Private owners also have unrestricted rights to the income or the capital from what they own, i.e., unlimited fiscal control. These rights include not only money from rents or leases but also the right to sell at a profit or to destroy what one owns. Private owners of resources, for example, may either sell them on the market or withhold them in order to raise the price. Also, private owners have the right to bequeath what they own or any part of it to whomever they please and with whatever conditions they please. Just as is the case with leases, in bequests the private owner may alienate only some of his rights or alienate them subject to restrictions. Thus, contrary to the rule against perpetuities which has evolved within common law, private owners can bequeath land or other ownables with entailments, for example, to be passed through the eldest heir of the eldest heir. Ownables bequeathed to a family in perpetuity are not privately owned because the family does not have the right to use them as they please. There is nothing anomalous about entailments in private ownership. Many persons who possess ownables such as lessees, bailees, or trustees, cannot exercise all of the private ownership rights.

The set of rights which constitute the content of the private ownership relation can be summarized in the term 'rights of all innocent uses.' Private ownership in the sense of all innocent uses may never have existed for all ownables in any society. It certainly does not exist in common law England or in the United States. Private ownership may be the ideal of only a few libertarians. Still, private ownership in the strict sense is a useful concept because it is at least clear and specific. Its primary usefulness is serving as conceptual base in order to define and compare forms of ownership which closely resemble it and are loosely called private ownership. There is another reason as well. The private ownership which functions in the economists' model of the free market is the strict sense of private ownership (except for entailments). Close approximations may not have the same economic consequences as does the strict sense. And, closer approximations may not always be better than less close approximations.

C. *The logical structure of ownership rules*

The necessary logical structure of all forms of ownership has remained hidden perhaps because the concept of ownership in general has not been widely discussed. Special attention has usually been given to one or another specific form such as private ownership or communal ownership. A discussion of ownership in general needs to be undertaken in order to understand the necessary logical structure of all specific forms of ownership and in order to construct a set of concepts to classify different specific forms of ownership both of which are essential to a compelling moral justification of a specific form.

Understanding the necessary logical structure of ownership is essential to moral justification since the logical structure places restrictions upon ownership rules by limiting possible forms of ownership only to those which are consistent with the logical requirements. It turns out, for example, that a system of ownership rules based upon the principle to each according to his needs is not a logically possible form of ownership since it violates the necessary logical structure. The classification of specific forms of ownership is also essential to moral justification since clear unambiguous specifications of forms of ownership are required to test how well forms of ownership meet the justificatory requirements of grounding moral principles.

All systems of ownership rules perform two essential social functions: they assign rights to individuals or groups of individuals, and they prescribe mechanisms for the acquisition, transfer, and alienation of these rights. The rights assigned to individuals by ownership rules are rights over things, where 'things' is maximally general, designating not only such material objects as oil fields and factories but also such incorporeal items as ideas and good will. It is possible to further explicate rights over things as rights against other persons, specifically, the right that others refrain from interfering with the owner's legitimate use of the thing.[8] Thus that a person owns something entails that he has rights over that thing with which others ought not to interfere.

Earlier it was demonstrated that ownership rules can be either legal or moral or both just so long as they are acknowledged; similarly no logical necessity requires that the rules assign any particular set of rights, or provide any particular way in which ownership rights can be acquired, transferred, or alienated. Rights must be assigned on some basis, but there are many possible criteria for doing this. Locke believes that in the state of nature the criteria for assigning rights are what a person labors to produce or what he receives as a gift or in exchange. Yet labor is not the only possible criterion for the assignment of ownership rights. Assignments can be made based upon status as a person or upon a democratically chosen social welfare policy. In addition, the extent or range of the assigned rights may also vary. Locke, again for the state of nature, believes that the rights assigned to owners are the rights of all morally innocent uses. Yet it is possible to assign rights which are more restricted and less extensive than those of Locke's system, e.g., rights over land use may be restricted by environmental protection standards. The rights actually assigned and the criteria upon which the assignments are based constitute the content of the set of ownership rules.

Whatever the content of a particular set of ownership rules happens to be, assignments of rights must be made and the rights so assigned must be specified. The term criteria of title can be used to refer to the ways sets of ownership rules assign rights over things to individuals or groups. Criteria of title are the rules which prescribe how ownership rights are assigned, that is, rules by which it is possible to determine who owns what and which are designed to answer the question: Does he own this? Every set of ownership rules must contain at least one criterion of title but this does not imply that every set share the same criterion nor does it imply that the same criterion be used for all possible ownables within a specific set of ownership rules. Criteria of title not only may vary from set to set but they may vary within a set from one kind of ownable to another, e.g., in early common law a freehold estate could only be owned if a clod of turf had been conveyed to the owner or it could be owned by inheritance, whereas chattel ownership could be based upon oral or written agreement and by bequest.

All sets of ownership rules must also contain rules which specify what can be called rights of title, that is, what rights an individual is assigned over what he owns. Rights of title within any set of ownership rules are rights against ranges of interferences by others, and these rights vest in owners as assigned by the various criteria of title. Rights of title also vary from set to set of ownership rules, and they may vary within a set depending upon the kind of ownable in question. In the United States today rights to sub-divide land can vary from community to community or within a community depending upon zoning ordinances.

Criteria of title and rights of title are both necessary elements in any set of ownership rules which constitute specific forms of ownership. Whatever implicit or explicit purposes and goals a society hopes to achieve through its specific form of ownership, it is the function of ownership rules to achieve these purposes and goals by assigning rights over things to individuals or groups. This is a conceptual truth; alternative ways of achieving social purposes and goals that do not function through the assignment of rights over things could not justifiably be considered ownership rules. The conceptual truth follows from the meaning of 'ownership' which is defined as a right constituted relation between individuals with respect to things. Section D of this chapter will consider the impossibility of a society without any form of ownership at all.

Criteria of title need to be discussed more fully. Criteria of title are the ownership rules which assign to individuals their rights over things.[9] Within a set of ownership rules the criteria of title are the basis for, or the reasons why, one individual may legitimately claim such rights. Even though there is no necessary content for all criteria of title, and a wide variety of criteria are possible, criteria of title must fulfill necessary logical requirements. The criteria of title must be consistent, determinate, and complete.

The requirement of consistency demands that the criteria of title be such that no individual or group of individuals can both own and not own the same thing at the same time and in the same way. Consistency does not exclude joint and common ownership nor does it exclude the possibility that some things may be unownable. What is required is only a consistent assignment of rights over things. The determinacy requirement demands that it must be possible, at least in principle, to unambiguously determine whether a person does or does not own some particular thing. Of course in practice, instances may arise in which ownership is unclear, e.g., there may be several different wills or parts of a deed may be missing. Still, determinate criteria of title would in principle supply an account of what would establish uncontestable title were it to exist. Third, the criteria of title must be complete. Completeness demands that if something is ownable according to a set of ownership rules then it must be possible for someone or some group to own it. This is not to say that every set of ownership rules must permit ownership of every kind of thing or that everyone own something. Completeness only requires that for everything which can be owned, relative to a specific set of ownership rules, the criteria of title must prescribe a procedure for ownership, or for non-ownership of that thing.

Two questions must now be answered. How do the logical requirements of consistency, determinacy, and completeness affect particular criteria of title? And why must the criteria of title fulfill these requirements?

The criteria of title must be consistent if the set of ownership rules is to fulfill its function. Inconsistent criteria of title imply that a person could both own and not own something which would be equivalent to a Hobbesian state of nature where no ownership rules exist and where no individual is prohibited from interfering with another's use of things. Owning something is to have rights against the interference of others, even if the range of rights is small; but where the criteria of title are inconsistent, conferring both ownership and non-ownership, it follows that one may own something and also fail to have rights against interference by others. In this case the concept of ownership is meaningless.

As a possible example of an inconsistent criterion of title consider "to each according to his needs." If interpreted as meaning that individuals own what they need, then two individuals who both need the same particular thing would each own it. Each individual would own the thing because he needs it and each would not own it because it is needed and hence owned by the other. Ownership in this instance is not joint or common ownership; it is assumed that each individual needs the whole of the thing in question. To each according to his need fails as a criterion of title because it places the two individuals in the same position with respect to each other as they would be if there were no rules of ownership or no criteria of title at all.

Gift and exchange are examples of consistent criteria of title if certain minimal background assumptions are made. Suppose that the members of a community already own things. How this ownership came about is irrelevant here. Once things are owned it is possible to use gift and exchange as criteria of title. A person owns what is given to him by another, or by a group, and he owns what he receives from others in exchange. The concept of giving precludes the giving of one thing, all of it and exclusively, to more

14

than one person. Of course, parts of a thing, e.g., a hundred acre plot of land, may be given to several persons; but then the thing each person is given, wholly and exclusively, is part of the whole plot of land. Thus no person could own the same thing in the same way and at the same time and not own it at the same time and in the same way.

Indeterminate criteria of title imply the possibility that no in principle determination could be made about who owns what. The possibility would always exist that nothing could prove or disprove ownership. Indeterminacy in this case is not equivalent to a "lost deed" where, were the lost deed discovered, ownership could be conclusively established; indeterminacy excludes the possibility of ever knowing uncontestably who owns what.

There are two ways in which criteria of title can be indeterminate. The first is person indeterminacy which concerns the individuals involved. The object or possible ownable in question is determinate, but it is unclear who owns the object or what share of it is owned by each of several individuals. Locke's criterion of labor can serve as an illustration, where a person's labor serves as a criterion of title. A person owns land, fruit, or a house, because he mixes his labor with unowned materials found pre-existing in their natural state. Once someone's labor is mixed with or spent on something he has valid title over it. Labor, then, is a criterion upon which title is based for those things which were once unowned (or at least not privately owned). But labor as a criterion of title is person indeterminate because it may be impossible to determine how much labor each of several individuals contributes to the completion of a joint project. Suppose two men work together to clear a field for cultivation. What share belongs to each? If the answer depends upon the proportional quantity of labor each expends, there are several difficulties in precisely and non-arbitrarily measuring the quantity of labor. The muscular energy each expends is not a sufficient measure because equal quantities of energy may be more or less efficient, skillful, or productive. The length of time each works is for the same reason also an insufficient measure. Therefore, it may not be possible to determine which of the two owns what proportional share of the land. The object to be shared is determinate enough, but since which individual owns what cannot be determined, the criterion is person indeterminate.[10]

Criteria of title can also be indeterminate with respect to

objects. The person involved may be determinate but the things he owns may not be. Suppose need is used as a criterion of title, i.e., a person owns, or ought to own, what he needs. While it is true that everyone needs food, clothing, and shelter, it may not always be possible to determine whether a person needs steak or soybean burger, or whether he needs this coat rather than one similar to it. In cases like these the criterion of need cannot by itself make the determination. Not all needs, however, are indeterminate. Someone may need this kidney, not this kind of kidney, for a kidney transplant, or a sculptor may need this piece of marble for his statue. It is possible to imagine that a starving man may need this particular morsel of food because no other is available. Thus need as a criterion of title may be object indeterminate in some instances but determinate in others.

The criteria of title for a set of ownership rules are incomplete if there are ownable objects and there are no criteria of title by which they can be owned. Locke's concept of labor as a criterion of title can once again be used to illustrate the requirement of completeness. Assume, as Locke does, that a person owns those previously unowned things he labors upon or mixes his labor with. But unlike Locke, assume that gift, bequest, and exchange are not permissible criteria of title. Thus persons may only own what they labor to produce. Now suppose that a man and his wife clear fields, build a house, and plant crops so that they own the land, house, and crops. No one, not even their children, can own any of it even after their parents' death. If the children were to help with the crop raising, then by their labor they would own some (indeterminate) share of the harvest. But the fields and the house could not belong to the children, since initially it contained none of their labor. The parents cannot give or bequeath the land and house to their children because by hypothesis only labor upon what is unowned and not gift or bequest are here considered as valid criteria of title. The house and fields are owned because the parents own them, but because there are no criteria of title by which ownership of the fields and house can be transferred to others they are unownable upon the death of the parents. The remedy within Locke's theory of ownership is to complete the set of criteria of title by the addition of gift, bequest, and exchange so that the parents may simply give the farm to their children. But Locke's method of making the labor criterion complete is not the only logically possible one. A criterion of title is conceivable which prescribes that, upon the death of the parents, the farm would revert to its prior unowned status and belong to the first person who labored upon it; a criterion of title is also possible which would prescribe that the farm transfer to the state to be reallocated according to a policy of social well-being. Whatever the additional criteria of title are which might be chosen, labor as a criterion of title is incomplete and must bè supplemented by one of them if the set of ownership rules is itself to be complete.

The criteria of title may be formal or material. With formal criteria such as gift, bequest, or exchange, it is impossible to deduce from the criteria what a person will own. In the case of material criteria of title such a deduction is possible. Given certain premises about what people need and about how plentiful goods are, the criterion of need permits deducing what collection of things a person will own. Similarly, knowing a society's social well-being policy will permit deducing what a person will own according to a socialist criterion of title. It should not be assumed that formal criteria of title always depend upon individual preference as do the criteria of gift, bequest, and exchange. Formal criteria of title may depend upon chance such as birth, where the eldest owns what his parents owned, or a crap game, where one owns according to one's number. Not all formal criteria permit individuals greater freedom of choice than do material criteria.

Joseph Raz, in *The Concept of a Legal System*, distinguishes between investive laws and divestive laws.[11] He says, "An investive law is a law which determines that when certain conditions obtain a certain person who did not have a certain right acquires it." And, "a divestive law is a law which determines that when certain conditions obtain a certain person who has a certain right loses it."[12] Investive and divestive laws function as do criteria of title in sets of ownership rules. Raz himself uses giving as an example of both investive and divestive laws, i.e., divestive for the giver and investive for the receiver. Not all criteria of title resemble giving in being symmetrical between investive and divestive functions. Feudal ownership rules of inheritance that prescribe which of one's heirs must inherit upon one's death might be viewed as exclusively investive laws, since the feudal land owner could not divest himself of his lands by gift, bequest, or exchange. At his death, his lands automatically vest in his heir without any further action. Locke's use of labor as a criterion of title is also only investive since labor functions as a criterion of title if the labor is expended upon what is unowned (or at least not privately owned). An example of a purely divestive criterion of title is the practice in some American cities of placing unwanted goods by the curbside the day before garbage collection. The placing by the curbside is considered a basis for divesting oneself of claim to title. Hobbes, in *Leviathan*, calls such acts renouncing a right rather than transferring a right. The difference between gift and strict inheritance rules also illustrates an important difference between kinds of criteria of title. Raz makes the point that "another law can determine that ownership in property of a certain type (which cannot be left by will) is acquired by a person upon the death of his spouse, who was the previous owner. Such a law makes the acquisition of ownership dependent not upon the performance of an act but upon the occurrence of an event."[13] Actually, it is the person's status as a spouse that is relevant to the inheritance, not merely the occurrence of the event, viz., death. It is therefore possible to distinguish two categories of criteria of title: performative criteria of title which depend upon the performance of some act by some individual, e.g., gift, bequest, exchange, and labor, and status criteria which depend upon an individual's status, e.g., being a spouse, being a member of a community, being himself. Status criteria may entitle an individual to a share of his spouse's belongings, a share of the land and resources of a community, or rights over his own labor, depending upon the relevant status involved.

The logical structure of criteria of title has been sufficiently explained.[14] It is now necessary to examine the rights of title which are the second element in the content of the ownership relation.

Rights of title, the rights conferred by ownership rules, prescribe what owners may do with what they own. There are two important issues concerning rights of title. The first is the question whether ownership entails necessary rights which all systems of ownership rules must contain. The second issue concerns the range of ownership rights, i.e., in what ways can the rights of title vary from one system of ownership to another.

It is sometimes thought that all systems of ownership rules, i.e., all specific forms of ownership, grant to owners the right to exclusively control all uses of what they own.[15] This is a twofold mistake. First, exclusivity is not a right at all. Second, although there is a sense of 'exclusivity' which is entailed by ownership, this does not extend to the right to control all uses of what one owns. Ownership does entail exclusivity in the sense that owners have rights over what they own which they alone, or their designees, may exercise; these are the rights over what they own which others, non-owners, simply lack. Exclusivity is not a right over and above the other rights of title; rather, 'exclusivity' in this context is only a summary expression for the idea that the rights of title vest only in the owner. Owners alone may exercise their rights of title because they alone have those rights. It is not as if owners have rights over what they own plus the additional right to exercise those rights. Were exclusivity another right, over and above the rights of title, then it would be possible to imagine other persons who have the same rights over a thing as does the owner except the right to exercise those rights. This is clearly absurd.

Even though owners may exercise their rights exclusively, this does not entail that the rights they exercise are unrestricted. A distinction must be drawn between exercising rights exclusively on the one hand, and the range of rights so exercised on the other. The range of owners' rights may be more or less inclusive, but this does not affect the owners exclusively exercising their rights within the permitted range. The range of rights is defined and established by the particular specific form of ownership within which the owners operate. Not all specific forms of ownership confer upon owners all rights to do whatever they wish (within the bounds of innocent use) with what they own.

A. M. Honoré argues that a right of recovery from unlawful appropriation is an essential right in the legal concept of 'liberal ownership.'[16] This idea which seems correct for the legal concept is too narrow for this discussion of ownership rules in general. All sets of rights of title must include proscriptions against the capricious appropriation of one's ownables by others. But what constitutes capricious appropriation is defined by each specific form of ownership and there is little reason to expect that equivalent definitions will occur in all specific forms. Besides, a proscription against capricious appropriation is only another way of expressing the truth that non-owners have an obligation to refrain from interfering with owners' legitimate rights. A right against capricious appropriation is not an additional right which owners have. The "recovery" aspect of Honoré's right is also too limited. In some instances, even in legal systems where liberal ownership is most closely approximated, the unlawfully appropriated ownable is not recovered but its money equivalent. In other specific forms of ownership it is possible to imagine additional ways in which owners could be compensated for capricious appropriation, e.g., by having the misappropriator perform services to the owners.

Since there appear to be no conceptually necessary sets of rights of title which specific forms of ownership confer, there can be numerous possible combinations of rights; still this is not to say that all specific forms are equally just, equally optimific, or equally efficient at stimulating production.

D.   *The impossibility of a society without ownership*

It has been suggested that a distinction needs to be made between a general justification of ownership which answers the question, "Why should there be any property rights at all – ever?" and the problem of specific justification which answers the question, "Given that there should be property rights of some kind, what kind(s) should there be?"[17] The distinction presupposes that a society without ownership in which there are no ownership rules at all is a logical possibility. While it is possible to imagine societies in which one specific form of ownership or another is absent, e.g., private ownership or feudal ownership, it is not possible to imagine a society in which there is no form of ownership whatsoever. If it can be shown that a society without any form of ownership is indeed inconceivable and impossible, then the only relevant moral issue is what specific form of ownership is morally justifiable and the question about the moral justifiability of ownership in general becomes moot.

The proof that a society with no form of ownership is impossible depends upon the inconceivability of a society in which there are no right constituted relationships, or sets of relationships, between persons with respect to things, i.e., that all societies must at least have some ownership rules prescribing rights of title and criteria of title. In order to establish this impossibility it is unnecessary to survey in detail all societies which have existed or which might possibly exist. It is only necessary to discuss two ideal types of society: societies based upon division of labor and exchange, and societies without division of labor and exchange, but in which scarcity requires production of what is needed.

'Exchange' must not be construed in the narrow sense of trading privately owned goods in a free open market but more broadly as the allocation or distribution of goods among members of society each of whom does not, by hypothesis, directly produce everything he needs. Showing that both types of society must contain ownership rules is conclusive because any actual or possible society must fall within either one of these two types.

All societies based upon division of labor and exchange must have some specific form of ownership because division of labor and exchange conceptually presuppose rights of title and criteria of title. Exchange, even in the broad sense used here, has no meaning apart from the idea of rights of title. Exchange is the transference of title to something, i.e., transference of rights over something from the person who has the rights to another who lacks those rights. Rights of title must at the minimum include the rights against capricious appropriation of one's ownables by others. Without this right there would be no reason to exchange since no one would be prohibited from taking what another possesses. Also, without rights of title being transferred, there would be no reason to exchange because nothing would be gained thereby. When exchange occurs, each exchanger, at the very least, assumes he will have rights over what he receives as a result of the exchange that he did not have before. It is not necessary, however, that the rights of title grant control of all innocent uses as does the private ownership specific form, e.g., not to be deprived of any use of one's ownables without one's consent. Rather, exchange only assumes as a minimum presupposition not being deprived of the rights over one's ownables except as permitted by the rules of the specific form. Exchange also presupposes rights of title which include the right to transfer title and permit exchange between individuals. It is not tautological to say this. The right of exchange is not necessarily contained in all rights of title since some specific forms of ownership limit the kinds of objects which can be exchanged, e.g., land, or limit the individuals with whom one may exchange, e.g., felons.

Criteria of title are also presupposed by division of labor and exchange. Since potential ownables do not enter the world with name tags on them, societies must have rules which permit identifying whose ownable something is. Exchange is possible only where it can be known with some degree of certainty who has title to what. This is true even in societies which lack market trading per se, but where the distribution of ownables, the hunter's kill, is determined by kinship ties. Even in this instance, there must be rules identifying whose kill it is (he who shoots the arrow or he who first reaches the kill), and rules identifying which kinsmen have rights to which parts. Criteria of title are also presupposed because exchange must confer title. If the acts of exchange were not recognized by the criteria of title as conferring title upon the exchangers, exchange would make no sense at all. Thus division of labor and exchange presuppose both rights of title and criteria of title which is a sufficient proof that division of labor and exchange presuppose some specific form of ownership.

Half the proof is established. All societies based upon division of labor and exchange are shown to presuppose some form of ownership. What has already been established is, however, really more than half of the proof. Since all modern societies are, and it is reasonable to suppose will be, based upon division of labor and exchange, it follows that all modern societies logically must have some specific form of ownership. This is a most important result for the purpose of morally justifying ownership since only the problem of specific justification need be considered. Still, to complete the proof that society without any form of ownership is impossible, societies not based upon division of labor or exchange, but in which people have to produce their livelihood, must also be shown to presuppose some form of ownership.

In order to prove that societies not based upon division of labor and exchange must have ownership relations, it is necessary to consider them from the external point of view, i.e., relations between members and non-members, and from the internal point of view, i.e., relations between members and members. From the external point of view, the crucial idea is that the society is aware of itself as a society or group which is differentiated and separate from other societies or groups. Where this idea of separateness is developed, a society will distinguish between members and non-members, and grant to the former rights of title over lands, herds, names, and perhaps religious objects even if these ownables are held in common by all members of the society. If non-members were to receive rights of title on par with the members of the society, it is hard to see what difference there would be, if any, between members and non-members. These rights of title must be vested according to some criterion of title; so it follows that there must also be criteria of title which confer these rights upon members, (e.g., by marriage) and by which they are denied to non-members.

Internal relations between the members will often lack the discriminations and complexity inherent in societies based on division of labor and exchange. Still, there will be right constituted relations between persons with respect to things. The society must have criteria of title prescribing which of its members have rights to appropriate its ownables. Even in the case where there is a status criterion of title which grants equal access to all members simply because they are members, or what is the same thing, the criterion makes no distinctions among members, there is a relation between individuals nonetheless. The status criterion which vests in each member the equal right to access would imply the condemnation of any member who interfered with another's right of access. Whether distinctions are drawn between members some of whom have rights while others do not, or no distinctions are drawn and all members have equal access, the criteria of title establish rights and correlative duties among the members. Rights of title are also present. Even in the absence of division of labor or exchange, societies must have some rules specifying members' rights over what they appropriate.

A collection of individuals without any shared criteria of title or rights of title, i.e., without any shared relations between themselves with respect to things, could hardly be called a society. The possible domain of the object of the ownership relation is so wide, it is difficult to conceive how individuals could interact enough, or how they could consider themselves as belonging together, without also having ownership rules over things.

The only possible objection to the logical necessity of some form of ownership existing in all societies must be based on criticism of the definition of ownership for being too broad. A more narrow definition of ownership, one that placed restrictions on the content of the ownership relation, would change the question about the existence of ownership from a conceptual one to an empirical one. It is doubtful that a more restricted content of the ownership relation could be specified in a non-arbitrary way; but all that a more restricted content could gain would be the ability to demonstrate empirically that some society lacked this restricted form of ownership. For example, if the ownership relations were restricted so that only forms which included the right to bequeath one's lands to whom one pleased were called ownership (or full ownership), then feudalism which lacked the right to bequeath would not be called a form of ownership (or this form of ownership). But for any restricted content to be relevant in a moral justification of ownership, there must be arguments which show how the restricted content meets the grounds of justification. Saying "This is what I (or we) mean by 'ownership'" is not a sufficiently good answer. The broad definition of ownership, i.e., the right constituted relation between persons with respect to things, leaves open the question which specific form or forms is morally justifiable. Specific forms must be examined to see whether they meet the grounds of justification. But no form of ownership is excluded because of an arbitrarily restricted content. The idea that some form of ownership must exist in all possible societies does not beg any questions. Societies never adopt ownership in general but always one or another specific form of ownership – thus justification is always of a specific form, never of ownership in general.

There is the possibility that no specific form of ownership is morally justifiable, although this is a highly unlikely possibility. Does this possibility, even as remote as it seems, pose a conceptual difficulty for the idea that some form of ownership must exist in all societies? It indeed seems odd to think that human societies must logically have an institution no variant of which is morally justifiable. But, in this case the oddity might be due to our idea of moral justifiability and not due to the definition of ownership. R. M. Hare, in *Freedom and Reason*, argues that people who make moral choices of necessity imply some moral principle or another.[18] It is possible, but again highly unlikely, that none of these principles are morally justifiable. Does this similar possibility mean that people who make moral decisions of necessity assume principles none of which are justifiable? Since the purpose of this work is to give a moral justification of a specific form of ownership (and of Hare's work to justify a utilitarian moral principle), the possibility that no specific form of ownership is justifiable is a possibility not to be taken seriously.

CHAPTER II

The Natural Perfectionists

A. Plato

The Natural Perfectionists are a trio of philosophers whose moral justification of ownership is grounded in the idea of virtuous perfection of human nature. They believe that the morally justified specific form of ownership for a particular society is the one which best enables its citizens to lead a virtuous life. Their idea is that some forms of ownership make living the virtuous life more difficult and other forms make it easier, so that a well ordered and harmonious society in which virtue thrives needs an appropriate form of ownership. Forms of ownership, as social institutions, can either facilitate or frustrate the rational governance of human desires. The philosophers' starting point is a conception of virtue which defines the good life to be fostered through the form of ownership. The justification is not utilitarian because there is not some good to be maximized; rather, social circumstances must enhance opportunities for virtuous behavior which is good in itself.

While the Natural Perfectionists employ roughly the same concept of virtue, what is interesting about them is that although they begin with the same idea about how ownership is to be morally justified they ultimately differ among themselves over the specific form which is believed to be morally right. Plato believes in a communal form of ownership, Aristotle argues primarily for private ownership and Aquinas advocates a mixed form. Why they reach such different conclusions is of interest, because, as would be expected from philosophers of this caliber, the reasons for their disagreement reappear in later justifications of ownership based upon other principles.

The Greek conception of virtue which is used by Plato and

Aristotle and in a modified version by Aquinas can be summarized by three principles of Greek practical reason. The first is know thyself, the second is nothing in excess and the third is the principle that each man should do in life that for which he is best suited. Aquinas will add to these three principles a fourth which is that the common good ought to be promoted. A very brief discussion of the three principles is useful at this point.

The principle nothing in excess is the most fundamental of the three principles of virtue in appreciating Plato's and Aristotle's arguments. The Greeks identified the virtuous with the rational and the limited. Virtuous reason restrains or places limits upon desires and appetites which permits humans to live properly. By contrast, vice, or the irrational, is identified with the unlimited. Thus any desire without limit or without rational control is not virtuous. One main function of reason is to control desires for accumulating goods and satisfactions. Accumulating too much is considered to be useless at the very least and too much may also be harmful because it increasingly stimulates desires so that they are more difficult to control. Moderation in the consumption of any particular good and of goods in general is the defining characteristic of Greek virtue.

The second principle of virtue is know thyself. Its most direct application is in the discovery of personal virtue. Since rational moderation is not the same for all people because of individual differences, each person must possess sufficient self-knowledge to know what moderation is for him. Self-knowledge is thus a prerequisite of virtue because virtue is personal and individual; it does not prescribe identical levels of consumption for everyone. There can be no single social standard applied identically and mechanically to everyone. Also, self-knowledge is essential in examining motives. Unless virtuous actions are performed for the right reason they are not really virtuous, i.e., a man is courageous only if he performs an act of bravery with a courageous motive.

The last of the three principles needing to be discussed is that each individual should do in life that for which he is best suited. Plato and Aristotle are not egalitarians. They do not believe that all people are fundamentally equal, so even if there are some ways in which people are equal, the ways in which people differ from one another are much more important. Social roles and responsibilities, therefore, ought to be distributed so as to best match the particular abilities of each person. Plato and Aristotle believe that social harmony and efficiency are thereby best promoted.

It will be best to begin with Plato's arguments now rather than discussing any further how the Greek principles of virtue are to be understood. His arguments to justify ownership can be sufficiently understood by understanding his specific use of the principles in context.

At different points in his career, Plato defends two different but closely related specific forms of ownership. In the *Republic*, the great work of Plato's mid-career, a form of ownership is described for what Plato calls the ideal political community. Later, in the *Laws*, he discusses a form of ownership which he believes is a lesser but possibly still attainable ideal. The two forms of ownership are consistent with one another; they follow from the same three Greek principles of virtue; they differ, as shall be seen, because Plato reverses his views about the limits to which human nature can be molded.

The *Republic*, notoriously, prescribes for the guardians or rulers of the ideal state communal ownership of a Spartan collection of ownables. The guardians are not to privately own any land, dwelling, gold or silver; they are to consider each other, i.e., all men and women, equally as husbands and wives with children in the same age cohort regarding each other as brother and sister. Guardians receive a daily salary for their services which Plato believes should just equal their expenses and which should be paid in food or in coinage having only local not intercity value.

> In the first place, none of them must possess any private property save the indispensable. Second, none must have any habitation or treasure house which is not open to all to enter at will. Their food, in such quantities as are needful for athletes of war sober and brave, they must receive as an agreed stipend from the other citizens as the wages of their guardianship, so measured that there shall be neither superfluity at the end of the year or any lack. And resorting to a common mess like soldiers on a campaign they will live together. . . . But for these only of all the dwellers in the city it is not lawful to handle gold and silver and to touch them nor yet come under the same roof with them, nor hang them as ornaments on their limbs nor drink from silver and gold. So living they would save themselves and save their city. But

whenever they shall acquire for themselves land of their own
and houses and coin, they will be householders and foemen
instead of guardians, and will be transformed from the helpers
of their fellow citizens to their enemies and masters, and so
in hating and being hated, plotting and being plotted against,
they will pass their days fearing far more and rather the
townsmen within than the farmers without – and then even
then laying the course of near shipwreck for themselves and
the state.[1]

The passage contains several of the elements through which
Plato connects communal ownership for the guardians to the principles of Greek virtue. Guardians are to perform one function in
the state, that of ruler-protector, much like a military general.
Having to care for lands and dwellings or oversee the manufacture
of crafts would distract the guardians from their tasks of ruling.
Further, Plato's passage illustrates his fear that too many material
comforts would make the guardians "soft" rather than temperate
and courageous since the life of a warrior places physical demands
on the mind and body which are different from the demands upon
the minds and bodies of farmers or craftsmen. Also illustrated is
Plato's overarching concern that wealth may come to be honored
rather than virtue.[2] Each of these elements is central in Plato's
thinking and each needs to be discussed in greater depth and
detail.

The communal ownership of the guardians both protects them
from the burdens of land ownership and protects them from the
destructive influence of wealth. Plato believes that managing a
state requires both skill and time, the first of which can only be
developed (in a few individuals) by a careful and lengthy education
in music, gymnastic, and dialectic. To also educate the guardians
in household management, husbandry, or crafts would, Plato
believes, strain the capacity of even the best endowed learners.
Besides, Plato believes that citizenship or governing is a full time
business that does not leave time for other vocations even if one
could possibly be knowledgeable in several of these arts.[3]

Communal ownership also protects the guardians from temp-
tations to oligarchy, the desire to prey upon the other citizens.
Were the guardians permitted private ownership and wealth, Plato
believes, they might become "enemies and tyrants."[4] First of all,
Plato thinks that "wealth and poverty" are two causes of the

28

deterioration of the arts. His example is the potter who, becoming wealthy, may no longer take the same pains with his art, becoming indolent and careless, and thus becoming a worse potter. A poor potter who cannot afford tools or instruments will not work equally well either.[5] By obvious analogy the guardians must also avoid wealth which would make them indolent and they must avoid abject poverty which would make them mean and vicious. Either extreme can cause social discontent by the guardians becoming at odds with the citizens.[6] Indolence destroys the desire to govern well while meanness destroys the capacity. Ill-government on the part of the guardians would lead to the destruction of the city.

Private ownership by the guardians might also set the guardians at odds with one another. For Plato, unity and harmony among the guardians is essential to unity and harmony in the state: "if these [guardians] are free from dissensions among themselves there is no fear that the rest of the city will ever start faction against them or against one another."[7] Common ownership prevents these causes of discord. Why does Plato hold the belief that common ownership leads to unity while private ownership leads to quarrel and discord? A belief which, by the way, Aristotle later questions. Plato thinks that unity is produced when citizens have common pleasures and pains in the sense that the citizens are glad or grieved on the same occasions of joys and sorrows.[8] That all citizens have one opinion about what is near and dear to them, all citizens will therefore strive towards a common end.[9] Since all opinions will coincide, as will the sources of pleasures and pains, Plato infers first that their interests will be harmonious and second that they will have the same opinion about what ought to be done. Each citizen, in Plato's view, ought to be affected in the same way. Here, the communality of children is probably the best illustration of what Plato is assuming. If no member of the guardian class is able to identify his or her child, then each child's achievements will be a source of pleasure for all guardians and each child's shortcomings will be a source of pain. There would be no possibility for parental envy and discord because no one could know which child he created. All children in the cohort would have the same relations. No parent would have any special pride or special shame from his own. Thus without these private sources of discord, envy, jealousy, and so on, the guardians would be united by the strongest of bonds.

Behind what Plato says about the communality of children is the assumption that privately owned shares – in this instance one's children – can be a cause of disunity and discord if the shares are different or unequal – in this instance the children's accomplishments. Plato is elsewhere more explicit about his assumption. Unequal private shares cause wealth for some and poverty for others. This creates "many states" with one state.[10] There will be (at least) two cities, a city of the rich and a city of the poor, dwelling together, and always plotting against one another.[11] Such a state cannot long survive because of its inherent instability. Of course, Plato's argument presupposes that private ownership inevitably leads to unequal shares or collections of good, i.e., some inevitably becoming wealthy, some becoming poor or perhaps propertyless. Plato has no difficulty making the assumption that private ownership will inevitably lead to rich and poor because Plato (unlike modern philosophers such as Hobbes, Locke, or Rousseau) does not assume the equality of all mankind. Nature, he believes, intends individuals for various different works and endows them with various different sets of abilities.[12] Thus it is not at all unreasonable for Plato to assume that a city which permits private ownership will inevitably be an unstable city of rich and poor.

Similar arguments are applied by Plato to justify his idea that the guardian's children ought to be considered communal property, i.e., all of the guardians considering all of the children their own. Plato does not assume that all of the children will be equal in beauty or ability (even though the guardians will be mated to produce the best off-spring) nor, therefore, will all of the children achieve equal levels of success. Parental pride or shame in their children could conceivably be a source of discord and strife amongst the rulers. Shakespeare, in *King Lear*, was not the first to understand the problem.

Although, in the *Republic*, Plato describes in great detail the form of ownership which is morally justified for the guardians, he writes virtually nothing about the forms of ownership under which the rest of the city ought to live. Plato gives us no information about land ownership, ownership of moveables, or even rights of bequest. To be sure, Plato decries either the city of too great wealth or too little wealth; but Plato gives no idea about what specific ownership institutions are needed to achieve virtue for the classes other than the guardian class. There are no clues in the *Republic* to explain Plato's omission. One possibility is that Plato thought that the guardians would decide upon the best form of ownership for their city depending upon geographic and economic circumstances and that he could not predict what their actual decisions would be. This is unlikely, however, given Plato's overall willingness to deal with such issues. Another explanation is simply that Plato was more interested in explaining the theory of the forms in the *Republic* than in explaining mundane rules for land ownership or retail trade. Plato later provides a full explanation of such ownership rules in the *Laws*, but it is unlikely that the omission from the *Republic* is due to any intention to discuss them in the later work.

In summary, ownership rules in the *Republic* are designed to avoid two evils. The first evil is the desire for wealth which Plato fears will overtake the desire for virtue as the primary human motive or goal. The second evil is social conflict or discord which inevitably results from unequal privately owned shares. Plato believes it is possible to fetter human desires by means of communal ownership in order to avoid the two evils.

In his later work, *Laws*, Plato continues to believe communal form of ownership is ideal, but perhaps it is too difficult to implement in the actual world because of habits already too well ingrained in Greek life:

> The first best society, then, that with the best constitution and code of law, is the one where the old saying is most universally true of the whole society. I mean the saying the 'friends' property is indeed common 'property'. If there is now on earth, or ever should be, such a society – a community in womenfolk, in children, in all possessions whatsoever – if all means have been taken to eliminate everything we mean by the word *ownership* from life; if all possible means have been taken to make even what nature has made our *own* in some sense common property, I mean, if our eye, ears, and hands seem to see, hear, act in the common service; if moreover, we all approve and condemn in perfect unison and derive pleasure and pain from the same sources – in a word, when the institutions of society make it most utterly one, that is a criterion of their excellence than which no truer or better will ever be found.[13]

The "second best" constitution of the *Laws* grants concessions to the realities of Greek life. The governors need not be philosopher kings specially trained in dialectic; rather they are chosen through a complicated election procedure by the four classes of citizens. Neither the governors nor the citizens are subject to the ideals of communal ownership.[14] Obviously, rulers who are elected to rule for a short, temporary period cannot be expected to give up what they own. Still, Plato condemns the effects of the desire for wealth on the individual:

. . . the passion for wealth [which] leaves a man not a moment of leisure to attend to anything beyond his personal fortunes. So long as a citizen's whole soul is wrapped up in these, he cannot give a thought to anything but the day's takings. Any study or pursuit which tends to that result everyone sets himself to learn and practice; all others are laughed at to scorn. Here, then, we may say, is one reason in particular why society declines to take this or any other wholly admirable pursuit seriously, though everyone in it is ready enough, in his furious thirst for gold and silver, to stoop to any trade and any shift, honorable or dishonorable, which holds out a prospect of wealth, to scruple at no act whatsoever – innocent, sinful, or utterly shameful – so long as it promises to sate him, like some brute beast, with a perfect glut of eating, drinking, and sexual sport.[15]

Clearly Plato has not abandoned the Greek principle of virtue nothing in excess. The form of ownership discussed in the *Laws* is well designed by Plato to limit wealth. "Now, a society in which neither riches nor poverty is a member regularly produces sterling characters, as it has no place for violence and wrong, nor yet for rivalry and envy."[16] Eliminating poverty remains a problem in the *Laws* for which colonization is Plato's ultimate answer although restricting the massing of wealth also commands Plato's attention. Nor has Plato abandoned the principle that each member of society should perform the task for which he is best suited; but, in the *Laws*, he has relaxed the idea of a single task so that the citizen land owner may also be a governor.

While it is true that in his *Laws* Plato no longer advocates communal ownership of land, wives, children, and so on, it would be incorrect to credit Plato with completely replacing communal ownership with a private system of ownership. There are some similarities between the form Plato advocates and private ownership. For example, at one point Plato speaks in a way that most strikingly anticipates what John Locke will say centuries later: "A simple rule, I take it, might be expressed thus. I would have no one touch my property, if I can help it, or disturb it in the slightest way without some kind of consent upon my part; if I am a man of sense, I must treat the property of others in the same way."[17] But there are also differences between ownership in the *Laws* and private ownership. The rights of title which citizens may exercise over the plots of land which they individually own are different from the rights of title in private ownership. Individuals have exclusive rights over land and houses which they alone may exercise, but the land and houses are divided into 5040 fixed, equal parcels which may be neither bought nor sold and which must be bequeathed without division to a male heir.[18] Each owner's allotment is divided into two segments, one to be near the center of the city and the other to be near the border. (This arrangement of land is adopted by Aristotle in his *Politics*.)[19] Plato gives no information about how the original allotments are appropriated, although it seems safe to assume that the decisions would be made by the city's elders. Land ownership cannot pass to women, who are simply married off, and surplus males, who do not inherit land, may either be adopted by childless landowning families or they may emigrate to the colonies. Plato's form of land ownership therefore differs from private ownership in that there are no rights to buy and sell land, no rights to bequeath land to other than male heirs, and no rights to sub-divide the land. To this extent land ownership more closely resembles the feudal rather than the private form. Plato does not discuss the right of leasing or renting land to others. These rights would, of course, have to be part of the rights of title in what is now considered private ownership. Plato's form of land ownership also differs from private ownership because only inheritance is a legitimate criterion of title.

Plato also limits the purposes to which individually owned plots may be put. "Little making of profit from mechanical crafts, or usury, or the raising of sordid beasts, but only as much as not force a man in his profit gathering to forget the ends for which possessions exist, that is to say, soul and body, which will never be of any account without bodily training and education at large."[20] As in the *Republic*, Plato still regards wealth and riches as an excess to be avoided because it may subvert the desire for virtue. Private individuals are not permitted gold or silver but only coinage for domestic use.[21] The products of the land, the "supplies and distribution of natural produce," must be made in equal shares to each class: citizen, slave and artisan; with each citizen receiving and distributing the share for his slaves.[22] For Plato the object of production is still to produce what is needed for living the virtuous life and not the maximization of the value of each share.

The rules of ownership for manufactured goods, in the *Laws*, more closely resemble private ownership than do the rules for land ownership. Buying and selling of manufactured goods is permitted, but Plato prohibits the landowner-citizen from following a trade, engaging in merchandise, or discharging menial service.[23] Only resident aliens and foreigners may engage in retail trade.[24] Plato's reasons for this are not only the principle that each individual ought to do what he is best suited for, but also to avoid the corrupting influence upon citizens of the desire for wealth.

Even under the control of foreigners, retail trade is limited. Unlike private ownership, buying and selling on credit is prohibited and a warranty, or more accurately a surety, is required from sellers of goods worth more than 50 drachmas. Plato requires sellers of such goods to remain within the territory for a space of ten days in order to satisfy the legal requirements of restitution.[25] Plato also anticipates the common law principle of adverse possession, although in this instance the principle is not applied to land but other ownables. According to Plato, the open and public use of a thing for a year guarantees title to it, unless the use is in the country and then the time is five years, or unless the use is indoors and then the time is three years.[26]

Plato's overarching aim is to avoid the harmful effects, conflict and corruption, of the desire for wealth upon human nature. He carefully constructs the forms of ownership for the *Republic* and the *Laws* to limit the amount citizens may own. Ownables must serve mankind in the search for virtue rather than virtue being the servant in the quest for ownables or wealth. A simple, but not uncomfortable, virtuous life is the goal ownership rules are designed by Plato to achieve.

Plato seems content to believe that the rules of ownership are adequate to achieve his goal. He believes the rules are sufficient to bridle the desire for wealth and steer it towards virtue. The question remains, however, is Plato correct in his assessment? Is the desire for wealth so easily controlled? Of course, there is the separate question whether the desire for wealth is so strong that all of Plato's restraints are necessary to control it. How destructive is the desire for wealth after all either for the individual or for society?

These questions will recur as we progress in our survey of the justifications of ownership. Answering them is one of the necessary prerequisites of any adequate moral justification of a form of ownership.

B. Aristotle

Aristotle, the second of the Natural Perfectionists, begins with the same principles of Greek practical reason as does Plato; but he reaches conclusions about ownership which differ significantly from Plato's views in the *Republic*, and, though they resemble Plato's position in the *Laws*, Aristotle has his own separate supporting rationale. Aristotle argues for what he calls private property. By contrast, Plato's ideal state requires communal ownership of land, spouses and children at least for the guardian class. Material possessions are limited only to what a warrior needs for survival. When Plato, in the *Laws*, retreats to a conception more closely resembling private ownership, he does so not because he abandons his belief in communal ownership as an ideal, but rather because he believes mankind is not yet prepared to live under those demanding conditions. To what extent Aristotle's conception of private ownership approximates the modern concept shall be discussed shortly; what is now important to understand is how Aristotle's assumptions lead him to such different conclusions.

Aristotle rejects Plato's ideal as misguided, and while Aristotle's own theory of ownership bears many resemblances to the form of ownership in the *Laws*, Aristotle does not consider private ownership second best or less than ideal. Aristotle has not abandoned any of the three principles of Greek practical reason nor has he abandoned justifying ownership by its contribution to human perfection. Aristotle's own notorious justification of slavery based upon the premise that some people by nature ought to be ruled is one of the best known examples of the Greek principle of practical reason that each person should do that for which he is best suited. The other two principles – know thyself and nothing in excess – are the cornerstones of Aristotle's account of virtue. The virtuous person must know what for him is the appropriate mean between the two possible extremes; he thus not only must know and avoid excessive extremes in general but also have sufficient self-knowledge to know what is his own appropriate mean since the mean is not the same for everyone. Aristotle's illustration is that the right amount of food for the accomplished wrestler, i.e., not too much nor too little, is not the right amount for the novice just beginning. By the same token, the virtue of liberality is a mean between giving too much and giving too little relative to individual wealth, e.g., a rich person who is liberal would give a greater amount to others than would a poorer, but equally liberal person. Clearly this is good evidence that Aristotle shares with Plato the three premises of Greek practical reason and thus Aristotle's preference for private ownership must have some other source.

At one point in the *Politics*, Aristotle offers an argument in support of private ownership which must perplex modern defenders of private ownership. He criticizes common ownership because it annihilates the virtue of liberality. "No one, when men have all things in common, will any longer set an example of liberality or do any liberal action, for liberality consists in the use which is made of (private) property."[27] Without private ownership, Aristotle believes people will not be able to give to their friends or to those who are in need. Private ownership is, therefore, valuable because of what it allows owners to do for others, not, as in more modern accounts, what private ownership allows owners to do for themselves. Aristotle does not develop this argument in any depth so it is difficult to assess how central it is to his overall attack upon communal ownership. He has other arguments which he develops in much more detail.

Aristotle bases his preference for private ownership over Plato's communal ownership on three grounds not shared by Plato. The first is Aristotle's understanding that what is privately owned will be better managed than what is communally owned. Second is Aristotle's understanding of what he names natural exchange. And third is Aristotle's understanding of human nature which implies the equalization of desires rather than the equalization of wealth through communal ownership.

Aristotle's first argument for private ownership is that what is privately owned is better cared for than what is communally owned. His argument is based upon two assumptions: one about the objects of knowledge and the other about human motivation and interest. In the *Nicomachean Ethics*, Aristotle supplies the following reasons for preferring private rather than public education:

> . . . private education has an advantage over public, as private
> medical treatment has, for while in general rest and
> abstinence from food are good for man in a fever, for a
> particular man they may not be; and a boxer presumably
> does not prescribe the same style of fighting to all his pupils.
> It would seem, then, that the detail is worked out with more
> precision if the control is private, for each person is more
> likely to get what suits his case.[28]

There are two inferences about ownership which can be drawn from this passage. The first is that those who would attempt to centrally manage communally owned lands might have great difficulty in acquiring all of the information necessary to make good judgments about how the communal lands should be utilized. Even if there were a community consensus about land management policy and purpose, which is not always likely, land managers of communally owned land would require a great deal of particular information about the varieties of terrain, drainage, fertility of the lands, about the natural resources, rivers, and about the weather. Such particular information might be very expensive to centrally acquire. Most importantly, if this kind of particular information is not available to the central administration, it hardly seems possible that they could issue wise or even competent decisions. And even if this information were available, as in a modern computerized country with its many information gathering organs, too much information might overwhelm groups of centralized planners who could not possibly assimilate and comprehend all of it or even (if known) all of it that is relevant. Mismanagement through ignorance seems an inevitable outcome.

The second inference from the passage is that each person is a better judge of what suits his interest than are others because each person is more likely to be better informed about the particulars of his own situation than are others who might participate in communal decisions. Aristotle here is not making the erroneous definitional claim that each person is the ultimate authority about what suits his interest. Aristotle is not a subjectivist who believes that what people want defines their interest because the function of reason is to evaluate the means to our ends but not to evaluate the ends themselves. Rather, Aristotle is a relativist who believes that virtue, which is the rational mean between extremes, is relative to each individual; but it is an objective relativity not a subjective one. Objective individual differences such as size or strength account for the different individual means. Thus while it is possible that people can be mistaken about their interest or their virtue because of a lack of judgment, Aristotle also believes that the more intimate knowledge of the particulars of his own situation affords each person an advantage in making good judgments which is not shared by those without this intimate knowledge. The implication for ownership is that each person can be better served by administering what he privately owns than he would be served by a more distant and impersonal administration. Each individual will more likely have his own unique needs fulfilled through his own rather than another's administration. Therefore, in the search for virtue an individual is better served by managing his own resources. He has more intimate knowledge of what he owns and how what he owns contributes to his successfully achieving his own individual virtuous means.

In the *Politics*, by contrast to the passage from the *Ethics*, Aristotle emphasizes human motivation as a reason why private ownership will result in better care being taken of what is owned than will communal ownership. Aristotle believes people think chiefly of their own and hardly at all of the common interest. "Everyone is more inclined to neglect the duty he expects another to fulfill. . . ."[29] Aristotle is not assuming psychological egoism, that self-interest is either the sole or primary human motive. Aristotle's account of virtue is incompatible with that theory of motivation. While Aristotle does say that ". . . love of self is a feeling implanted in nature and not given in vain," he also believes the vice of selfishness is "rightly censured." Aristotle has no difficulty adhering to these two beliefs because he separates self-love from the vice of selfishness which is self-love in excess. All men, or almost all men, can keep self-love within the proper measure.[30] Thus caring for what one privately owns is not a vice according to Aristotle, nor is preferring one's own biological children. Granted that sometimes there are situations in which care or preference for one's own would be rightly censured self-love in excess, e.g., a judge deciding with favoritism towards his own

38

relations; in many other situations care or preference for one's own is morally appropriate, e.g., in giving birthday presents. Kept within the proper measure, self-love for, concern with, or partiality towards what is privately owned is a virtue not a vice. Aristotle argues that because of the special love and care for what is privately owned the thing owned should benefit from the special concern.

Aristotle is unwilling to accept Plato's contention that love and concern may be extended to the large numbers of people which would be required by communal ownership of land or spouses and children. Aristotle differs with Plato about the actual and possible extent of human love and concern. It seems that the disagreement between them lies in an empirical estimation of human love and concern although there may be non-empirical elements involved. Later on, Marx will side with Plato about human love and concern while Locke seems to side with Aristotle.

Turning now to Aristotle's definition of private ownership, it can be seen to resemble the modern conception in some respects and to differ from it in others. The most extreme difference occurs with Aristotle's concept of private ownership of land. Unlike the modern conception of private land ownership, Aristotle does not consider privately owned land to be alienable by either bequest or exchange. Land is to remain connected to each family to serve as a means of producing the family's subsistence. Each family is actually to have two plots, one near the city and the other near the border in order to inspire unanimity among the people in their border wars.[31] While Aristotle sometimes seems to advocate communally owned land which can be cultivated in order to support common meals and religious worship, Aristotle does not locate great importance in the idea.

> Property should be in a certain sense common, but as a general rule, private; for when everyone has a direct interest, men will not complain of one another, and they will make more progress, because everyone will be attending to his own business. And yet by reason of goodness, and in respect of use, 'Friends', as the proverb says, 'will have everything in common.'. . . For although every man has his own property, some things he will place at the disposal of his friends, while others he shares the use of them. . . . It is clearly better that property should be private, but the use of it common. . . .[32]

That individuals may privately own things, both land and goods, for Aristotle implies they will be better cared for by the person who owns them, i.e., the management right of title is best exercised by private owners. Presumably, better management benefits everyone because of increased efficiency. Rights of use must be shared by owners with others who can make use of what is owned. Aristotle's example is that of a man needing provisions to go on a journey. He may appropriate what he finds in fields belonging to others throughout the country. Aristotle does not give this idea more detailed discussion nor does he wonder about its efficiency, i.e., would land owners continue to cultivate land if others frequently appropriated its fruits. It is likely that Aristotle considered each citizen to be a land owner so that using of the fruits of another's lands would be an infrequent occurrence. Common rights of use or appropriation despite their inefficiency still have the advantage of helping those who are in need. Privately owned lands, therefore, are to be used in order to support the family at a comfortable level and not to create an excess of wealth. Selling the land for money is frowned upon by Aristotle.[33]

Ownership of goods, which are the products of labor upon land and resources, much more closely resembles the modern concept. Aristotle includes the rights of alienation by bequest or exchange in the concept of privately owning goods so long as the purpose of the exchange is the acquisition of what is useful in a life of moderate desires.[34] Of course, when Aristotle refers to a life of moderate desires he means a life of virtue. Thus the rights of title for goods, in Aristotle's scheme of private ownership, differ in purpose from the modern concept: gift, bequest and exchange are all permitted and all confer title. The difference between them lies in Aristotle's more restricted notion of natural exchange compared to what he calls retail trade.

> The source of the confusion is the near connection between the two kinds of wealth-getting, in either, the instrument is the same, although the case is different, and so they pass into one another; for each is a use of property, but with a difference: accumulation is the end in one case, but there is a further end in the other. Hence, some persons are led to believe that getting wealth is the object of household management, and the whole idea of their lives is that they

ought either to increase their money without limit, or at any rate not to lose it.[35]

Natural exchange, which for Aristotle is the true function of household management, is a means of gaining wealth, but limited only to what is useful in a virtuous life, i.e., a life of moderate desires. Natural exchange is contrasted to retail trade which is not a virtue. Aristotle claims that the purpose of retail trade is that of acquiring coin or money without limit and for no additional purpose. Even though Aristotle, himself, seems to locate the problem with retail trade in its aiming at coin or money, it is a mistake to consider coin or money the real problem. What is really salient in Aristotle's condemnation of retail trade is its aiming at unlimited accumulation; what underlies his objection to retail trade is that it is unlimited, and therefore a non-virtuous acquisition of goods of any kind at all not merely coin or money. In order to understand this, it is first necessary to take a closer look at what Aristotle means by natural exchange.

Aristotle states that natural exchange occurs because "some have too little and others too much."[36] This possibility (of having too little or too much) is a consequence of private ownership since, even if it were assumed that all land holdings were equal in size or in value, it could not be assumed that all land holdings are identical in natural resources, fertility, and so on. Some exchanges will be inevitable. Suppose there are two households, Green's and Black's, and that Green has too little of X and Black has too much of X. That Green has too little of X and Black has too much of X is a necessary condition of natural exchange but it is not sufficient. Green and Black need to own some other commodity, Y, also in unequal amounts in order for natural exchange to be possible between them. If all of Green's and Black's possessions were equal except for X, then Green would have nothing to exchange with Black for additional X. Thus natural exchange presupposes not only that Green has too little X and Black has too much X but also, in addition, that Green has too much Y and Black has too little Y. Green can, therefore, exchange his extra Y's for Black's surplus X's. The limit of their natural exchange is reached when either Green or Black or both have the right amount of X and Y. By "right amount," Aristotle means the amount useful in a life of moderate desire where too many goods are useless or harmful.

For example Black's land may be more conducive to the production of olives while Green's land may have better pastures. Black may produce too many olives and Green too much feta cheese for their own use. Olives and feta would be exchanged until Green and Black have more nearly what they need.

By contrast, according to Aristotle, retail trade aims at the unlimited acquisition of coin or money. But is it the coin or money purpose or the unlimited acquisition purpose which is the more fundamental evil? At one point Aristotle does say that retail trade makes unnatural use of things because things are traded for coin or money. He distinguishes between the natural use and the unnatural use of a thing. The natural use of shoes, for example, is to protect the feet. Aristotle goes on to say that exchanging shoes with someone who needs shoes to protect his feet is a natural, although secondary, use of shoes if what shoes are exchanged for, say a blanket, is something which itself will be put to a natural use, e.g., as a sleeping cover. Aristotle says that retail trade, by contrast, makes unnatural use of things because things are traded for coin or money.

But this objection to retail trade, that it makes unnatural use of things, turns out to be nothing new. That the object of the exchange is coin or money cannot be the sole basis for condemning retail trade as an unnatural use of things. It is only Aristotle's earlier objection to retail trade, that it is without limit, but in different words. The idea of unnatural use is a restatement in different terms of the idea of unlimited and hence non-virtuous acquisition beyond one's needs. A land holder who exchanges shoes for money and subsequently uses the money to exchange for a blanket is no different from another who makes the shoes–blanket exchange directly without the use of money. Exchanging shoes for money and then for the blanket is not unnatural in Aristotle's sense because the blanket fulfills a genuine need. Mediating the exchange through the use of money leaves unchanged the ultimate purpose of the exchange which is fulfilling one's need for the blanket. Within virtuous exchange the use of coin or money makes no difference. There is no reason why retail trade cannot be practiced within virtuous limits. A person who engages in retail trade only to fulfill his genuine needs or the needs of his family rather than with the purpose of acquiring as much money as possible would be indistinguishable from the land owner who exchanges to fulfill moderate desires. By the same token, a land owner who produced shoes or olives without limit in order to exchange for as much money (or as many blankets) as he could, would be engaged in retail trade. In either of the two illustrations retail traders and land holders are indistinguishable. What does distinguish them in fact is not the desire for coin or money, but the limited or unlimited nature of their desires. Retail trade therefore must be considered as exchange without limit for money or for any other commodity. Aristotle condemns these unlimited desires because they aim at what is useless or harmful. This is simply Aristotle's earlier objection. Thus trade for coin or money, if pursued within rational limits in order to fulfill moderate and virtuous desires, is no less natural than direct commodity exchange. The idea of natural use turns out upon analysis to amount to nothing more than the idea that virtue is identified with limited and rational desires while unlimited and irrational desires are vices. The unnatural use of things is to use them to acquire more than is needed to satisfy moderate desires.

Thus, the right of exchange in Aristotle's concept of ownership is not the private ownership unfettered right of title to exchange goods in order to acquire riches. His concept of natural exchange is much more restricted being limited to exchanges necessary in order for each household to have the material prerequisites of a virtuous life. To this extent Aristotle's concept of private ownership of goods differs from the modern concept.

The last of Aristotle's reasons for preferring private to communal ownership is his belief that communal ownership will not prevent the discord and disharmony which Plato hopes to avoid. Aristotle agrees with Plato that a city in which the distribution of wealth promotes discord is a city ripe for sedition or revolution. Dissatisfaction with one's wealth may be a powerful source of dissatisfaction with one's city. This source of dissatisfaction Plato believes can be prevented by equalizing wealth through equalizing ownership. If wealth and possessions are equalized, Plato believes, everyone will be satisfied with their allotment.

Aristotle challenges the idea that equalizing wealth and possessions removes the discord which may arise out of inequality. Aristotle does not argue, as one might, that other sources of discord exist in addition to inequality of wealth and possessions such as the absence of liberty or self-determination which are at least as significant as causes of sedition or revolution. The absence, in Plato's *Republic*, of freedom and autonomy is one of its main detractions. Later discussions of the justification of ownership emphasize just this point.

Aristotle, however, pursues a different objection. Even if wealth were equalized, Aristotle sees no reason to assume that discord will cease because people's desires are not equal. Equality of wealth and possessions can be as much of a source of dissatisfaction as inequality of wealth, although the class of those who may be dissatisfied will be different from those who are dissatisfied with inequality:

> The equalization of property is one of those things that tend to prevent the citizens from quarreling. Not that the gain in this direction is very great. For the nobles will be dissatisfied because they think themselves worthy of more than equal shares of honor, on this is also found to be a cause of sedition and revolution.[37]

Aristotle's objection is not limited to perceived inequality or relative deprivation. While the nobles' dissatisfaction as a cause of revolution may be a disadvantage to "equalization of property," there are other difficulties which do not depend upon the mere perception or sense of inequality. Thus, Aristotle argues that:

> . . . where there is equality of property, the amount may either be too large or too small, and the possessor may be living in luxury or penury. Clearly, then, the legislator ought not only aim at the equalization of properties, but at moderation in the amount. Further, if he prescribes this moderate amount equally to all, he will be no nearer the mark; for it is not the possessions but the desires of mankind which require to be equalized, and this is impossible unless a sufficient education is provided by the laws.[38]

Real harm or real injustice can result from equalization of ownables, not merely perceived injustice or harm. Aristotle, as other opponents of equalization, notices that the concept of equality by itself cannot prescribe at what level of well-being – rich, moderate, or poor – everyone ought to be treated. A society in which everyone is equally well satisfied would, from the perspective of equality, have nothing to commend it over a community in which everyone is equally poorly satisfied. Equality

44

needs to be supplemented by an additional principle which would prescribe the level of equality.

The second half of the above quotation points to a more fundamental objection to the "equalization of property." Even if the "correct" level of equalization could be found, equalizing everyone's property would be unjust because people are not equal. Aristotle refers to unequal desires but people also have unequal needs, unequal deserts, and unequal entitlements. Thus, treating everyone equally will miss the mark and be unjust because some need more, desire more, or are entitled to more. Unequals, for Aristotle, ought to be treated unequally; and to the degree to which people in a society are not equal the "equalization of property" will be unjust. As an ideal, equality of unequals is wrong.

Aristotle goes on to argue that people's desires can be equalized by moderation in possessions, habits of temperance, and philosophy.[39] But is there reason to believe that equalization of desires reduces the chances for sedition or revolution? Earlier, the absence of liberty and self-determination were also understood to be causes of sedition and revolution as well as inequality either real or perceived. So even if the desire for wealth were equalized it would not remove all of the causes. Still, is Aristotle right in thinking that equalizing desires reduces the chances from that specific cause?

Much depends upon what Aristotle has in mind by the idea of educating desires. If Aristotle means by that educating people to desire the same kinds of particular things, e.g., light meats or a certain kind of bed, then equalizing desires may not reduce the sources of discord. This is because conflict may be spawned out of scarcities in the objects of desire. If everyone, or most, desired to consume only light meats because they are healthful, there may not be enough light meat to satisfy all. While if there were a diversity of desire for both light and heavy meats, there could well be sufficient meat to go around. Diversity of desires may make satisfaction easier because specific items may be in less demand. Similarity of desires may actually increase dissatisfaction rather than reduce it.

Aristotle may not mean that people will have the same desires for the same things. Perhaps what Aristotle is referring to here is the idea of virtue as a mean between extremes, so that by educating people to become virtuous their desires are made more equal, i.e., less extreme, by aiming at the mean. Desires of the virtuous will be more limited and will more closely resemble one another than will the desires of the nonvirtuous. Scarcity, while always a source of conflict and discord, may be less so where all citizens practice virtue as moderation.

In the final analysis, and most simply stated, Aristotle is convinced that private ownership promotes virtue and that communal ownership does not. One factor is that private ownership is supposedly more productive so that people can live better. Aristotle further identifies private ownership with virtue because private ownership is just, i.e., unlike communal ownership unequals are not treated equally. And, finally, Aristotle believes that private ownership provides the opportunity for virtue insofar as individuals must make choices about the use of what they own.

Even though there are similarities between how Aristotle conceives of private ownership and later conceptions, his concept is importantly different. While land is under individual family control, land is not alienable from the family either by gift and bequest or by exchange and sale. Aristotle's concept of land ownership therefore much more closely approximates feudal land ownership than it resembles what now is called private ownership. Also the products of the land may be sometimes appropriated by non-owners who need not ask the owner's permission. Ownership of goods, for Aristotle, differs less from the modern concept. Title rights of use, management income, gift, bequest, and exchange vest in owners much as they do now. It is virtue which for Aristotle limits the rights of owners to use their ownables to try to increase their wealth and income. Virtue prescribes moderation in wealth as well as in desires. Thus the later justifications of private ownership grounded upon free market maximization of wealth and efficiency are in opposition to the virtue by which Aristotle justifies private ownership.

C. Thomas Aquinas

Thomas Aquinas is the third of the philosophers classified as a Natural Perfectionist. Like Plato and Aristotle, his justification of ownership is grounded upon the idea of human perfection. Aquinas' idea is that a form of ownership is morally justified to the extent that it provides for everyone's good. While his discussion of ownership occurs in the specific context of examining the injustice of theft, it is sufficiently general to constitute a fairly complete theory.

Aquinas borrows heavily from Aristotle both in the content and the form of ownership which is defended and in the arguments by which the defense is made. Aquinas even incorporates some of Aristotle's own illustrations. This does not mean that Aquinas merely reduplicates Aristotle; there are significant differences between them. First of all, Aquinas places greater emphasis upon the idea that the products of labor upon the land as well as other produced necessities should be made available to anyone who needs them. In Aristotle's example, a traveler who occasionally needs provisions for a journey may take what he needs from fields which do not belong to him. Aquinas, by contrast, generalizes from the example to argue that anyone ought to receive what he needs from the common pool of material goods. In cases of necessity, Aquinas says, "everything is in common."[40]

Aquinas' idea that those who are in need have a right to receive what is needed has more than just historical interest. The idea of a duty to help those who are in need has recently been called into question by philosophers such as Robert Nozick who claim that the idea is incoherent. Their main objections seem to be that anyone who has plenty would have to be judged immoral if he were not constantly helping all who are in need and that it makes no sense to conceive of duties unless there are assignable individuals to whom the duty is owed. Nor could anyone be blamed for failing to help a particular person because the so-called general duty does not specify exactly who should be helped out of all who are in need. A general duty to help those in need, they conclude, does not exist because people would have to be blamed for failing to fulfill a duty which cannot be kept. Aquinas' assertion, that in necessity everything is in common, can be interpreted in a way which avoids these objections against a duty to help others. The interpretation alters the duty to help from a general one to a specific duty to help assignable persons. Those in necessity, i.e., those who do not have the food and such needed to survive, have a right which they may invoke against specific persons who possess a surplus. Suppose each person has a right to what he needs for survival, an assumption which plausibly may be attributed to Aquinas. This right could then be invoked by someone in need against those others with plenty who the person in need believes can help. Those with plenty have a duty to help only when someone in need invokes his right to be helped. The idea of invoking one's right to be helped should not be taken too literally. In a situation where a person cannot for physical reasons invoke the right but where it is reasonable to assume he would invoke it were it physically possible, a specific duty would be created. A starving person lost in the forest, for example, who finds a house containing food would have a right against the owner of the house to enter it and consume the food he needs. The owners, because of the specifics of the circumstance, would therefore be under a duty to help. The duty would be toward the particular person who, at the moment, is in need of help.

Much more could be said about how the right to live entails a right to the necessities of life and about the circumstances in which the right can be invoked. In Chapter VI the topic shall be developed in much greater depth and detail. For now, it suffices to see how Aquinas differs from Aristotle in the strength of the duty to help others.

A second way Aquinas differs from Aristotle is that he seems to be more of an egalitarian than Aristotle. Not that Aquinas believes all people as fundamentally equal in the way a modern liberal democrat would view them, but, because he ascribes to the Christian principle, love thy neighbor as thyself, Aquinas places less emphasis upon differences between people based upon talents, skills, or learned abilities.

Aquinas' theory of ownership is based upon his belief that man has a two-fold competence with respect to material things. The first is what he calls the "title to care for and distribute the earth's resources" and the second is the "use and management" of the same.[41] The title to care for and distribute vests in individuals for Aquinas and to this extent he is much closer to Aristotle than to Plato. Aquinas' arguments by which he supports vesting the title in separate individuals rather than in a corporate communal body are virtually identical to the arguments which Aristotle uses to argue for private ownership:

> First because each person takes more trouble to care for
> something that is his sole responsibility than what is held in
> common or by many – for in such a case each individual shirks
> work and leaves the responsibility to someone else, which is
> what happens when too many officials are involved. Second,
> because human affairs are more efficiently organized if each

person has his own responsibility to discharge; there would be chaos if everybody cared for everything. Third, because men live together in greater peace where everyone is content with his task.[42]

Title over things is to be individual, not communal or social, because Aquinas thinks there would be greater efficiency and less discord if everybody cared for his own. Individual owners are vested with the right to use what they own in ways they believe are most productive and individual owners are vested with the right to make the decisions about how what they produce is to be distributed. As Aquinas reasons, there would be greater productive efficiency and less discord if everybody cared for his own.

It is a mistake, however, to describe Aquinas' form of ownership as private ownership. While individual owners exclusively have the rights of title to decide how what they own is to be used and managed, individual owners do not have unlimited rights of title to use what they own as they please or to accumulate wealth without regard for others. The second competence over material things mentioned by Aquinas drastically limits the rightful uses which may be made of what is individually owned. The "use and management" of the earth's resources must promote the common good. Individual owners are obligated to make decisions governing what they own so that everyone, non-owners included, may benefit. Thus for Aquinas, the morally justified form of ownership must be so constituted that the poor and those in need are provided for from the goods produced by individual owners. "A man's needs must therefore still be met out of the world's goods even though a certain division and apportionment of them is determined by law."[43] Those who are in need cannot legitimately be prevented from using the surplus owned by others; as Aquinas says, "in the case of necessity everything is common."[44]

Private ownership, at least under a number of its descriptions, does not grant to non-owners the right to take what they need without permission. Nor do most descriptions of private ownership include any requirement that owners use their abundance to enrich those who are poor or in need. For Aquinas, the rules of ownership obligate individual owners to manage what they own so as to meet the needs of those who are suffering from poverty. Owners do not have the right to manage what they own simply for their own benefit or advantage. Aquinas even permits a person, who himself is not in need, to take what is owned by another in order to give it to a third person who is in need.[45]

Aquinas does not discuss, nor does he seem to be aware of, the economic tension between the two competencies. His arguments in support of individual title to "care for and distribute" are based upon considerations of economic efficiency, i.e., individually controlled production and distribution are more efficient than communally directed production and distribution. The second competency, "use and management," includes the right to take what someone else owns if it is needed. This right to take what is owned by another will, however, if frequently exercised, result in productive inefficiency because producers may be unwilling to work hard if they cannot be assured of a secure outcome. Further, non-producers may find it easier to take from producers rather than trying to produce for themselves. Farmers, for example, may be unwilling to take care of their crops, or to plant at all, if others who are in need have the right to appropriate what the farmer has produced. Similar economic disincentives would occur in manufacturing if manufactured goods also could be appropriated by those in need. Thus the efficiency Aquinas believes would be generated by individual title to care for and distribute goods is reduced to the extent that the rights of the needy create disincentives to production.

Aquinas never calls the form of ownership which he defends private ownership. He speaks only of "property" and "possession" without ever using the modifier "private." This might seem surprising because Aristotle, from whom Aquinas heavily borrows, explicitly argues for private ownership. Further commentators such as Jacques Maritain see in Aquinas a justification for private ownership.[46] Nevertheless, the form of ownership which Aquinas defends could be called private only by exaggerating its similarities to and minimizing its differences from private ownership. In this context it is most useful to break the comparison down to right of title and criteria of title for each of the forms in order to see how Aquinas' form differs in particulars from private ownership.

The criteria of title for land and goods in Aquinas' form of ownership resemble private ownership because the criteria vest in individual owners the rights of use, management, care, distribution and so on. But land ownership criterion of title, for

Aquinas, vests only by inheritance.[47] Land may not be alienated by gift, bequest, or sale. The criteria of title for goods, by contrast, include gift, bequest, and exchange; further unowned found goods such as gemstones or treasure troves become owned by the finder.[48] In this way, Aquinas' criteria of title for goods resemble the criteria of title for private ownership. The difference between the two sets of criteria lies in Aquinas' principle that those in need may legitimately appropriate what they need but do not own, which creates a criterion of title that each may own what he needs.

The rights of title in Aquinas' form of ownership resemble the rights in private ownership only in some respects. While it is true that individual owners have the right to make their own decisions about how what they own is used, managed, distributed and so on without anyone else's permission as is the case in private ownership, unlike private ownership, Aquinas requires that these decisions be "in the interest of all."[49] Each individual owner may make his own decision but what he is deciding about is how best to benefit all. In this sense each individual owner is, for Aquinas, only a manager or trustee of a collection of resources which he is obligated to manage for everyone's benefit. This is quite different from private ownership in which each owner may use and manage what he owns entirely as he sees fit.

Aquinas' principle to help others is not undercut by the free market argument that individual choices in a free market economy ultimately work out to benefit everyone. Even apart from the issue of a fair or just distribution, Aquinas' form of ownership obligates each owner, himself and individually, to be directly concerned with and to contribute to the interests of all. Each owner may not rely upon indirect market methods to fulfill his obligation.

This completes the survey of the Natural Perfectionists who justify ownership by its contribution to virtue. While the three philosophers differ among themselves about which form is best, they agree about what ownership is to facilitate. The next group of philosophers, the First Appropriationists, do not share any substantive goal. They believe what justifies ownership is the manner by which land and goods come to be legitimately possessed.

CHAPTER III

The First Appropriationists

The First Appropriationists have provided the historically most influential justification of private ownership. Beginning with Locke (although he is not the originator) and passing through Rousseau and Kant, first appropriation is probably the most cited justification of private ownership. Recently, Robert Nozick has revived first appropriation as the foundation of his entitlement theory of justice. First appropriation is not only the most frequently used argument, it is the most powerful of the arguments for private ownership. In a state of nature, i.e., before positive law regulates such matters, the first appropriation of an unowned object is considered to be sufficient reason to justify the private ownership of the object by the first appropriator. In some instances what underlies first appropriation is a deontological presupposition; in other instances utilitarian considerations are invoked as support.

The central idea in first appropriation is that the object is unowned. The appropriator performs an act which constitutes his claim to the object, i.e., which functions as the criterion of title for the object. Then, according to first appropriation theory, all rights of title vest in the appropriator.

Each of the three aspects of first appropriation theory needs examination. One of the first questions which shall be raised is why appropriation vests private ownership rights of title rather than some other set of rights of title. Are there good reasons for thinking that first appropriation of what is unowned justifies private ownership and no other? The second important question concerns the conditions of the state of nature in which first appropriations are carried out. Some, but not all, first appropriation arguments limit the conditions of justified appropriation in the state of nature to those where there is enough and as good

52

remaining for others or where no one is made worse off. What implications do these state of nature conditions have for the plausibility of the argument? Some of the ways that the state of nature is conceived may make ownership of any kind unnecessary. Also, it is difficult to translate what is right in a more or less unrealistic state of nature into what is right in the actual state men must live their lives. Finally, the question arises: what is meant by 'unowned'? First appropriation arguments may all be question begging because of the sense of 'unowned' which the argument requires. It may be that first appropriation can serve as a criterion of title within a form of ownership but that it cannot serve as a reason for believing that one specific form of ownership is morally justified.

Locke, Nozick, Rousseau, and Kant are discussed as First Appropriationists. Locke will take up most of the discussion because not only is he the most influential but his discussion is the most subtle and complete. The Nozick and Kant discussions best illustrate the question begging in first appropriation arguments. Rousseau is mentioned primarily for the negative effects upon society he believes are caused by private ownership. Rousseau thus serves as a good transition to Marx. The discussion of Rousseau also serves as a good transition to the Conventionalists because for Rousseau social convention is needed to legitimate first appropriation.

The four First Appropriationists are not discussed in historical sequence. This is necessary in order to best explain the strengths of first appropriation theory as well as its severe limits.

A. Locke

John Locke's chapter in *The Second Treatise* on ownership is perhaps the most influential of all first appropriationist tracts. Locke argues that laboring in the state of nature upon some unowned object, land, resources, or goods, makes that object privately owned by the laborer if enough and as good is left for others to appropriate.[1] Locke's metaphor is that a person privately owns the unowned objects he mixes his labor with. Thus a fruit picked from a tree by Black contains some of Black's labor because climbing the tree, grasping the fruit, and returning to the ground in order to eat the fruit are all labors of Black which become somehow mixed with the fruit. If the land and tree are unowned, the fruit is privately owned by Black. Of course, if Green already owns the land and tree, then Black may be a thief.

There are several different interpretations of Locke's state of nature justification of private ownership. One is that Locke is really a utilitarian and first appropriation is justified by the good consequences of first appropriation private ownership. More good, more agricultural production, and greater incentive to hard productive work, is produced by people working upon privately owned plots. The utilitarian interpretation resembles some of Aristotle's reasons for preferring private ownership. A second interpretation of Locke's state of nature argument is that it is deontologically grounded in each person's right over his personal labor. Here the mixing metaphor is apt. The right over one's labor becomes mixed with the object by one's labor so the object then becomes one's own. Each of these interpretations will be carefully analyzed to draw out its implications and presuppositions. Neither of the interpretations of Locke's argument succeeds in the task of justifying private ownership in the state of nature. The reasons for this will be apparent as the discussion progresses.

One aspect of Locke's theory of ownership which has not received sufficient attention is the relation between the form of ownership Locke defends for the state of nature and the form he believes is justified for civil society. Locke believes that a morally justified form of ownership for civil society is a legislatively regulated variant of private ownership in the state of nature. The relationship between the two forms shall be discussed at the end of this section.

One final introductory note: no attempt will be made to try to uncover what Locke really intended or meant to say. He was not aware of the distinctions which underlie the differences between utilitarian and deontological moral theories and he was not aware of the necessary logical structure of all forms of ownership. While these ideas are useful in interpreting what Locke said and in making what he said more coherent, they cannot remove Locke's textual ambiguities. The following discussion tries to remain as true to Locke as possible; however, it is not intended to be a definitive interpretation of Locke, but to follow out the implications of his thought.

The specific form of ownership which Locke attempts to justify in the state of nature is private ownership. The criteria of title for this form are labor upon what is not already (privately) owned, gift, bequest, and exchange. The rights of title are what has come to be called the rights of innocent use. This range of rights of title is implied by Locke's statement that, "I have truly no property in that, which another can by right take from me, when he pleases without my consent," which is interpreted as meaning that owners may do whatever they wish with what they own within only those limits which are imposed by natural law.[2] A possible specification of the rights of innocent use would include at least the following: the right to possess, the right to use, the right to manage, the right to income, the right to the capital, the right to security, and the rights of alienation by gift, bequest, and exchange.[3] No other specific form of ownership has such a broad range of rights of title.

Locke's system of private ownership fulfills the requirements of the necessary logical structure of all forms of ownership. The criteria of title are consistent, the criteria taken as a whole are determinate (although the labor criterion by itself is not), and the criteria as a whole are complete (although the labor criterion is not complete by itself).

The deontological interpretation of Locke's theory of ownership for the state of nature is based upon Locke's alleged use of a deontological justification of private ownership in the state of nature. J. P. Day offers the following rendering of Locke's state of nature argument:

	(1)	Every man has a right to own his person
therefore	(2)	Every man has a right to own the labor of his person
therefore	(3)	Every man has a right to own that which he has mixed the labor of his person with.[4]

Day seems to think that the inferences between (1) and (2) and between (2) and (3) are immediate. This view cannot be correct because both inferences depend upon Locke's basic assumption that all men in the state of nature are de jure equal and free from subordination to others.[5] It is usually assumed that the word 'own' in premise (1) is used in the sense of private ownership. This sense of 'own' is consistent with Locke's assumption of de jure equality and freedom from subordination. The criterion of title is the status criterion of being oneself which everyone equally possesses and the rights of title are the rights of all innocent use. If, however, some individuals were the natural subordinates of others (perhaps some God created these natural subordinates), then either premise (1) is false because some men are privately owned by others or there is another sense of 'own' in premise (1) and the inference to premise (2) might be blocked because the rights of title over one's person for natural subordinates might not include the right to direct all of their labor. The feudal corvée system illustrates this possibility since the nobility had rights over some but not all of the subordinates' labor. Subordinates within the corvee could be said to own their own person because they had the right to direct the bulk of their own labor free from interference by the nobility. The corvée system only required a certain number of days' labor by the subordinates for the nobility. In the corvee system, it would not be true that every man had rights to all of his own labor even though it is true in some sense that each person owned his own person. Thus the inference from owning one's person to owning one's labor depends upon Locke's assumption of de jure equality and freedom from subordination to others.

The inference from premise (2), owning one's labor, to premise (3), owning what one mixes one's labor with, is also not immediate but again depends upon Locke's assumption of de jure equality and freedom from subordination. Locke's description of the state of nature in which each individual privately owns his own labor includes the hypothesis that an individual's labor of appropriation upon what is unowned does not affect anyone else because enough and as good remains for others to appropriate. In these circumstances, anyone who claims a right over what another labors to appropriate must base his claim upon some form of rightful superiority. No other basis for such a claim is even possible because the enough and as good hypothesis vitiates any justification based upon utility or need since it is a simple matter for others to appropriate what they need or want.[6] Now a natural superior, if one were to exist, might have a right to what another labors to produce even though the superior has no right to direct or control the inferior's labor. The superior might have the right occasionally to take something the subordinate produces. While such a right might indirectly control the subordinate's labor because he might refrain from producing what the superiors want to take from him, this indirect control differs from ownership of the subordinate's labor. Thus to argue that another might own what one labors to produce, assuming private ownership of one's labor, is equivalent to denying that all men are de jure equal and free from subordination to others. The inference from owning one's labor to owning what one mixes one's labor with therefore is not immediate but depends upon Locke's general assumption.

Private ownership of what one labors to produce or what one mixes one's labor with is therefore a possible conclusion of Locke's deontological argument. But private ownership is not the only form of ownership which the deontological argument justifies. Even when Locke's general assumption that all men in the state of nature are de jure equal and free from subordination is explicitly included, it is nevertheless possible that at least one other specific form of ownership is implied by the deontological justification. This other specific form of ownership can be called, for convenience, private usufruct ownership. It can be shown that private usufruct ownership is consistent with the equality and freedom assumption and that it is consistent with the conclusion of the deontological justification and thus private ownership is not the only form which Locke's argument justifies.

For simplicity, private usufruct ownership of land will be considered. While other ownables might also fall under private usufruct, assuming the conditions of Locke's deontological justification, the content of the ownership relation for these ownables is too complex to be easily discussed here. Besides, in order to show that other forms of ownership are consistent with Locke's deontological justification, it is sufficient to argue the case for private usufruct of land. Even if all other kinds of ownables were privately owned, the specific form of ownership whose content included private usufruct of land would differ from a specific form in which all ownables were privately owned. The argument for the private usufruct of land does not depend, as do many arguments against Locke's private ownership of land, upon the idea that land exists independently of labor and is not produced by labor. While the idea has merit and causes some problems for Locke's theory, it is not the line of criticism used to support the private usufruct form.

Consider a private usufruct ownership of land in which laboring upon the land is a criterion of title for land which is not presently owned. The rights of title over the land in this specific form include the rights to use and manage the land, the right to income from the land and its products, the right to possess the land and rights against trespass by others. But this specific form of ownership does not include within the range of rights of title the rights to alienate the land by gift, bequest, or exchange, although the land may simply be abandoned. A person who clears the land and uses it for farming, cattle raising, a home, etc., would have title to that land for as long as he continued to use it. If, however, his use of the land discontinued for some period of time, the land would revert to its unowned, common state. Only those who are laboring upon or using the land may claim title to it for the period of their use.

Private usufruct differs from the private form of ownership in that its more restricted range of rights of title and that only labor and not gift, bequest, or exchange is a criterion of title over land. Individuals only temporarily have rights over the land a id when the land is no longer used; it then becomes available for others to appropriate. There may be difficulties in determining what constitutes land use, e.g., a field which is left fallow in order to increase its fertility, but the difficulties are no worse than those which plague Locke's own theory. The private usufruct form of ownership causes no greater inconveniences in the state of nature where enough and as good remains for others than the inconveniences in the state of nature surrounding private ownership.

Private usufruct ownership is consistent with the conclusion of Locke's deontological argument and it is consistent with Locke's assumption of de jure equality and freedom from subordination to others. Those who work upon unowned land or mix their labor with unowned land come to own the land. They have a range of rights over the land which they may exercise because the private usufruct form of ownership uses labor upon what is unowned as a criterion of title. De jure equality and freedom from subordination are also respected. Individuals who own land in the private usufruct form of ownership are not less equal nor more subordinate to others than private owners would be. So long as no individual has more extensive rights over land than any other individual, the private usufruct form is consistent with Locke's assumption. No one would have the right to alienate land by gift, bequest, or exchange. Clearly the deontological interpretation of Locke's justification not only justifies private ownership but at least one other different form of ownership.

Locke probably did not perceive this implication. But Locke's thinking is not the relevant issue here. What is important to understand is that privately owning one's labor does not imply that private ownership of other ownables is the only morally justifiable form of ownership. Private usufruct ownership is also consistent with ownership of one's labor. The only difference between these two forms of ownership is that private usufruct does not include the right to alienate the land by gift or exchange or the right to control by bequest who may use the land once the original appropriator is no longer using it. It is not at all obvious why owning one's labor should create rights which endure after land use has ceased. Private usufruct ownership might not stimulate the accumulation of large quantities of land by single individuals or by families as would bequeathable private ownership, but then ownership should not be based upon what has been called "the divine right of grab."[7]

That the deontological interpretation of the Lockean justification of private ownership is also compatible with private usufruct ownership suggests there may be additional forms of ownership which are compatible with the idea that each man owns his own labor and are compatible with the assumption of de jure equality and freedom from subordination. Such forms might differ from private ownership in criteria of title or rights of title and in the domains of ownables to which they apply. Subsequent arguments shall show both that such forms of ownership are possible and that they are morally justifiable.

One more aspect of the deontological interpretation needs to be discussed before moving on to the utilitarian interpretation of Locke's state of nature argument. The hypothesis that enough and as good remains for others is absolutely essential to the deontological argument. The inferences in the argument about owning what is mixed with one's labor are plausible only given Locke's assumption that individuals in the state of nature are de jure equal and free from subordination to others. But if land appropriation does not leave enough and as good for others to appropriate, then it is possible that earlier appropriators will leave later ones without any land at all to appropriate. It is difficult to conceive how private ownership could create a completely landless class and still maintain over time de jure equality and non-subordination. Only by the hypothesis that sufficient unowned land exists is it therefore possible for individual appropriations not to upset Locke's assumption.

The utilitarian interpretation of Locke's state of nature justification of private ownership is usually based upon the passage which says:

> God, who hath given the world to all men in common, hath also given them reason to make use of it to the best advantage of life and convenience . . ., yet being given for the use of man, there must of necessity be a means to appropriate them in some way or other before they can be of any use, or at all beneficial, to any particular man.[8]

This passage can be interpreted to mean that ownership rules are needed for the useful or beneficial appropriation of ownables. It is only a short additional step to the idea that the form of ownership itself ought to be most useful or most beneficial. Locke, in fact, repeatedly argues that great value is produced by labor upon privately owned lands.[9]

If Locke's justification is utilitarian, then a specific form of ownership is morally justified if and only if the consequences of adopting and operating it are better than the consequences of adopting and operating any other specific form. However, no utilitarian justification can be unconditional or abstract. It cannot be abstract because there is little reason to believe that one specific form of ownership will maximize valuable consequences in all circumstances. Equal ownership of wealth, for example, would have consequences in a society lacking capital intensive industry different from its consequences in a society already heavily capitalized. A utilitarian justification cannot be unconditional because as circumstances change so may the value of the consequences produced by a specific form of ownership. A utilitarian justification, therefore, must either stipulate some set of conditions in which the form of ownership is to apply, or it must empirically examine conditions as they presently exist and as they are likely to exist in the future.

Locke's description of the state of nature can be understood as stipulating a set of initial conditions in which private ownership is to operate. Once these conditions have been specified it is then possible to predict what the likely consequences are of adopting and operating the private ownership form. The salient features of the state of nature as Locke describes it are: first, that all men are de jure equal and free from subordination to others; second, that individual acts of appropriation leave enough and as good for others to appropriate; and third, that men by and large are capable of following the same natural law. The second and third features avoid the Hobbesian war of every man against every man. The first feature guarantees that no one may claim all ownables as his by right. The second feature, additionally, although Locke most likely did not have it in mind, eliminates the necessity of making interpersonal comparisons of utility since one individual's appropriation and the utility he derives from it does not affect what another individual may appropriate and the utility he derives.

Private ownership can be proven morally justified for the state of nature if the private ownership form produces greater utility than any other possible form. The utilitarian justification will, first of all, require an examination of the consequences produced by the private ownership criteria of title and rights of title in Locke's state of nature conditions. Second, these consequences must be compared to other forms to see if greater value is produced. The labor criterion of title contributes to high levels of utility and satisfaction in the state of nature. That a person can acquire rights over the unowned things he labors upon or mixes his labor with can augment the utility of the person who appropriates by his labor. If the laborer accurately estimates the value to him of what he is laboring upon and he accurately calculates whatever disutility may be involved in his laboring as well as his chances of failure or success, then it is reasonable to assume that the laborer's utility will increase if he successfully completes the task he freely sets for himself in appropriating some object. For example, it is reasonable to assume that a person who freely chooses to clear a field, plant crops, and successfully harvests the crops will judge himself better off, even considering the toils of labor, than he would have been otherwise. Not only does the labor criterion increase the utility of the laborer appropriator, it does not result in any disutility for others. No one suffers by a laborer appropriating what he labors upon, because, by assumption, in the state of nature there is enough and as good remaining for others to appropriate. The appropriation by one individual does not affect the ability of others to make a similar appropriation. The labor criterion of title thus fulfills the requirements of a Pareto improvement condition. Some individual benefits and no one else suffers from the laborer's appropriation of land and other possible ownables.[10]

The gift, bequest, and exchange criteria of title must now be considered. If a person is given something or receives it as a bequest, it is reasonable to expect that his utility will be increased. Of course, some gifts or bequests may lower the recipient's utility, e.g., a debt ridden business. Also other persons may suffer a loss of utility because of their disappointment over not receiving a certain gift or bequest. But where enough and as good remains to be appropriated by anyone who cares to, these two sources of disutility may be negligible. Exchange, where freely entered into by two or more participants who each have access to goods through their own labor, is sufficient evidence that the free participants view themselves as benefiting. Again, any non-participants should not suffer loss of utility where enough and as good remains for them.

The private ownership rights of title also produce high levels of utility in the state of nature. Since the only limits upon the rights of title in the state of nature are a non-injury restriction and the limits of natural law, there is no morally permissible way that owners could have greater freedom to do what they wish with what they own. The non-injury restriction comes from what can be called Locke's principle of measure. Alan Ryan calls Locke's principle "the spoilation limitation."[11] What Locke says at one point is that no one ought to appropriate more than he can make use of before it spoils.[12] But it is difficult to understand what is impermissible about spoilage if there remains still enough and as good for others to appropriate. Where unowned land and goods are not abundant, spoilage or waste could very well injure others who may thereby be deprived of what they need. Locke later does substitute not injuring others as his explicit measure of what may be appropriated.[13] This latter measure seems more general in that it applies to both the superabundant state of nature as well as to the less abundant but more realistic conditions in which men find themselves. Within the area of action delimited by the non-injury condition and by the natural law, it is difficult to see how what an owner does with what he owns can diminish the utility of others. Just as long as enough and as good remains for others to appropriate, all other persons retain an undiminished capacity to appropriate what they please and augment their own utility.

Private ownership of all categories of ownables produces a high level of utility in the state of nature conditions which Locke envisions. But in order to prove that private ownership in these circumstances is morally justifiable it must be shown that no other specific form of ownership produces greater utility. The private usufruct form of ownership discussed in connection with the deontological interpretation may not produce as high a level of utility in the state of nature as does the private ownership form. Since the two forms differ only in the criteria of title and the rights of title over land, only the levels of utility for land ownership need be considered. Since both forms of ownership permit appropriation of land by a labor criterion of title and both forms permit the owner to keep whatever is produced by the land, the utility for owners ought to be similar in each form. The difference between the two forms lies only in the absence of rights to alienate the land by gift, bequest, or exchange in the private usufruct form. Lower utility levels might be produced if land owners desire to give or bequeath their land to someone and are prevented from doing so by the rules of the private usufruct form. How much lower the utility is depends upon how strong the desire is to bequeath or give the land to others and the amount of dissatisfaction which results if the desire is unfulfilled. Absence of a right to exchange land for money or other ownables is also a source of lower utility because free exchange raises the utility of the participants, at least from their subjective perspective, and land owners in the private usufruct form would not be able to avail themselves of this source of utility. A lower level of utility might also occur because land owners might have less incentive to improve the land or maintain its fertility because the land has value to them only over their life span. This loss of utility would be significant in actual circumstances where land is not superabundant; but in Locke's state of nature where enough and as good other lands exist, the commercial value of land will be low as will be the demand for maintaining fertility. Thus in these circumstances this source of disutility will be small.

That private ownership produces a higher level of utility than the private usufruct form shows that private ownership is preferable but not that it is morally justified in the state of nature. It still must be shown that no other possible specific form produces greater utility. Various forms of socialist ownership of land and resources might produce high levels of utility, but they cannot be considered at this point because no government or political authority exists in the state of nature. It is unnecessary, however, to try to imagine what the utility is of all other possible specific forms in the state of nature. There is only one imaginable form of

ownership which might seriously challenge Locke's private ownership. The state of nature superabundance of unowned land and
resources implies that the only limit upon utility is one's physical
ability to labor. A specific form of ownership based upon a
criterion of title which avoids the limit placed by the physical
capacity to labor might produce greater utility. The only imaginable criterion is a criterion of title that a person owns those
unowned things he wants. But an examination of the want
criterion of title shows that it fails to meet the necessary logical
requirements of determinacy and consistency.

The want criterion of title fails to meet the consistency requirement because individuals can both own and not own a thing at
the same time and in the same way. The criterion is inconsistent
because if Gray wants X then Gray owns X, but if Black wants
X then Black also owns X. X will be owned wholly by both Gray
and Black, or, which is the same thing, Gray will own X because
he wants it and Gray will not own X because X is wanted and
hence owned by Black. The want criterion of title is also indeterminate. This is because wanting something is intensional or occurs
under a particular description so it may be impossible in principle
to determine who owns what or what collection of things a person
owns.

No possible specific form of ownership produces greater utility
in the state of nature as defined by Locke than does private
ownership. The only other competition, based upon the want
criterion of title, even though it avoids the disutility of labor,
cannot meet the necessary logical requirements of ownership.

There is, however, a serious problem with the utilitarian
interpretation of Locke's state of nature justification of private
ownership. Locke, unlike Hobbes whose description of the state
of nature does not include any unrealistic assumption about abundance, abstracts away scarcity of land and resources. If Locke's
hypothesis is interpreted to mean that no scarcity literally exists
for land and resources, including food and raw materials, it is
difficult to imagine what ownership rules at all would be required
in such circumstances. Assuming that there is no scarcity whatsoever in land and resources, appropriation would demand virtually
no effort because the amount of effort required to appropriate
something seems to be conceptually tied to how abundant it is.
What makes something scarce is the effort required to locate it
or the effort required to appropriate it once located. Consider the

effort required to locate. Some streams and rivers contain gold-bearing gravel. Working away the lighter stones is all that is required once the stream or river is found. But because there are so few of these streams, and so few sections of these streams, a great deal of effort is required in order to locate them. This is why gold is said to be scarce. In much the same way the abundant unowned land in America which Locke himself mentions can illustrate the point. For those living in England the trip to America and the travel beyond the already settled eastern coast to appropriate unowned land would be expensive, difficult, and time consuming. Thus because of the effort in locating the unowned American land, in England, unowned American land would be scarce.

Even if the effort required to locate something is small, if a great deal of effort is required to appropriate it, once found the thing is also scarce. There may be many trout in a stream and they may be easy to find. But on a day when the trout are not biting and they are difficult to catch, caught trout are scarce. Even in Locke's America where unowned land is abundant, land suitable for farming would be considered scarce if a great deal of effort were required to clear the land and prepare it for cultivation. Farmable land to that extent would be scarce even if unowned land were not.

There would be little reason to claim rights over things which excludes others' use of them if there were literally no scarcity of land, resources, food and so on, and if appropriation were literally effortless. One of Locke's own examples can again serve as an illustration. Locke asks if the water drawn from a river does not belong to whomever draws it, to be used for his own purposes, assuming enough water and as good remains. Drawing water from a river may involve considerable effort if some distance must be traveled in order to reach it. This effort might justify a person's rights over the drawn water. However, if no effort at all is required to draw the water (perhaps drawing water required less effort than breathing), it is difficult to understand why ownership rules would be adopted creating rights over the water. There could be no reason to deny to others what one has effortlessly appropriated and could continue to effortlessly appropriate. Nor would there be any reason for others to demand what they could effortlessly appropriate; but if they did ask, what possible reason could there be for refusing. Things which are literally not at all scarce, i.e., things which require no effort to locate or to appropriate, need not be the object of any ownership relations.

Locke's actual description of the state of nature does not seem to imply the absence of all scarcity. He assumes that labor, i.e., effort, is required to appropriate possible ownables. But, in order for either the utilitarian or the deontological interpretation of Locke's state of nature justification of private ownership to be plausible, there must be at least sufficient abundance so that one's acts of appropriation do not affect the utility levels of others or create inequality and subordination.

It might be possible to conceptually distinguish between the two levels of abundance. The first level would be that of extreme abundance where no effort at all is required for appropriation. The second level of abundance would be the one which Locke might have in mind, where effort is required to appropriate land, resources, and so on but where others are not affected at all by individual acts of appropriation. To distinguish between the two levels, in practice, is far more difficult. Practical concerns force a collapse of the second level into the first. This can best be seen by considering the appropriation of land. Once some land becomes privately owned, others may have to travel farther and expend more effort in order to appropriate unowned land. The utility levels of the later appropriators are therefore affected because they must incur greater costs in order to appropriate. The enough and as good hypothesis is therefore not satisfied because later appropriators find land appropriation more costly. In order to maintain the enough and as good hypothesis which is necessary to both deontological and utilitarian interpretations, Locke would be forced to adopt the first level of abundance in which no effort is required for any appropriation. But in the first level of abundance ownership rules seem to make little sense at all.

The analysis of Locke's state of nature justification of private ownership has yielded two very important results. The deontological interpretation of Locke's argument fails to produce a conclusive justification for private ownership. Locke's premiss that each individual has rights over his person and thus rights over his labor does not imply that private ownership is the only morally permissible form of ownership in the state of nature. Private usufruct is also implied by the deontological argument and its presuppositions. Gift, bequest, and exchange are not essential rights of title for land in the state of nature. That a private usufruct form of ownership is also morally permissible in the state of nature undercuts the criticism that Locke's arguments lay the foundation for possessive individualism, great concentrations of wealth, and indefeasible permanent rights to land and resources.[14] Whatever Locke might have intended, the deontological interpretation of his argument admits the possibility of several morally justifiable forms of ownership in the state of nature. The second important result is that the utilitarian interpretation of Locke's argument may not be conclusive either. While there is some reason to believe that the more inclusive range of rights of title in private ownership produces higher levels of utility than the more restricted range in private usufruct, confusion over what Locke could mean by abundance, i.e., enough and as good, raises doubts about why private ownership or any form of ownership would be adopted in the state of nature.

Even if these difficulties in understanding just what sort of abundance and absence of scarcity exist in the state of nature could be overcome, it is plain that the conditions Locke envisions for civil society are manifestly different from those of the state of nature. The question naturally arises, can private ownership in the state of nature be a benchmark or model for civil society where there is certainly no abundance of unowned land, resources, food, and so on? There is no reason to assume that ownership rules for civil society ought to approximate as closely as possible those for the state of nature. The presence of scarcity might require major changes in the range of rights of title or the criteria of title, e.g., by taxing bequests. Scarcity might require a form of ownership which is radically different, a form, for example, in which all land is socially owned. There is nothing in the state of nature argument which would imply that the closer the approximation is to private ownership in civil society the more morally justified it will be. The real function of the state of nature may be one of contrast rather than one of comparison.

Locke believes it is the responsibility of the legislature to make laws regulating ownership in civil society where the conditions of the state of nature are not fulfilled.[15] The legislature decides what form of law to create guided by the consent of the people and by what is for the common good. There are several difficulties in Locke's discussion of legislatively regulated ownership in civil society. First of all, he does not seem to take very seriously the possible conflict between what the citizens want and what is for the common good.[16] Second, Locke says almost nothing about the kind of alternatives to private ownership which would be required in order to adjust to the conditions of civil society. Locke's silence on this may be perhaps understandable because of the difficulty in predicting what legislation citizens would consent to and in predicting what conditions of relative scarcity or relative abundance are for the civil society. The idea that "life, liberty, and estate" ought to be protected is not specific enough to exclude a variety of ownership forms, e.g., it might be plausibly argued that some forms of socialism protect everyone's life, liberty, and estate where estate is appropriately defined.[17]

The laws which the legislature makes to regulate ownership would define the subject, object and the content of the ownership relation. Legislative regulation of the criteria of title might, for example, require that certain types of exchanges are carried out by written agreement rather than by oral agreement or regulation might require three witnesses to a will. These regulations would be a legislative response to one of the "inconveniences" of the state of nature, namely, the absence of a known and settled law.[18] Other legislative regulation might be a response to the conditions of scarcity extant in civil society. The legislature might restrict the range of rights of title by excluding perpetuities in order to increase the commercial viability of land by making it freely exchangeable.

That the legislature ought to be guided in regulating ownership by both consent and the common good precisely mirrors the twin deontological and utilitarian elements in Locke's justification of private ownership in the state of nature. The idea that the legislature is guided by consent follows from the deontological right of de jure equality and freedom from subordination. This right requires that political processes weigh everyone's preferences equally. The utilitarian interpretation of the state of nature justification easily translates into the common good. Thus the laws regulating ownership which the legislature ought to adopt admit of the same interpretations as Locke's state of nature arguments. If the deontological right to de jure equality and freedom from subordination were emphasized, the legislature might enact laws which limited the accumulation of wealth or which prohibited bequest or inheritance of land. If the utilitarian interpretation were emphasized, laws might be enacted which promoted large public corporations which compete with one another for consumers' purchases.

Locke may have intended to justify private ownership for both the state of nature and civil society even though his actual arguments fail to do so. What Locke did not see, and could not have seen, was the development of industrialized capitalism founded upon private ownership of land, resources, and the means of production in which great wealth and great poverty were simultaneously produced. It is as unfair to blame Locke for the evils of nineteenth century capitalism as it is unfair to blame Aristotle for the dark ages. Whatever Locke may have intended, his arguments cannot justify the excesses of capitalism. His arguments concerning ownership in the state of nature fail to prove that private ownership alone is justifiable. And, there is little reason to believe private ownership is always justifiable in civil society. The legislature in making laws for civil society must respect the consent of the people and the common good. It is perfectly conceivable that the legislature guided by consent and the common good could adopt a form of ownership radically different from private ownership. There is nothing in Locke's arguments which would exclude a form of democratic socialism which both promotes the common good and respects the right to de jure equality and freedom from subordination.[19]

B.   Kant and Rousseau

Kant and Rousseau are the next of the First Appropriationists who shall be discussed. Kant is important because he, of all the First Appropriationists, is aware that private ownership must be logically presupposed if first appropriation is to confer private ownership upon those who appropriate. Unfortunately, many of Kant's other contributions to first appropriation theory are either unoriginal or misleading. Rousseau is important here because he focuses upon some of the more adverse consequences of private ownership and upon how first appropriation is supplemented by social contract. Rousseau is thus in a transitional position to the ideas discussed in the next two chapters.

Kant shall be discussed before Rousseau even though Rousseau historically precedes Kant. This makes the continuity of thought easier to follow. The discussion will concentrate almost exclusively upon land ownership because their ideas about this topic are more fully developed and more influential.

Kant considers his primary enterprise in the Private Law section of *The Metaphysics of Justice* to be that of explaining how sensible internal possession becomes intelligible external possession, i.e., how actual possession and control of an object becomes authority over or rightful control of the thing. The essence of ownership for Kant is the right to something one owns even though the object is not, at the moment, in physical possession of the owner. Owners have rights over what they own which they may exercise even if what is owned is not within their immediate physical control, e.g., rights one has over a book which is lent to and thus in the possession of a friend. How such rights are possible, for Kant, is equivalent to the justification of private ownership which is grounded in first appropriation. And first appropriation grounds private ownership because of the presupposition which Kant calls "The Juridical Postulate of Practical Reason."

How Kant's Juridical Postulate of Practical Reason functions in the justification of private ownership can best be examined if the details of first appropriation are explained. By first explaining the details, the logical gap which the Postulate must bridge can be most dramatically laid bare.

Kant describes first appropriation in the following passage:

> In this way, taking possession of a secluded piece of land is an act of private will without being an arbitrary usurpation. The possessor bases his act on [the concept of] innate common possession of the earth's surface and on the a priori general will corresponding to it, which permits private possession of land (since otherwise unoccupied things [e.g., land] would in themselves and in accordance with a law become ownerless things). Thus the possessor originally acquires a piece of land through first appropriation and withstands by right anyone else who might interfere with his private use of it.[20]

Following the tradition of Locke, Kant views first appropriation as occurring in a state of nature before civil government. Kant also explicitly says that first appropriation establishes a natural right with which no government may interfere. According to Kant, men need private ownership, especially of land, for otherwise they would have no reason to quit the state of nature. Kant is much more narrow on this point than is Locke. The three inconveniences which Locke mentions as reasons for quitting the state of nature, while they may have to do with ownership in a broad sense, do not depend for their force upon each person in the state of nature privately owning land or other goods. Kant is also more narrow on the role of civil government. While Locke permits civil government to regulate the form of ownership to promote the common good, for Kant the only change that civil government may make in private ownership is to impose a law prohibiting bequests of land to succeeding generations for all time. Even so, Kant requires compensation to be paid to owners from whom this right is taken.[21]

The novel aspect of Kant's characterization of first appropriation is that it is based upon "an act of private will" rather than upon labor or some other act. Kant does not argue that laboring upon or adding value to what is appropriated is what legitimates first appropriation. Kant's "acts of private will" require neither laboring upon nor adding value. All that is required for appropriation is a declared intention to appropriate. "When I declare (by word or deed), 'I will that an external thing be mine,' I thereby declare it obligatory for everyone else to refrain from [using] the object of my will."[22] Laboring upon land can, of course, serve as a deed which expresses or declares an intention to appropriate; but for Kant, clearly, it is the intention to appropriate which is primary and for which labor is only one of a variety of different ways of declaring.

Kant's act of private will seems to be compatible with, e.g., Balboa's claiming the whole Pacific Ocean to be privately owned by Spain simply by declaring it to belong to the king. It is not even obvious that one would have to do what Balboa did, namely to actually set foot upon or place his staff in the ocean, in order to claim it. There does not appear to be anything in Kant's formula to preclude someone from declaring the planet Uranus to be his own. Unlike Locke's criterion of title in which the ability to labor is a limiting condition on how much may be appropriated, Kant's criterion contains no such limitation.

Labor as a criterion of title would avoid several other difficulties which plague Kant's idea of an act of private will as the basis of first appropriation. Labor upon a plot of land is one possible way of interpreting physical possession of the land at least to the extent that the metaphor of mixing labor with the land makes sense. But, how is it possible to understand the idea of possession if it is based solely on declaration by word or deed? Is there any change in the thing which is claimed or any other mark that would demonstrate possession? It is not even clear that an appropriator need be in proximity to what he is declaring to be his. There is far too much indeterminacy in acts of will as a criterion of title. Further, because possible appropriators need not be in proximity of what they claim and because there need be no physical contact with what is claimed, acts of will can be inconsistent as a criterion of title. Two appropriators could claim the same object, perhaps under different descriptions of the object, and both have title over the object to the exclusion of the other. Thus, Kant's criterion of title for first appropriation fails to satisfy the requirements of the necessary logical structure. While the indeterminacy might in theory at least be corrected, the possible inconsistencies cannot be removed. Kant's criterion cannot function as part of a coherent theory of ownership.

Kant's discussion of first appropriation also makes no provision that enough and as good remain for subsequent appropriation. Kant does say each appropriator makes ". . . an acknowledgment of being reciprocally bound to everyone else to [exercise] a similar and equal restraint with respect to what is theirs."[23] But the context seems to imply that Kant is concerned with respecting others' rights over what they already have appropriated and he is not here discussing what is to remain for others to use. It is surprising that he makes no such provision since equal freedom, which is contained in the Juridical Postulate of Practical Reason, ultimately grounds and legitimates ownership for Kant. How can a person be free if all available land has already been appropriated? There is no limit on appropriation in Kant's theory which precludes the possibility that one or a small number of individuals appropriate everything which might be owned. This is a real possibility because, as noticed earlier, appropriation for Kant is almost effortless since only a declaration is required. There is no reason to believe that Kant thought his readers would simply assume he makes the same provision as Locke did. Nor is there any evidence in *The Metaphysics of Justice* that Kant realized there is a problem about how much a person may legitimately appropriate.

It is now time to examine in detail the function of the Juridical Postulate of Practical Reason in Kant's justification of private ownership. The problem Kant faces is how to infer that someone privately owns something from the act of private will declaring the thing to be owned. Kant must be able to justify the inference from Green declaring he owns Blackacre to the conclusion that

Green privately owns Blackacre. Ignoring for the moment the previously discussed difficulties with declaring as a criterion of title, there is still the logical gap between "Green declares this to be his," and "Green privately owns this." This gap actually has two chasms to be bridged. The first is the one from "Green declares this to be his," to "Green owns this," where the form of ownership is left unspecified. The second one is from "Green owns this," in some sense of ownership, to "Green privately owns this." It is essential to remember that there are many possible forms of ownership, so that "Green owns this" cannot be automatically construed as meaning Green privately owns the thing in question.

How can "Green owns Blackacre" be inferred from Green declaring he owns Blackacre? First of all, as Kant realizes, if Green is to appropriate Blackacre, no one may have any prior claims to Blackacre. There is, of course, a degree of ambiguity here. That no one has any claims to Blackacre may mean that within a system of private ownership no one has, as a matter of fact, any private ownership rights over Blackacre. That no one has any claim may also mean that there is no private ownership in place and thus no one has any prior claims. There is a third possible interpretation in which Blackacre is owned in common and everyone may use Blackacre so that no one has any special claims. Kant seems to favor the last interpretation when he speaks of "innate common possession of the earth's surface."[24]

Kant's Juridical Postulate of Practical Reason asserts, ". . . it is possible to have any and every object of my will as my property. In other words, a maxim according to which, if it were made into a law, an object of the will would have to be itself (objectively) ownerless . . . conflicts with Law and Justice."[25] Kant calls this a postulate because it cannot be demonstrated on theoretical grounds:

> It confers upon us an authorization that we cannot derive from mere concepts of justice in general, namely, the authorization to impose an obligation upon all others – an obligation that they otherwise would not have had – to refrain from using certain objects of our will because we were the first to take possession of them. Reason requires that this postulate be taken as a basic principle, and it does this as practical reason extending itself a priori by means of this postulate.[26]

The function of the Postulate is to rationally ground private ownership through first appropriation. This is clear in the passage where Kant argues for private ownership from first appropriation:

> In relation to all others, this possession is (as far as one knows) a first possession and as such is consistent with the law of external freedom and is, at the same time, implied in the original community of possession, which in turn, implies the a priori ground of the possibility of private possession.[27]

The Postulate is to be presupposed in order to justify private ownership. Only by assuming that an object of one's will can become privately owned is it possible to justify taking from the common stock for permanent private use. Without the assumption contained in the Postulate there would be no reason, for Kant, why first possession of what is in common would create permanent rights to exclude others rather than simply continuing a common use and availability. Without the Postulate, first appropriation might only imply temporary use of what is appropriated, e.g., Green might only have rights over Blackacre while he is using it.

In any case, Kant correctly sees that first appropriation can legitimate rights over what is appropriated only if it is already postulated that first appropriation creates rights. While Kant's criterion of title for first appropriation is an act of private will, it is possible to reformulate Kant's Postulate in order to have it reflect Locke's criterion of title for first appropriation. The Postulate would then read: It is possible to have any and every object of my labor as my private property. Clearly Locke's argument from first appropriation requires the postulate just as much as does Kant's. Kant's recognition of the need for the Postulate in order for first appropriation to legitimate private ownership reinforces the criticism to be made against Nozick, and now by implication against Locke, that their arguments justifying private ownership are question begging. First appropriation, by itself, is insufficient to justify private ownership or, for that matter, any other form of ownership. First appropriation must be supplemented by additional rational considerations if any inference is to be made about what form of ownership is morally justified.

While Kant does not provide a theoretical demonstration of the Postulate, he does argue its reasonableness in terms of the freedom. First of all, an absolute prohibition against using unowned objects would be a "contradiction of external freedom with itself."[28] Second, using what another owns without his permission is also a limitation on his freedom. Private ownership does provide great freedom for owners over what they own. But Kant, like most other defenders of private ownership, ignores the lack of freedom for non-owners. In the case of land and resources which exist independently of labor and are in finite supply, appropriation by one individual or a few can greatly limit the freedom of non-owners especially if there is no unowned land to use. This point has been made before and shall be more fully developed in Chapter VII, so it needs no further development here. Still Kant's theory of first appropriation, because it is not limited by any provision that enough and as good remain for others, most starkly illustrates the loss of freedom which non-owners suffer.

Jean Jacques Rousseau, in contrast to Kant, is acutely aware of how non-owners fare under private ownership. While Rousseau believes that first appropriation, what he calls first occupancy, grounds ownership through rights created through the social compact, he does not believe that everyone's well-being or that everyone's freedom is promoted by private ownership. Non-owners, as well as the other poor, may be virtually enslaved by an ownership form which permits great accumulation of wealth.

That there are those who own nothing or little, especially land, is part of the very nature of ownership for Rousseau; it is not an accidental by-product. The quotation which serves as the front-piece to this book illustrates the point: "Every man has naturally a right to everything he needs; but the positive act which makes him proprietor of one thing excludes him from everything else."[29] Rousseau seems to be referring here to the transition from a stage of human society in which all was owned in common to a later stage, brought about by the social compact, in which individuals have rights over things that exclude others. White becomes proprietor of Greenacre when the social compact turns his possession into ownership. But, of course, what happens for White happens for others. They get rights over what they possess which exclude White. The rights which one gains over what he possesses he loses over what all others possess because they gain the right to exclude him. Individuals who possess little or nothing may lose a great deal or everything.

Rousseau's idea that every man has a right to everything he needs is much the same as Aquinas' idea that in necessity everything is in common.[30] It is not clear how this right to what is needed functions in civil society. Rousseau does not argue that the rich have a duty to help the poor. The right is therefore best understood as describing a goal for society, i.e., a society in which everyone has what he needs. This shall be made clear shortly. Rousseau's ideal society, were it possible, is a small democracy in which everyone knows everyone else, in which there is no very rich nor very poor, and thus there is little conflict and rivalry.[31]

Ownership, for Rousseau, is grounded in first possession. The process of first possession or first occupancy is described in the *Social Contract*:

> In general, to establish right of first occupier over a plot of ground, the following conditions are necessary: first, the land must not be inhabited; second, a man must occupy only the amount he needs for his subsistence; and in the third place, possession must be taken, not by an empty ceremony, but by labor and cultivation, the only sign of proprietorship that should be respected by others in default of a legal title.[32]

The "right of first occupier" is not for Rousseau a full moral right in the state of nature. In *The Social Contract*, he argues that morality and indeed rationality arise only with the compact to enter civil society.[33] But were morality and rationality both absent it is difficult to say what the right of first occupier could possibly entail. Again in *The Social Contract*, Rousseau compares the right of first occupier to the right of the strongest, saying that the right of the first occupier is more of a right, but he has also just argued that the right of the strongest is not a right at all because it is self-contradictory.[34] In his *Discourse on the Origin of Inequality*, Rousseau views rationality and morality as possibly existing in extended families of "savages."[35] In these circumstances the right of first occupier could readily be construed as a moral, but not yet legal or civil, right. The different conceptions of morality in the state of nature before the social compact may only be apparent, resulting from the different purposes of each work, the *Discourse* being more of a historical than a moral, logical examination. Thus whatever the precise interpretation is put on the right of first occupier in the state of nature, full moral rights of ownership arise, according to Rousseau, only in a civil society founded by compact.

Rousseau's thinking on this point places him both with Locke,

Nozick, and Kant who believe that ownership rights exist in the state of nature and with Hobbes and Hume who believe ownership arises only with social convention. Rousseau's thought thus places him as a transition to both the Conventionalists and to those who argue against private ownership.

The second clause in Rousseau's description of first occupancy, that one may only appropriate an amount needed for subsistence, reflects a strong anti-wealth posture which he shares with the Natural Perfectionists. Rousseau would limit riches so that "no one shall ever be wealthy enough to buy another, and none poor enough to be forced to sell himself," although he realizes that in fact the limitation is unlikely to obtain.[36] Rousseau shares, throughout his writing, Aristotle's ideal of virtue as moderation. There is also an echo of Locke who limits how much a person may appropriate to what the appropriator may use without injuring others.

The third clause, that appropriation be based upon labor and cultivation, functions both as a criterion of title for land and also as a supplementary principle of measure. As a criterion of title, labor and cultivation avoids Kant's difficulty over inconsistency if it is assumed that no one would begin to labor upon or cultivate a field which someone else has already begun to work. Rousseau does face the problem of determinacy which confronts any labor criterion of title. Not only is there the problem of what constitutes labor and cultivation, e.g., a field left fallow to improve its fertility, but there is also indeterminacy if several people co-operate to labor upon or cultivate a field.[37] Labor and cultivation can also function in Rousseau's theory as a principle of measure to limit how much someone may appropriate. To labor to appropriate more than one can use is irrational. Labor consumes both time and energy. If labor is spent upon appropriating more than can be used by the appropriator (including using what is appropriated as a gift or for exchange) it is wasted labor. Such labor consumes a costly outlay without any additional return. To that extent, the additional labor is irrational.

For Rousseau, moral rights and ownership are only fully established in a civil society founded by the social compact. The compact requires each person to give up all of his rights to what others possess if they reciprocally give up all of their rights to what he possesses.[38] Thus the social compact legitimates first occupancy because each possessor retains what he possesses now with the addition of compact and law. Whatever rights first occupancy may have given in the state of nature, whatever their moral force, the social compact agreements give those rights full moral and legal status. Still, for Rousseau, the rights established by the compact from first occupancy are not absolute and do not place non-defeasible limits upon society's regulation of ownership. The rights which an individual exercises over what he owns are subordinate to the rights of the community as a whole: "the right which each individual has to his own estate is always subordinate to the right of the community over all. . . ."[39] Rousseau is farther from Kant on this point and closer to Locke and to Hobbes. Even though some rights to ownership exist in the state of nature, they are alterable in a society based upon a legitimate social contract. Rousseau realizes this is necessary in order to maintain social stability especially regarding the rich and the poor.

The wealth of the rich and the poverty of the poor are both perpetuated by the social compact which legitimates state of nature holdings. Rousseau does not argue, as do the Conventionalists, that the poor and landless benefit from the agriculture, commerce, and industry which are made possible through legitimizing possession into ownership. Both in *The Social Contract* and in the *Discourse on the Origin of Inequality*, Rousseau argues that the poor suffer. Even in the simple societies discussed in the *Discourse*, natural inequalities will lead to unequal holdings and wealth because some individuals have lower skills and abilities.[40] Competition, rivalry, and conflicts of interest will inevitably result between rich and poor. And, thus, the social compact will enslave the poor because it legitimates the position of both the rich and the poor.[41] It is only logical for Rousseau to conclude that ongoing stability is possible only if the society has the right to regulate ownership. Rousseau, unlike Kant, is acutely aware of the problems which first appropriation causes the poor.

C. Nozick

Robert Nozick, in his deservedly much discussed book *Anarchy, State and Utopia*, defends a system of private ownership as the backbone of an entitlement theory of justice which is historical and unpatterned. Justice is historical, for Nozick, because "a distribution is just if it arises from another (just) distribution by legitimate means."[42] The legitimate means are called "principles of justice in transfer," and Nozick offers gift, exchange, and bequest as examples of legitimate means. The entitlement theory is unpatterned because just distributions need not "vary along with some natural dimensions, weighted sum of natural dimensions, or lexicographic ordering of natural dimensions."[43] People may justly transfer things to one another by gift, exchange, or bequest in ways which do not correspond to any natural dimensions. Principles of justice in transfer presuppose some original distribution which Nozick supplies by what he calls "the principle of justice in acquisition."[44] Nozick's principle of justice in acquisition, which he believes closely approximates the principle defended by John Locke, is that an appropriation of an unowned object is just if the appropriation does not worsen the situation of others, i.e., there is plenty left for others to use or they benefit from the appropriation.[45] The two principles supplemented by a principle of rectification, which corrects for past injustices, completely define his entitlement theory of justice.

There is a great temptation to discuss many of Nozick's ideas about justice because they are so richly and provocatively presented. But focus permits only consideration of his arguments for just acquisition and just transfer of private ownables. Private ownership is an absolutely essential component of Nozick's own entitlement theory of justice. Nozick correctly understands that "the central core of the notion of a property right in X, relating to which other parts of the notion are to be explained, is the right to determine what shall be done with X; the right to choose which of the constrained set of options concerning X shall be realized or attempted."[46] Moreover, he believes that "the constraints are set by other principles or laws operating in the society. . . ."[47] Private ownership is not the only possible form; there are others with less extensive rights of title, and, as Cheyney C. Ryan points out, "where my rights in something I came to hold do not include the right to sell or exchange it, then preventing me from doing so hardly constitutes a restriction of my liberty."[48] Nozick therefore must prove that private appropriation and transfer of ownables is morally justifiable in order to find firm ground for his entitlement theory.

The procedure Nozick must follow in his moral justification of private ownership is first to establish the moral rightness of a criterion of title for original private acquisition and then prove that the range of rights of title in private ownership is also morally justifiable. This procedure must be followed because of the historical character of his entitlement theory. Non-historical theories, such as utilitarianism, can dispense with the question of original acquisition and restrict consideration to whether the form of ownership presently fulfills the justificatory requirements, e.g., whether private ownership as a societal institution presently produces the best consequences. Nozick, however, must show how original private acquisition is morally justifiable because unless original acquisition is just, transfers and subsequent possessions will not be just.

Nozick, following Locke, argues that acquisition or appropriation of an unowned object is just if there is plenty left over, and for Nozick, "The crucial question is whether the appropriation of an unowned object worsens the condition of others."[49] Several questions arise concerning this criterion of title for original appropriation. Nozick, himself, worries about what constitutes appropriation (is it labor?) and he worries about what constitutes the base line for determining being made worse off. Further, it is not clear whether Nozick conceives actual particular acts of private appropriation as improving the condition of (all?) others or whether he conceives a system of private appropriation as improving the condition of (all?) others. There is also the most important question of what is meant by 'unowned.'

For Nozick's state of nature justification it is essential that the object to be appropriated is unowned. But 'unowned' has several possible meanings which must be clarified and distinguished from one another. First, 'unowned' might mean not privately owned by anyone within a system of private ownership rules. In this sense a plot of land is unowned if no one has private title according to a system of private ownership. This is the sense of ownership implicit in Nozick's argument. Second, 'unowned' might mean not owned by anyone according to a system of ownership rules Y, where for Y could be substituted feudal, corporate, communal, private, and so forth. This sense of 'unowned' implies that any claim about something being unowned always refers, implicitly or explicitly, to a specific form of ownership (although it need not always refer to private ownership or any other particular form). In this sense of 'unowned' a plot of land may or may not be owned by anyone depending upon the specific form of ownership used as a referent. This is the sense of unowned which is relevant to any attempt to justify ownership by first appropriation. The third sense of 'unowned' is that the object is not owned by anyone according to any (actual, possible or conceivable?) form of ownership. This third sense may upon analysis turn out to be incoherent. If these senses of 'unowned' are kept clearly in mind, Nozick's argument for original private appropriation in the state of nature is question begging.

If Nozick means by 'unowned' that no one owns the object according to a system of private ownership rules, the question begging is obvious enough. If 'unowned' in the original appropriation argument means not owned by anyone according to a system of private ownership, the argument already presupposes private ownership as the form of ownership in which the appropriation takes place and thus is obviously question begging. Unowned land, for example, which is appropriated becomes privately owned precisely because private ownership rules are already presupposed. It is the second sense of unowned which must be used in any first appropriation argument, i.e., unowned according to a form of ownership Y. What rights vest in a first appropriator, if any rights vest, then depends upon the specific form of ownership which is substituted for Y. If private ownership is substituted then private ownership rights vest, but if private usufruct is substituted for Y then private usufruct rights vest.

Suppose Nozick were to use 'unowned' in the sense that no one privately owns the object, but nothing is implied about the form of ownership. This sense of 'unowned' is perfectly compatible with the idea that something is communally owned by a tribe, a community, or all of mankind. Suppose further that such a form of communal ownership has a status criterion of title according to which each member of the (human) community has an equal right to participate in decisions about how land is used. A person who then privately and permanently appropriates some of the 'unowned' land and who claims the rights to exclude others' use of it, to give, exchange, or bequeath it to whom he pleases, or to otherwise exclusively control what use is made of the land, would thereby be in conflict with the rights of the communal owners. There is nothing in Nozick's discussion of private appropriation which demonstrates why the actions of the appropriator nullify the rights of possible communal owners.[50]

Consider a sailor who is shipwrecked upon an unknown island. He is a believer in private ownership and therefore after a time views himself as privately owning the parts of the island he improves and develops. He might even improve and develop the whole island if it is small enough. At some later time a group of explorers discover him and the island. Suppose that these explorers believe that all land is communally owned by all of mankind, i.e., that all people have an equal right to participate in decisions about how land is used. It is not at all clear why the explorers have to recognize the claim that the island is privately appropriated. That the sailor has appropriated the land and improved it and that the explorers had not known of the island's existence does not suffice, by itself, to establish the sailor's private ownership rights. There is no reason why the explorers cannot legitimately claim that they, too, as members of the human community, have rights over the island. Even if the sailor's private appropriation has not made the explorers worse off, they are not irrational in arguing that their rights over the island are violated by the sailor's private appropriation. There must be additional considerations in order for the argument about private appropriation to be plausible.

Nozick might correctly reply that the sailor does have some rights over what he improved and developed which it would be wrong for the explorers to violate. But there is little reason to believe that these rights must be coextensive with bequeathable, alienable private ownership rights. One factor which might influence what rights the explorers are willing to concede to the sailor is their own system of ownership rules. They might concede to the sailor private usufruct rights over his improvements if their communal form of ownership recognizes individuals' rights to control their own labor. If, however, the explorers' form of communal ownership prescribes communal participation in decisions about land usage, then they may not have reason to make any concessions.

It is not clear how Nozick's qualification that no one is made worse off by state of nature appropriation bears upon the sailor-explorer confrontation. His weaker requirement is not violated because the explorers had not been able to freely use the island until they discovered it.[51] The explorers, nevertheless, would consider their communal ownership rights violated by the sailor's proclaimed private ownership. The sailor's claim that he alone can control the improved island is a denial that the explorers can exercise what they believe to be their rights even though the sailor has not made them worse off. Nozick might claim that the sailor's private appropriation is still justified because he can pay compensation to those whose boundary rights he has crossed, i.e., the sailor might recognize the explorer's communal ownership rights, admit he violated them, and pay the explorers compensation from the benefits he has gained by his private appropriation. There are severe problems with this counter move. The first problem is how to measure the value of the compensation paid for violating the communal rights. If the explorers believe that communal rights over land are inalienable, there will be no market price for these rights. Unlike the loss of an automobile which is frequently bought and sold, therefore having a market price, communal ownership rights may have no established price. Even if a compensation price could be established a second problem arises. If the explorers believe that land is communally owned by everyone, or everyone in some sizable community, the sailor may never have sufficient assets to actually compensate all whose boundary rights he has crossed. Finally, the idea that the sailor admits the existence of the communal ownership rights and can violate those rights if he can pay compensation gives the justification of private ownership rights a utilitarian flavor which Nozick may not wish to stomach. The idea that compensation can be paid for violating ownership rights implies that those with the greatest assets, or those with the most profitable use for land, may violate the rights of others so long as compensation is paid. In such a system a person's rights over things would only include the right to use it in the most profitable way, since if someone else could use it more profitably, he could appropriate it himself, pay the compensation, and still be better off. The result might be Kantianism for persons and utilitarianism for ownership rights.[52] Utilitarianism for ownership rights can, however, dispense with the issue of original appropriation and allocate things in any manner which, at present, maximizes profits or well-being. Of course Nozick does not believe that all border crossings are permissible even if compensation is paid, but his arguments for this are difficult to separate from utilitarian ones.[53] The introduction of compensation does not help; Nozick is in the position where either the communal rights must be recognized and compensation paid (in which case the justification of private ownership becomes utilitarian and the issue of original appropriation is irrelevant) or the communal rights must

83

be recognized and the boundaries respected (in which case the moral justification of original acquisition fails).

It should be noted that the above argument does not favor communal ownership compared to private ownership. The example can be reversed, i.e., the sailor can be a believer in communal ownership and the explorers can be believers in private ownership, without changing the force of the argument. If 'unowned' is interpreted simply to mean not privately owned, Nozick's argument is question begging. Thus, because Nozick is unsuccessful in justifying a criterion of title for original appropriation, no questions about the extent of the range of rights of title can legitimately be raised. The rights to give, bequeath, or exchange make no sense unless there is an independent criterion of title.

Nozick's justification of private ownership must also fail if the word 'unowned' is interpreted as meaning not owned according to any specific form of ownership. Could appropriating what is unowned, in this sense of unowned, justify private ownership rights? Asking such a question demonstrates as clearly as possible the question begging inherent in state of nature arguments for original acquisition. What rights of title are conferred by a criterion of title for original appropriation depends entirely upon the specific form of ownership one has in mind. Original acquisition cannot by itself be used to decide which form is morally justifiable. Even if, as is perhaps the case for Nozick, one were to apply the "correct" moral principle to a state of nature situation where things are unowned in the sense of not being owned according to the rules of any forms of ownership, it is difficult to understand what cogency such arguments would have.

The idea that things might be unowned according to any conceivable form of ownership may be empty because it is possible to conceive of a communal form of ownership in which everything is considered communally owned. If 'unowned' were given a more narrow interpretation such as not being owned according to the rules of any actual system of ownership rules, it is possible that some things may be unowned. The fact that something is unowned in this narrower sense, however, undercuts the moral force of original appropriation. Actual forms of ownership now existing may be morally justifiable or they may not. Thus that something is unowned according to actual forms of ownership is morally arbitrary and there may be no justifiable right to appropriate it.

A few tentative conclusions can be drawn at this point about first appropriation justifications in the state of nature. Nozick's state of nature justification of private ownership fails because it is question begging. Locke's state of nature justification question begs and also fails because of his unrealistic assumptions about the conditions of abundance in the state of nature. Kant recognizes this but his solution is to simply postulate. Must all state of nature justifications of private ownership be either unrealistic or question begging?

The question is too complex and far reaching to be fully discussed here. Yet it is possible to sketch out some reasons for an affirmative answer. State of nature theorists, typified by Hobbes, Locke, and Rousseau, disclaim any historical reality for their state of nature. However, they all tend to view their states of nature as plausible descriptions of life in a stateless existence without government. One problem lies in the level of generality which is necessary if any state of nature is to fulfill a justificatory function given the wide range of conditions in which humans live. A too general description of the state of nature may not be sufficiently determinate to prove that one form of ownership rather than another is morally justified. And, if the state of nature conditions are too specific, e.g., assuming abundance or assuming narrow self-interest, the proposed justification might have a too limited application because the justification might not be plausible in conditions at variance with the narrow specific range described. But even if the difficulties of realism could be surmounted by an ingenious philosophy, a second problem of question begging still remains. The possible range of senses for the term 'unowned' make the charge of question begging inescapable for anyone who, unlike Hobbes, believes it is possible to justify a form of ownership by original appropriation in the state of nature. Depending upon the sense of 'unowned,' state of nature justifications are question begging, they are non-sensical, or they are morally irrelevant. State of nature arguments might be useful for some purposes but the justification of a form of ownership is not one of them.

CHAPTER IV

The Conventionalists

The Conventionalists, Hobbes, Hume, and Rawls, believe that forms of ownership are justifiable through political or legal conventions. The convention may be an act of social contract, as with Hobbes and Rawls, where a social contract establishes the authority who will enact ownership legislation. But the convention also might not be based upon any explicit contract, as is the case with Hume where ownership is only justified within the laws and authority of civil society. The justification does not depend upon any rights that are alleged to exist in a state of nature before civil society arises.

Conventionalists believe that the justifiable form of ownership results from political and legislative decisions within civil society; but this does not imply that the decisions are ultimately arbitrary, amoral, or extra-rational. Some Conventionalists are positivists who believe that legal rules including the rules which constitute ownership have no necessary moral content or are not the result of moral deliberation.[1] Hobbes would fall within this category if he were narrowly interpreted.[2] Other Conventionalists believe that the laws which constitute forms of ownership must have a moral content or be the result of legitimate moral deliberation. These Conventionalists support their views with moral arguments about which specific form of ownership ought to be adopted and practiced by civil society. The arguments may be utilitarian or deontological: Hume is an example of a utilitarian justification while Rawls illustrates a deontological approach.

It is remarkable that the Conventionalists, Hobbes, Hume and Rawls, all have a very different view of the material conditions of human life than do First Appropriationists such as Locke, Rousseau, and perhaps Nozick. Hobbes' state of nature, as an illustration, is not a state in which appropriations can readily be made which leave enough and as good for others. Hume goes even further and argues that without scarcity there would be no reason at all to have any form of ownership. The different conclusions these groups of philosophers draw about how ownership is morally justified seem to be based upon their different views of the material conditions of human existence. The idea that first appropriation vests rights of title may make sense in abundance; but 'first come first served' is not plausible where there is not enough to go around, especially where some cannot help arriving later than others.

The Conventionalists need not be wedded to private ownership in the way in which First Appropriationists are. Actual civil societies differ from each other and from the First Appropriationists' state of nature in such material circumstances as population density, fertility of the land, length of the growing season, rainfall, mineral deposits, degree of industrialization, capital, and so forth. Thus, there may be little reason to believe that one form of ownership alone is morally justifiable in all such widely divergent circumstances. Regulation of the rights of owners or regulation of how ownables are acquired and transferred may have morally welcomed results.

A final introductory note: the greater realism of the three Conventionalists needs to be stressed. With the exception of Hobbes' exaggerated egoism, the Conventionalists much more than the First Appropriationists have a realistic view of the conditions in which the question of the moral justifiability of a form of ownership is now raised. Whatever the conditions of human life might have been in some distant (or fictitious) past, those conditions do not still obtain. It is therefore difficult to understand the continuing influence of the First Appropriationists. The position of the Conventionalists, whatever their other shortcomings, is at least formed out of an appreciation of the material circumstances which are relevant to any contemporary attempt to morally justify a form of ownership.

A. Hobbes

Thomas Hobbes' description of the state of nature is almost the antithesis of John Locke's. Hobbes believes that without political authority to coerce people into obeying the natural law, there would be a war of everyman against everyman in which life would be "solitary, poor, nasty, brutish, and short."[3] Because there can be little cooperation among people in these conditions of distrust and competition, there will be little industry, commerce, or agriculture so that the material conditions for life will be in very short supply only further compounding the competition. Even those who might be satisfied with their small lot are forced out of fear or diffidence to be at war with their neighbors.[4]

In this state of nature, Hobbes believes that there is a "Liberty each man hath, to use his own power as he will himself, for the preservation of his own Nature; that is to say, of his own Life: and consequently, of doing any thing which in his own Judgment and Reasons, he shall conceive to be the aptest means thereunto."[5] Individuals in the state of nature may have reason not to obey the precepts of natural law if there are others who are also disobeying them. A corollary of this liberty which exists where there is no law or authority is that no form of ownership will exist. If two individuals believe they need the same thing for survival, then each of them will have the liberty to try to possess that thing. For Hobbes, having rights over things which others do not share requires the existence of laws which define and establish such rights.[6] Thus in the state of nature anyone may try to use whatever he judges he needs, but once laws are enacted by a political authority or sovereign, then exclusive rights over ownables can be created. The sovereign will have the power and authority to enact laws constituting a form of ownership which will be acknowledged by the members of the commonwealth.

On the point that law is possible only if enacted by political authority, Hobbes is much more open to criticism. Locke most certainly questions Hobbes' assumption. If men were capable of knowing what the natural law is without too many disagreements and if men could follow those laws without too many delinquents, then according to Locke it would be possible to have a form of ownership in the state of nature. Where people acknowledge and follow the same laws ownership is possible. Hobbes would not disagree with this; he only would contest the possibility of commonly acknowledged and followed laws in the state of nature without a sovereign who coerces obedience to the laws by punishing transgressors. Hobbes and Locke do not disagree about the need for commonly acknowledged laws in order for forms of ownership to be possible; they disagree about the conditions in which such laws are possible.

It is no easy task to decide whether Hobbes or Locke is correct about the connection between law and authority. These concepts have so many different but still legitimate senses that it is difficult to construct any tests which will decisively verify either Hobbes' or Locke's point of view. Some so-called primitive societies may have had forms of authority which fall short of Hobbes' sovereign and still had laws; but the laws in these societies have more closely resembled moral rules than the legal rules Hobbes has in mind.[7]

What is important to understand at this point is the connection between ownership and commonly acknowledged rules which Hobbes correctly identifies. The other controversy concerning the existence of laws including ownership rules in the state of nature is not relevant to a justification of ownership which must be plausible for large modern industrialized nation states. The possibility of a state of nature is so remote, and the conditions which define it (either Hobbesian or Lockean) are so unlike life as it now exists in most parts of the world, the relevance of state of nature arguments to the moral justification of ownership is minimal even if the inherent question begging could be avoided.

For Hobbes, then, ownership arises as a result of the convention which creates law. As is well known, the sovereign is authorized to enact laws as a consequent of the social contract by which everyone transfers to the sovereign his own individual rights:

> . . . made by Covenant of every man with every man, in such
> a manner, as if every man should say to every man, I
> Authorise and give up my Right of Governing my self, to this
> Man, or to this Assembly of men, on this condition, that
> thou give up thy Right to him, and Authorise all his actions
> in a like manner.[8]

The sovereign, who may be an individual or a group of individuals, is authorized to enact laws in order to establish and preserve peace and security within the commonwealth. Hobbes believes that because the sovereign is authorized to provide peace and security, he also has the right to whatever means he judges necessary to achieve that end.[9] Certainly one of the primary means to peace and security is the creation of laws defining a form of ownership:

Seventhly, is annexed to the Sovereigntie, the whole power of prescribing Rules, whereby every man may know, what Goods he may enjoy, and what Actions he may also do, without being molested by any of his fellow Subjects: And this is it men call Propriety.[10]

The justification of ownership rules, for Hobbes, is that they are enacted by an authorized sovereign in a manner to preserve the peace and security of the commonwealth. It seems unlikely that only one particular form of ownership would be appropriate for all commonwealths. Commonwealths differ from one another in their material circumstances as well as in the judgments of their sovereigns. Thus, there will be a variety of different justifiable forms of ownership, since in different circumstances rights of title and criteria of title will have different effects upon peace and security. This is not to say that Hobbes would believe that any form of ownership a sovereign enacts is justifiable. Sovereigns may legislate well or poorly and their laws may be more or less conducive to peace and security, so that laws would not be morally justifiable if they fail to promote peace through the regulation of ownables.

Hobbes does not say a great deal about the form of ownership he believes most conducive to peace. His discussion of specific sets of rules is restricted to Chapter XXIV of *Leviathan*, "Of the Nutrition and Procreation of a Common-wealth."[11] Hobbes does not go into as many details as would be helpful. He is sometimes suggestive and often incomplete. Hobbes says, for example, that the sovereign assigns, as he sees fit, a portion of land to everyman.[12] Yet Hobbes does not discuss whether or not the land is alienable by gift, bequest, or exchange. Nor does Hobbes explain what other rights vest in land owners. He does say that "Properiety in lands constitute a right to exclude all other subjects from the use of them, and not exclude their Sovereign, be it an Assembly, or a Monarch," but Hobbes is silent upon the uses to which the land may be put or whether it may be sub-divided.[13] Hobbes does consider the possibility of some land remaining under the direct control of the sovereign in order to fund governmental operations, but, for various reasons, he believes the arrangement is unstable.

Hobbes discusses exchange of goods; but as in the case with his discussion of land, some of the more interesting issues are not fully developed. Hobbes' discussion of exchange begins in much the same way Aristotle's does with the inequality of both the land holdings each person has and the skills and abilities they have to develop them. Some individuals will produce more of one kind of good while other individuals will produce more of some other kind. Thus, Hobbes says it is necessary that men distribute what they can spare to one another by mutual contract.[14] Hobbes does not, as does Aristotle, distinguish between retail trade which is the amassing of as much wealth as possible (in whatever form that wealth takes) and exchanges in order to fulfill the natural needs of the exchangers. Hobbes neither praises nor condemns exchanging goods merely to increase wealth without limit rather than to help fulfill each other's needs.

Hobbes does believe foreign trade, "What commodities the subject shall traffique abroad," is to be regulated by the sovereign.[15] But Hobbes' reasons here have nothing to do with wealth accumulation. He is concerned primarily with exporting commodities which might enable enemies to hurt the commonwealth, although he is also concerned about the importation of goods which might be "pleasing men's appetites" but are also harmful or noxious.[16]

Whatever kinds of exchanges are or are not permitted, the sovereign regulates the form of contract. Hobbes says that the sovereign is to decide the manner in which all kinds of contract between subjects are to be made, e.g., buying, selling, borrowing, lending, letting, and hiring.[17] Also the sovereign is to prescribe by what words and signs contracts are made valid.[18] It is not at all clear from the context whether Hobbes believes the sovereign is to regulate both the content of contracts, i.e., the kinds of agreements which may be entered into, as well as the form of the contract, e.g., whether it be written or oral, and whether consideration must be transferred. It is a plausible reading of Hobbes to suggest that he has only the second in mind, namely, regulating the form contracts must have if they are to be valid. The alternative reading, that the sovereign may regulate both the form and the content of contracts, is also consistent with Hobbes' concept of sovereignty in which the sovereign has the right to whatever means are necessary for preserving peace. Surely the peace and security of the commonwealth are affected by the kinds of contracts its members may enter into. Hobbes' concept of the sovereign's rights would imply he has both rights; limiting the sovereign to only one of the rights would be inconsistent with Hobbes' general thinking about the sovereign who has the right to all of the possible means of establishing and preserving peace.

There is one aspect of ownership about which Hobbes is surprisingly clear and precise. He says that ". . . a man's Labour also, is a commodity exchangeable for benefit, as well as any other thing."[19] This is radically at odds with the Natural Perfectionists. They believe that labor, human activity, constitutes part of the virtue or perfection of human nature. To exchange labor just as any other commodity would be a depreciation of human nature. Hobbes is much closer to a modern conception of labor. It is important in this respect to remember that Hobbes wrote *Leviathan* well before any of the First Appropriationists who were discussed in the last chapter. Even Locke refrains from calling labor a commodity exchangeable as well as any other. Hobbes does not discuss any of the implications of viewing labor as a commodity, implications which become important in later criticisms of private ownership.

Hobbes has made two significant contributions to the justification of ownership. His first is his description of the material conditions of human life which depict the scarcity of what is needed. Second is his insistence upon the need for commonly acknowledged rules if ownership is to make any sense at all. While it may not be possible to decide whether Hobbes is also correct in thinking that such rules require political power for their existence, it is important to understand that the rules arise from some sort of convention. Hume discusses both of these points in greater depth and detail, so it is best to turn the discussion toward him.

B. Hume

Hume is the second Conventionalist who believes that ownership rules are not grounded upon natural rights which exist in a state of nature independently of civil society but that ownership rules are a creation of civil society and draw their validity from their social usefulness. Hume's theory of ownership is presented both in his *Treatise* and his *Enquiries*.[20] While there are a few significant differences between Hume's two presentations which shall be noted, most of the differences appear to be differences of emphasis rather than differences of substance.

Hume classifies ownership rules as a sub-set of the rules of justice which arise as a tacit convention among the members of society. The rules of justice and the rules of ownership resemble the rules that constitute the rules of language or of promising which are practiced by society not as a result of any explicit promise or contract but are practiced as a result of many separate understandings within society that become engrained habit and custom, i.e., a convention. Hume devotes much of the *Treatise* to explaining why justice, and by implication ownership, is an artificial virtue and not a natural one. Although this issue has some importance, it is not vital to understanding Hume's conception of ownership and his method for morally justifying a particular form of ownership. A thorough discussion of Hume's conception of justice as an artificial virtue has recently been published by Jonathan Harrison.[21] Not only is Harrison's book worth consulting about justice, but his ideas about Hume's theory of ownership have also influenced the discussion in this section.

The clearest way to approach Hume's theory of ownership is to divide it into three separate topics. The first topic is Hume's appraisal of the conditions which give rise to the need for having ownership rules. This is, perhaps, Hume's most important contribution. The second topic concerns Hume's method of justification, i.e., the moral considerations he employs in his attempt to justify a form of ownership. The last of the three topics is the actual form of ownership Hume believes to be morally justified.

In the *Treatise*, Hume isolates the two sets of conditions he believes give rise to the need for establishing ownership rules:

> The qualities of mind are selfishness and limited generosity:
> And the situation of external objects is their easy change
> join'd to their scarcity in comparison of the wants and desires
> of men.[22]

Beginning with Hume's second condition, the scarcity of goods and their easy change, it is possible to understand why ownership is necessary. There are three kinds of goods according to Hume: the satisfactions of our minds, the external advantages of our bodies, and the enjoyments of such possessions we have acquired by our industry and good fortune.[23] Hume believes that it is only the third of these goods, external possessions, which need be the object of the ownership relation, i.e., the only kind of goods which need to be regulated by ownership rules. His reasons are that the first goods, the satisfactions of our minds, are perfectly secure and that the second goods, the advantages of our bodies, cannot be to the advantage of others.[24] Hume is not entirely correct on this point. The satisfactions of the mind, or at least future satisfaction, can be disrupted by others and by the environment in which people live. Similarly, while parts of one person's body may not benefit others (transplants must be discounted because Hume could not have foreseen them), conditions such as a dangerous factory where loss of limb is likely may create an incentive or benefit to one person's disregarding the bodily safety of others. Dangerous conditions in a factory may financially benefit its owners while the workers suffer from increased hazards. Thus ownership rules may be required to protect and regulate the first two goods as well as regulating Hume's third kind, external possessions.

Hume believes external goods need regulation because of their "easy change" and their "scarcity." The scarcity condition is the more important of the two because if goods were abundant rather than scarce the easy change condition would not be sufficient by itself to give rise to the need for ownership rules. If goods were sufficiently abundant, no problems would arise; whatever one wanted or needed could easily be appropriated. "Easy change" may not even be a necessary condition for having ownership rules. Where goods are scarce but not easily changed, such as ownership of land where titles are recorded or deeds securely kept, ownership rules would still be required to define rights and duties even though appropriation of land was a rare occurrence. Even in a society where land is communally owned and thus not transferable, alienable, or changeable, there still would be a need for ownership rules which define rights and duties of land use so long as there is any scarcity of land.

The scarcity Hume has in mind is moderate and not extreme scarcity. Extreme scarcity, or what in the *Enquiries* Hume calls extreme necessity, makes ownership rules as useless as extreme abundance.[25] Hume does not explain what he means by extreme necessity nor does he indicate how scarce goods must be, but it is reasonable to assume that what he has in mind is that below a certain level of goods needed for survival people cannot be expected to follow the social convention which defines ownership. Goods would be in such limited supply that no one could reasonably expect good consequences to follow from obeying ownership rules.[26]

The argument that ownership rules are unnecessary where there is abundance is clearly intended by Hume to counter arguments by First Appropriationists, such as Locke, which try to establish natural rights to ownership. In the *Treatise*, Hume says, "Increase to a sufficient degree . . . the bounty of nature . . . and you render justice useless . . . ," meaning as well to include within justice the rules of ownership.[27] Hume elaborates in the *Enquiries*:

> For what purpose make a partition of goods, where everyone has more than enough? Why give rise to property, where there cannot possibly be any injury? Why call this object mine, when upon the seizing of it by another I need but stretch out my hand to possess myself to what is equally valuable?[28]
>
> We see, even in the present necessitous condition of mankind, that, whenever any benefit is bestowed by nature in an unlimited abundance, we leave it always in common among the whole human race, and make no subdivisions of right and property.[29]

Hume's own examples of goods which exist in this rich abundance are air, water, and land in some countries.

It should be noted in this context that Locke uses as one example of first appropriation establishing private ownership a person who takes a "good Draught" of water from a river leaving "enough and as good" abundance for others.[30] Locke believes that the taking of this abundantly flowing water establishes ownership rights. Hume, however, is correct in doubting that ownership rights would vest under such circumstances. There is no possible purpose which could be served by creating ownership rights over water which exists in such abundance. If, as Hume suggests, no effort is required in order to appropriate, "I need but stretch out my hand," establishing and enforcing ownership rules would not only serve no purpose but would be more trouble than appropriating without regulation what exists in such abundance.

Whether this kind of abundance has ever existed in the past, it is unlikely to exist now or in the future. While the abundance Locke envisions makes ownership unnecessary, the realities of the scarcity of goods in human life make all assumptions about abundance purely speculative. Hume's condition of moderate scarcity is the correct perspective from which to consider the need for ownership. Moderate scarcity seems to be an inescapable part of human circumstance, and therefore ownership too is inescapable.[31]

The second of the two conditions Hume considers necessary to give rise to the need for ownership rules is what he calls the qualities of mind: selfishness and limited generosity. Hume does not take great pains to sufficiently clarify these concepts. He does not seem to identify selfishness with egoism in the sense that self-interest is identified as the sole or primary human motive.[32] Closer, perhaps to what Hume seems to mean is Aristotle's idea that selfishness is self-love in excess, a passion which Aristotle believes can be modified by virtue. So even though Hume believes that all human passions including love and benevolence are ultimately grounded in pleasures, he also believes the sources of these pleasures are broad enough to include the well-being of others. That Hume also recognizes the possibility of even limited generosity shows his concept of selfishness is not so narrow as egoism.

Hume believes that removing selfishness by increasing benevolence to a significant degree would render ownership rules useless.[33] In the *Enquiries* he says:

> Why raise land-marks between my neighbor's field and mine, when my heart has made no division between our interests; but shares all his joys and sorrows with the same force and vivacity as if originally my own? . . . And the whole human race would form only one family; where all would lie in common and be used freely, without regard to property. . . .[34]

In order to test that increased benevolence without selfishness makes ownership rules useless, increased benevolence must be examined in conjunction with scarcity and in the absence of scarcity. While Hume always discusses increased benevolence in tandem with the absence of scarcity, it is informative to consider both possibilities because the condition of increased benevolence where scarcity exists still gives rise to the need for ownership – a possibility Hume may have failed to see.

A benevolent person, it can be supposed, is generous towards others who are in need and will desire to be giving to his friends and relatives. Assume that goods are moderately scarce and not at all abundant. Someone with increased benevolence will have to know what he owns in order to know what he may rightfully give to others. Ownership rules will therefore still be necessary because a person may only give away what he owns. It might be thought that if everyone, as Hume assumes, were to have increased benevolence, one benevolent person would not complain if another took what belongs to him in order to give it to a third person who is in need, e.g., if Green takes food which belongs to Black and gives it to White who is in need. A benevolent person such as Black, it might be thought, should not mind if Green takes his food to give it to another who is in need.[35] But Black may have reason to complain, not because he is selfish and wants to keep the food for himself which would be contrary to the assumption of increased benevolence, but Black may complain because there is a fourth person, Brown, whom Black may desire to help. If scarcity exists, Black may not own enough food to help both White and Brown; so Black may complain about Green's taking the food in order to give it to White instead of Brown who is Black's preferred recipient. Ownership rules are therefore needed even if there is increased benevolence so long as scarcity exists because benevolent givers need to know what they own and what is owned by others. Disagreements over who is to be helped rather than selfishness is the cause in this situation which gives rise to the need for ownership rules.

Dropping the assumption about scarcity changes the example. If there is more than enough for everyone, then Black will have no grounds for complaint about Green's taking food to give to White. Black may have more than enough for both White and Brown as well as enough for himself. But the assumption that goods exist in sufficient abundance so that a person need only "stretch out his hand" implies that no one ought to be in a situation of necessity. No one ought to need help. Certainly people will still desire to make gifts to friends or loved ones, but in abundance the value of such gifts will be small and should not be the cause of disagreements. Hume has already proven that in abundance no ownership rules are necessary. It follows that whether or not increased benevolence is assumed, no ownership rules are needed in abundance.

Hume's examination of increased benevolence is not without value even though he is not entirely correct in believing that the need for ownership rules vanishes simply as a consequence of increased benevolence. Both unlimited abundance and unlimited benevolence are not practically possible, and Hume is aware that they are only conceptual possibilities. Some goods will always be in limited supply if only because human labor and effort are not unlimited. Unlimited benevolence may not be, upon close analysis, a coherent concept. Even so, both the material circumstances of human life and the psychological dispositions engrained in human nature are factors which generate the need for ownership rules. Both vary by degrees from time to time and place to place. The conceptually possible extremes which Hume's examples illustrate may, at least, give guidance and direction in deciding which form of ownership ought to be chosen for adoption. In societies where love and concern are bestowed over a wide range of people, ownership rules may be different from societies in which love and concern range less widely. Adjustments also should be made depending upon the availability of material goods. Societies which are more abundantly productive should have a form of ownership which differs from those which are less productive. Chapters VI and VII explain how abundance and scarcity as well as how human motivation affect the rules of autonomous ownership.

Hume's appraisal of the actual conditions which give rise to the need for ownership is much more helpful than that of the First Appropriationists, such as Locke, who envision a justification of private ownership in conditions of material abundance. Their attempt at justification only appears compelling because no form of ownership is really necessary at all. Hume's own try at morally justifying a form of ownership, whatever its ultimate inadequacies, has the virtue of being grounded upon a plausible understanding of the conditions which give rise to the need for ownership rules.

Hume's method of justification for a form of ownership depends upon the contribution of the rules of ownership to everyone's interest.[36] Hume's position is that "Our property is nothing but those goods, whose constant possession is established by the laws of society; that is by the laws of justice."[37] In what is probably the most frequently cited passage by Hume concerning ownership, he says:

No one can doubt, that the convention for the distinction of property, and for the stability of possession, is of all circumstances the most necessary to the establishment of human society, and after the agreement for fixing and observing this rule, there remains little or nothing to be done towards settling a perfect harmony and concord.[38]

Hume believes everyone can benefit from having rules which define ownership. Further, he believes that these rules are produced by society; they are not natural rules existing apart from any social convention. In the *Treatise*, he writes as if ownership rules are moral, founded upon justice, yet contrasted with natural virtues.[39] But in his *Enquiries*, Hume treats ownership rules as "civil laws" which he believes may "extend, restrain, modify, and alter the rules of natural justice according to the convenience of each community," because of differences in the manners, climate, commerce, and situation of each society.[40] There appears to be some inconsistency between the two works about the status of ownership rules. The *Treatise* seems to construe ownership rules as what in Chapter I were called moral rules while the *Enquiries* construes them as what were called legal rules in H. L. A. Hart's sense of the two kinds of rule.[41] The difference between the two senses of rule, though to some extent real, is not as significant as it might otherwise be because of Hume's method of justification. The contribution to everyone's interest of following rules depends upon the "situation of each society". Thus whether the rules have moral or legal status, their content must be dictated by the conditions in which the rules are practiced and the content may have to change as conditions change. This is clearly seen by carefully examining Hume's method of moral justification.

Hume is insistent that ownership is rule constituted, and thus the justification of ownership is the justification of rules which are adopted by a social convention, specific rules, that is, which are acknowledged by the members of society. Hume's reasons for insisting upon rules are not the logical conditions discussed in Chapter I, but practical considerations which, however, closely resemble those logical conditions. The key consideration, for Hume, is that material possessions be as stable as possible so that owners may peacefully enjoy the goods they acquire.[42] Ownables should be secure in the sense that owners ought not be deprived of them except as a result of exchange (or as with debts, be deprived of what one owns as a result of agreements entered into).

In order to secure possessions and ownables, Hume believes a method must be adopted to "distinguish what particular goods are to be assign'd to each particular person," while excluding others from the enjoyment of them.[43] Hume considers two principles which ultimately he rejects that might be thought capable of making the assignment. The first of this principles is what now would be called act utilitarianism; the second is the principle of equality.

Hume considers the principle that people ought to be assigned goods which would benefit them most.[44] "Particular judgments" about the utility of assignments of ownables would be made in each case.[45] It does not stretch Hume's intent to construe this as act utilitarianism.

Hume's criticism of this act utilitarian method of assigning ownables to owners is that relying upon particular judgments about individual assignments makes ownership "too loose and uncertain."[46] He does not elaborate upon what he means by "loose and uncertain" but a plausible interpretation of these terms can be supplied by extrapolating from the necessary logical structure of ownership rules. An act utilitarian principle for assigning ownables to owners could conceivably produce incomplete assignments. If two persons would each equally benefit from owning some particular good, then an act utilitarian criterion of title might imply that each owns the good to the exclusion of the other. The act utilitarian maneuver for responding to ties in utility, that either of the actions is right to perform with the choice up to the agent, is not possible in assigning ownables. An additional principle is required to complete the assignments by prescribing who is to be granted the authority to make the determination. Leaving the decision in the hands of any agent or agents is too "loose" a procedure. A second difficulty with act utilitarianism as a criterion of title is that assignments could only be determinate if it were possible to make precise, conclusive calculations of utility. This seems an unlikely possibility. Any owner who has to rely upon utilitarian calculations to determine what he owns may well be unable to reliably know what he owns. Ownership in this sense would not be certain. Even if precise and conclusive utilitarian calculations could be made, there is an additional sense in which ownership based upon an act utilitarian criterion of title would be uncertain. Since there is no reason to suppose that the utility of one owner owning some object will remain constant with respect to other possible owners, what objects a person owns will change as often as do changes in the utility people might receive from owning the object. Suppose that Brown owns Greenacre, a farm, because at one point in time utility is best enhanced by his owning it. At some later time, White may need Greenacre more than Brown does, perhaps because White has a larger family. An act utilitarian criterion of title would "judge" that Greenacre become owned by the needy White, assuming that more utility overall is produced by satisfying the greater need. No one could be "certain" about the stability of what they own because utility levels fluctuate.

Hume's criticism of the loose and uncertain stability of ownership based upon act utilitarianism is similar to the criticism made in the preceding chapter of Nozick's position that boundary crossings may permissibly violate rights in circumstances where the benefits to the violator are sufficiently large to compensate owners whose rights are violated.[47] Nozick's position would also imply that ownership is too loose and uncertain.

Hume could not have intended all of these logical difficulties when he rejects act utilitarianism because it is "too loose and uncertain." Still, there is little distortion to Hume's thought caused by interpreting his concept in this way. Hume is on solid ground in rejecting act utilitarianism as a principle for the ongoing assignment of ownables to owners.

The second of the two principles Hume rejects as an ongoing principle for assigning ownables to owners is the principle of equality. His discussion of equality occurs in the *Enquiries*. Hume has some sympathy with the idea of an equal distribution of what can be owned:

> It also must be confessed, that whenever we depart from this
> equality, we rob the poor of more satisfaction than we add
> to the rich, and that the slight gratification of a frivolous vanity
> in one individual, frequently costs more than bread to many
> families or even provinces.[48]

A more equal distribution is more desirable because it benefits more people. But, Hume also argues that imposing an equal distribution is both "impracticable and pernicious."[49] It is impracticable, according to Hume, because men's different degrees of art, care, and industry will immediately upset equality.[50] It is pernicious, he believes, because the authority to enforce equality must degenerate to tyranny.[51]

Hume considers these two objections against equality to be

conclusive. He has, however, a third reason for rejecting equality. People ought to own what they produce or improve by their own industry in order to encourage useful habits and accomplishments.[52] Hume sees this labor criterion of title as contributing to the common interest. It is best to postpone further discussion of Hume's labor criterion of title until the rules which constitute the content of his ownership rules are discussed. The addition of a labor criterion of title by Hume in his *Enquiries* is a needed supplement to the rules he advocates in his *Treatise*.

What remains for Hume to use as a grounding moral principle for ownership rules once he has rejected act utilitarianism and equality? Appearances aside, Hume must attempt to justify a particular form of ownership and not merely ownership rules in general. Hume realizes that ownership rules must be specific if possessions are to be stable, and thus, although it is true that having rules of some sort stabilizes possessions better than the absence of rules, it is always particular specific rules which stabilize ownables and are in need of justification. The moral principle Hume uses to justify one specific form of ownership is the principle that everyone's interest ought to be promoted.[53] Ownership rules must promote the "general interest" if they are to be morally justifiable.

Hume is sometimes said to use a rule utilitarian justification of ownership because he argues that following the rules produces benefits and he also argues that the rules must be followed even if some (immediate) gains in utility could be produced by occasionally breaking the rule. One reason for thinking this is a misreading of Hume, perhaps influenced by later conceptual developments, is Hume's appreciation that ownership must be rule constituted. Hume's insistence that ownership rules not be broken for gains in utility may be better understood as an appreciation by Hume of what is required for a society to govern its behavior by rules than by interpreting Hume as arguing that following rules produces higher utility. It is sufficient for Hume to argue that breaking the rules for gains in utility would make possession too unstable even if enough extra utility were produced to compensate for the instability. Even though utility were promoted, members of society could not be certain about what they own. Thus, Hume's insistence upon observing the rules of ownership need not depend upon interpreting his justification as rule utilitarian.

Another reason for doubting that Hume employs a rule utilitarian justification of a form of ownership is that he never argues that ownership rules ought to be constituted in a way which maximizes the benefits of following them. He does not argue that ownership rules are justified only if 'they produce as much utility as possible.[54] Hume is content to point merely to the advantages society gains by regulating ownables by ownership rules, i.e., people's interests are advanced by following the rules. He does not argue as would a rule utilitarian that people's interests are promoted as much as possible.

Hume supplements his primary argument that rules are needed for stability with considerations, primarily presented in extended footnotes, appealing to his theory of the association of ideas. It might be thought that, by these considerations, Hume demonstrates, inadvertently and not intentionally, the maximum utility of observing ownership rules. Observing ownership rules might be construed as being maximally useful because the rules correspond to people's psychological associations which are impressed upon their minds as a consequence of repeated experiences. People might be thought to be benefited because the rules which assign ownables best satisfy their psychological expectations.

To interpret Hume's argument in this fashion would require assumptions about the causes of satisfaction which are too tenuous to attribute to Hume. Hume would have to maintain that mental habits of association, which are the basis of a form of ownership rules, are so thoroughly engrained that the adoption of any other set of ownership rules would produce so little satisfaction or be so psychologically disruptive that any increased benefits could not compensate for the loss.

Nowhere does Hume write anything which approximates such arguments. In fact, in several places, he argues that the association of ideas is not sufficiently determinate or rigid to settle all questions about what ownership rules should be.[55] Hume actually believes that how the mind associates ideas leaves room for several alternative ways of assigning ownables to owners. A rule utilitarian interpretation, therefore, cannot be supported by the association of ideas. Hume cannot argue both that one particular set of ownership rules maximizes utility because it best satisfies the pre-established association of ideas and that the association of ideas is loose enough to accommodate several different sets of rules.

There is little more about Hume's justification of ownership which needs to be said beyond noting that he believes ownership must be constituted by a set of rules whose observance tends to promote general utility. One might rehearse the problems confronting a rule utilitarian justification which Hume would face were he arguing in this way; but little would be added to understanding Hume's own thought. It is now appropriate to discuss the actual content of the ownership rules which Hume defends.

The content of the form of ownership which Hume discusses in the *Treatise* is defined by five rules. The rules are: present possession, prescription, accession, succession, and transference by consent. In the *Enquiries*, Hume adds a sixth rule, a labor criterion of acquisition that people own what they labor to produce or improve. These rules constitute a form of ownership which resembles the form of private ownership explained in Chapter I. All of these rules are criteria of title and, therefore, must be examined to see if they are compatible with the necessary logical structure of ownership rules. While Hume's discussion of these rules is lengthy and thorough, he does not devote much attention to the rights of title which vest in owners so that it is difficult to know with any precision the degree to which Hume's rights of title approximate private ownership rights of title. Hume's criteria of title shall be discussed first and a brief examination of his few comments upon rights of title will follow.

Present possession is the criterion of title responsible for the original assignment of ownables to individuals. The original assignment is made immediately after the general convention to establish society in order to achieve "constancy of possession."[56] This rule assigns to each individual the particular portion of goods he is to initially enjoy. Hume acknowledges that present possession is not a clear and precise concept since situations may arise in which the decision about who possesses what cannot avoid arbitrariness. While Hume believes that the imagination and the association of ideas may help make decisions about who possesses what more precise, he also acknowledges there may always be the need for authority to decide the issue.[57] Hume defends present possession as a "natural expedient" for assigning to each what he is "at present master of" so that each person has ownership rights over what he initially possesses.[58] This original assignment functions as the basis upon which the other criteria of title begin and presuppose. Accession, succession, and transfer by consent presuppose that individuals already have ownership rights over things.

There is an obvious question why Hume settles upon present possession as a criterion for the original assignment rather than some other criteria such as equality or utility. Why not, for the purpose of original assignment only, give each person an equal share of the goods to be assigned or assign goods upon the basis of their utility to the initial owner? Hume's reason for rejecting equality as an ongoing criterion of title for distributing goods, that equality is "impractible" and "pernicious," would not apply to equality limited only to original assignment. The impracticality Hume there refers to derives from the difficulty in perpetuating equality which becomes disrupted by individual differences, art, care, and industry.[59] But restricting equality only to an original assignment would not generate any of those impractical difficulties. Similarly, the perniciousness Hume refers to derives from the likely abuses of authority he believes arise from continually enforcing equality. Abuses of authority might not arise were equality only used as a criterion of original assignment. The poor, those with few or no possessions, certainly stand to benefit from an original equal assignment of goods. Whether the poor could sustain their equal share certainly depends upon the art, care, and industry they exercise over the goods they might be assigned. Still, whatever would happen after the original assignment, Hume is aware that the poor would gain more than the rich might lose if goods initially were equally distributed.

Much the same line of argument can be used to ask why Hume fails to use utility as a criterion of original assignment rather than using present possession. While Hume is right in believing that utility as a criterion of title for ongoing possession makes possession too unstable, there is no reason to believe that utility as a criterion for original assignment would be less stable than present possession.

Hume defends present possession as a natural expedient for original assignment of goods because people are in the habit of enjoying what they possess. Hume may believe that to rearrange possessions would cause much dissatisfaction in those who would be deprived of rights to what they already possess at the convention to establish society. If this were Hume's line of thought, he would have to argue that the dissatisfaction brought about in those who are dispossessed, e.g., the rich, is greater than the gains to others who would benefit from the rearrangement of original possession made on the basis of equality or utility. Hume makes no such argument. Certainly, using present possession as a criterion of title for original assignment of ownables avoids the need to create possibly cumbersome governmental authorities to make any redistribution. Yet, it is not at all obvious that the gains to the poor fail to compensate on balance.

The present possession criterion of title for the original assignment of ownables is possibly consistent, but it fails to fulfill the necessary logical requirements of determinacy and completeness. Present possession would be consistent if it were possible unambiguously and without vagueness to determine in principle who possesses what collection of goods. Hume is well aware that present possession is not sufficiently determinate. In a series of footnotes he offers several examples illustrating how possession lacks determinacy.[60] Hume has a method for removing this indeterminacy which is to authorize the civil laws and judges to make the rules more precise and to make decisions in hard cases. There is no logical difficulty in using additional criteria of title to remove indeterminacy. Locke (perhaps not intentionally) makes a similar correction by using agreements and exchange of labor to overcome the indeterminacy of labor as a criterion of title.[61] This needed addition is also one of the reasons why present possession is not complete; it requires other criteria of title to remove the indeterminacy. There is another, more important, way in which present possession is incomplete. If at the convention to transform possession into ownership there were ownables, especially goods, which were not in anyone's possession, these ownables might not ever become owned because no one possessed them, and Hume's other criteria of title, discussed in the *Treatise*, may not guarantee that these goods can be owned. Hume's criteria of prescription and accession may not cover cases such as goods which are not long lived. This incompleteness shall be more fully discussed when the five criteria of the *Treatise* are considered as a whole.

The second of Hume's criteria of title is prescription. A person who possesses land or goods for a long period of time gains ownership rights.[62] One function prescription plays is to vest title in goods which were not possessed at the original assignment. In order for goods to be acquired by prescription they would have to be fairly durable. A second function of prescription, the one Hume emphasizes, is to replace original possession as an ongoing criterion of title, since Hume believes that memories fade and knowledge of who is original possessor may be lost. Valid title would therefore vest in someone who has possessed the good in question for as long as anyone could remember. A similar principle has long been a part of common law.[63] Plato also recognizes a principle with the same effect.[64]

Prescription as a criterion of title shares many of the problems which confront possession. It lacks determinacy insofar as it cannot be clearly determined who has had sufficiently long possession of a collection of goods. Prescription could be consistent if it were possible to clear up indeterminacy and if it were not possible for more than one person to possess goods at a time. Prescription is not complete, but Hume does not intend it to function by itself as a single criterion of title.

Accession and succession are criteria of title by which rights over ownables are acquired and transferred. They should be discussed together because Hume's explanation of them relies upon his theory of association of ideas as well as upon utility. Objects become owned by accession if they are connected in an intimate manner with objects which are already owned.[65] Hume's examples are the fruits of one's garden, the off-spring of one's cattle and the work of one's slaves. The connection is made by the imagination which "connects two objects by means of an intermediate one which is related to both."[66] In the example of the fruits of one's garden, the fruits are owned because the plant which is the intermediary belongs to the owner; the owned plant is the imaginative connection between the owner of the plant and its fruit. One rationale for accession as a criterion of title is that it reflects the way in which the mind works.

Two comments need to be made about accession. First, the criterion adds a criterion of title which is missing, or is unstated, in Locke's discussion of ownership. Locke's criteria of labor, gift, and exchange are not complete unless Locke assumes something similar to Hume's accession. Second, it is not clear that utility is always promoted by accession. While in many cases it is beneficial to the society that the farmer owns the produce of his crops, both Aristotle and Aquinas mention circumstances in which this might not be so. In some forms of social organization communal ownership of the fruits might be more advantageous.

Hume also appeals to the association of ideas as part of his rationale for succession viewed as a criterion of title which vests rights over ownables in the "son after the parents decease. . . ."[67] Because the imagination naturally passes from parent to child, Hume believes ownables should also so pass. With succession, as with accession, the association of ideas is not Hume's only reason supporting this criterion of title. Hume also believes that it is in the general interest of mankind that parents be able to give what they own to their children because it makes the parents "more industrious and frugal."[68] To what extent Hume is correct that this right of inheritance does stimulate industry and conservation shall be discussed more thoroughly in Chapter VI. Suffice it for now to note that common law entailments may have thwarted economic development of land. There may be some reason for thinking Hume is correct, but other factors such as the concentration of wealth and power in a relatively small number of persons, as Marx argues, may change the desirability of an unfettered right of inheritance.

It is difficult to understand how limiting the association of ideas is in defining the two criteria of title accession and succession. Societies with social structures and traditions different from the English society in which Hume lived might generate different associations of ideas in their members. A society in which all young people of the same age cohort were considered to be children in common of all the parents, for example as in Plato's *Republic* or in some so-called primitive cultures, might create different associations of ideas. Hume appears to be aware of these possibilities, at least in his *Enquiries*, where he admits that ownership rules ought to be modified to meet the particular convenience of each community, e.g., its manners and religion.[69] Similarly, it should be expected that if any particular society's associations of ideas change, so should the rules of ownership. While Hume frequently contrasts the association of ideas with utility as separate supporting reasons for his criteria of title, he also thinks that the two kinds of reasons point in the same direction. It is a mistake to collapse the two reasons solely to utility. Hume probably did believe that basing criteria of title upon the association of ideas augments utility, yet he always maintains a separation between the two kinds of reasons. It is plausible to interpret Hume in this way; unfortunately neither the *Treatise* nor the *Enquiries* is sufficiently precise to remove all uncertainty about what Hume's actual position is.

The last of the criteria of title in the *Treatise* is "transferrence by consent." Hume's reason for including this criterion is clearly utility. He says that the other criteria of title may place under people's control goods they neither need nor desire, "persons and possessions may very often be ill adjusted."[70] People's needs and desires can be better satisfied if they are able to transfer to one another what they own. Transferring title by gift, bequest, or exchange is complete, determinate, and consistent.

The five criteria of title Hume proposes in the *Treatise* are consistent and can possibly be made determinate. Completeness is still a problem because first possession, prescription, and accession do not guarantee that all ownables can be owned. Goods which are quickly perishable may not last long enough to become owned by prescription, and if they are not originally possessed or if they are not products of goods already owned, there are no criteria in the *Treatise* by which they are owned. Locke's well used example of fruit picked off a tree exemplifies the problem. The fruit is too short lived to be owned by prescription. If the tree and the land upon which it grows are not owned and are not closely related to anything which is owned, the fruit cannot be owned. None of the criteria proposed in the *Treatise* apply to this situation.

In the *Enquiries*, Hume proposes a criterion of title which is not included in the *Treatise*. "Who sees not . . . that whatever is produced or improved by a man's art or industry ought, for ever, be secured to him, in order to give encouragement to such useful habits and accomplishment?"[71] The addition of labor (presumably upon what is unowned) as a criterion of title makes Hume's whole set complete. Fruit from unowned trees becomes owned by he who picks it.

Hume's criteria of title closely resemble the criteria of title for private ownership. Labor, gift, bequest, and exchange vest rights in owners. Although Hume says little about the range of rights which vest in owners, he seems to have in mind a range of rights of title which closely approximates private ownership. Hume says that owners' rights over what they own are absolute and entire.[72] In the context which this appears, Hume may only be making the observation that ownership rights either completely vest or fail to vest (whatever their range) in owners and that there are no degrees of vesting. Yet he also states that owners have, "full right to make use," of what they own which suggests a wide range of ownership rights.[73] To this extent Hume's concept of rights also approximates private ownership. To another extent, Hume recognizes the need for civil laws to both regulate and define ownership rules which conceivably could legitimate a range of rights of title less broad than private ownership. Neither the *Treatise* nor the *Enquiries* permits a more definite conclusion about the rights Hume actually has in mind.

Of Hume's theory of ownership, his most significant contribution is the analysis of the conditions which give rise to the need for ownership rules. Without any scarcity of goods or labor there is no need for any ownership rules at all. Hume is also correct in insisting that ownership is rule constituted and created. The remainder of Hume's theory is not very remarkable. His moral justification of ownership is not sophisticated enough to address the issues which have been raised in recent investigations into the relation between act and rule utilitarianism, although Hume deserves credit for many original insights. The content of Hume's form of ownership differs little from other defenders of private ownership, although, again, he has some important insights into the plight of the poor.

C. Rawls

John Rawls is the last of the Conventionalists who need to be discussed. Rawls can be classified as a Conventionalist because he believes that ownership rules, as well as the rules which define justice, are a product of deliberation in an original position that decides upon the rules for society. Rawls explicitly accepts Hume's description of the conditions which give rise to the need for ownership.

Rawls' theory is well known and too far reaching to summarize here. There is, however, one contribution he makes toward the justification of ownership which is unique and will be the focus of this section.

In his book, *A Theory of Justice*, John Rawls presents a most radical account of ownership of oneself. He argues that the distribution of natural talents must be regarded as a common asset[74] and also that the distribution of natural abilities must be regarded as a collective asset.[75] Since Rawls does not place any emphasis on the difference between natural talents and abilities, it is best to consider them as freely interchangeable stylistic variants of one another. What is radical in Rawls' concept of self-ownership is that at least a part of oneself, i.e., one's share of the distribution of natural talents or abilities, is not privately but collectively or communally owned. This conception of self-ownership differs from all others discussed so far: private ownership of oneself is central to the theories of Locke and Nozick, while even Marx must hold a view of self-ownership which is remarkably close to private ownership. Before discussing why Rawls believes his concept of self-ownership is morally justified it is first necessary to understand what he means by regarding the distribution of natural talents and abilities as common or collective assets.

The necessary logical structure of all forms of ownership can help make sense of Rawls' concept of self-ownership. Communal or collective ownership can be contrasted with private ownership. Private ownership of oneself is constituted by a status criterion of title that each person is himself and by performative criteria of gift, bequest and exchange as well as by rights of title which include the rights to possess, to use, to manage, to the income, to the capital, to security, and to transmit by gift, bequest, or exchange. Self-ownership, according to Rawls' view, would have to differ from private ownership in the rights of title, criteria of title, and also in the subject and object of the ownership relation. Consider first the criteria of title and rights of title for Rawls' conception of ownership of natural talents. There would have to be criteria of title for the natural talents or abilities which are collectively owned and there would have to be criteria of title for those aspects of a person which are not collectively owned but owned in some other way. In each case the object of the ownership relation would have to be differentiated from the other aspects of a person. It is not at all clear how to draw the line between natural talents and the other aspects of a person. Rawls seems to think that such inherited qualities as intelligence or body build and dexterity are to be included in the category of natural talents. Acquired talents such as learning French might be excluded, but Rawls sometimes includes skills developed by education and training in the category of natural assets or powers.[76] Rawls is never really clear about the distinction. If the criteria of title over natural assets is to be determinate, a more careful distinction has to be made. The subject of the ownership relation would also have to be specified. Assuming that a clear distinction could be drawn between natural abilities which are collective assets and the other aspects of persons which are not, the problem remains of defining the community in which the rights over the collective assets vest. Rawls, reluctantly, identifies the community in which the rights vest with nation states for the purpose of simplicity in the exposition of his theory. The criterion of title over natural talents and abilities would be a status criterion that each member of the nation has rights (yet to be specified) over the natural talents and abilities of all members of the nation. However, limiting the community (or collective) to national boundaries may be morally arbitrary or capricious. The accident of living or being born on one side of a boundary rather than another might dramatically affect the collective assets over which one has rights. If this criterion of title can be made determinate, since it appears to be consistent and complete, the rights of title over natural talents and abilities can be discussed.

The rights over the collective assets which vest in the members of the community would be a proper sub-set of private ownership rights determined by the nature of natural talents or abilities and by the two principles of justice as fairness. It is the nature of natural talents and abilities that they cannot be possessed except by the person whose talents they are. So it makes no sense to include the right to possess or the right to transmit by gift, bequest, or exchange in the rights of title which vest in the community. The right to security, i.e., the right to be protected against unlawful taking of or damage to what one owns by others, would make sense only if construed as duties upon members of other nations or if the right could be construed as a duty of the community to promote, or at least not reduce, the pool of natural talents. What remains are the rights to use, to manage, to the capital and to the income. The difference principle, the second of Rawls' three lexically ordered principles used to establish justice as fairness, implies that the greater well-being of those who are well off is justified only if it is required to improve the condition of the lesser (or least) well off. Income therefore may need to be transferred to those with small incomes from those with large incomes. The difference principle implies that possessors of natural talents have no special right to the income their talents may earn in an economic system. Rights over the income from natural talents vest in all members of the community. Rawls does not suggest that the income be distributed equally, because that may lower the well-being of those who are less well off. Rawls believes that justice requires incentives to stimulate production. He further believes that the difference principle captures the idea of a just distribution in that all members of the community would agree to the distribution if they considered the idea from the proper position.

While it is clear that the right to income is part of the rights of title which vest in the community, it is not clear where Rawls' principles of justice place the rights to use, to manage, and to the capital. On the one hand, the principle of liberty, that each person has an equal right to the most extensive basic liberty compatible with a similar liberty for others,[77] seems to require that the rights to use, to manage, and to the capital vest in the individual possessor of natural talents. Were others or the community as a whole to have the right to decide how one's talents are to be used, e.g., the kind of employment one is to seek, the liberty of the community would take precedence over the liberty of the individual. The same could be said for the rights to manage and to the capital. If the community could dictate to the possessor of a talent that he manage his talent in a certain way, e.g., by going to law school, or that he refrain from consuming the capital, e.g., by smoking cigarettes, the possessor of the talent would not have the same freedom to control as would the community. On the other hand, the difference principle which redistributes or transfers income does limit how individuals use their natural talents. The difference principle might require those who desire large incomes to work harder than they would have to work without income transfers. To the extent that limits on income are imposed, the rights to use, to manage, and to the capital would vest in the community as a whole which imposes the income transfer and redistribution.

Collective ownership of natural talents or abilities, however, can most straightforwardly be understood as a right to the income from the talents or abilities which vests in each member of the community simply because of membership in the community. The specific form of ownership for the other aspects of a person, i.e., those aspects not included as natural talents or abilities, is not discussed explicitly by Rawls but it seems safe to assume that it closely resembles the private ownership form. Thus the form of self-ownership which is implied by Rawls' theory of justice is a composite. Part of the self is owned by rules which resemble those which constitute private ownership and part of the self is owned by rules which vest in the community the right to income from natural talents and abilities.

Before addressing the question whether Rawls' conception of self-ownership is or is not morally justifiable, there is a certain vagueness in the idea of a right to income from talents which needs to be considered. Income is typically earned through work. Natural talents or abilities have no value unless they are coupled with effort in the attempt to do something. People are not paid for their talents or abilities but for what they do with them. A person's income is therefore a function of his talents or abilities and the effort he makes.[78] It is not clear whether the collective ownership of natural talents includes the right to all income produced by talents plus effort or whether it includes only the right to that part of the income which is attributable to the natural talent factor – assuming that it could be isolated and computed. It is sometimes suggested that the willingness to make an effort is itself a natural talent or ability and, therefore, the problem does not arise. But if the willingness to make an effort is not a natural talent or ability, then only that part of the income which is attributable to natural talents or abilities would properly be the object of communal rights. How large or small a portion of the income this part is cannot be discussed here.

The moral justifiability of Rawls' conception of self-ownership can be evaluated from two perspectives. First, from an internal perspective of consistency with his own theory, and second, from an external perspective which brings into question the justifiability of the theory of justice as fairness. From an internal perspective, the idea that a part of the self is communally owned seems *ad hoc* and not essentially connected to other parts of Rawls' theory. Why are natural talents and abilities collective assets, while natural resources and land are not? One of Rawls' reasons for considering natural talents as collective assets is to mitigate the influence of social contingency and natural fortune on distributive shares.[79] Would not the same reasoning apply to natural resources and land? Private ownership of natural resources and land may not mitigate but exaggerate the influence of social contingency and natural fortune. Suppose Brown privately owns a parcel of land upon which oil is discovered. This good fortune will dramatically increase Brown's income. Does Brown deserve the increased income? Suppose further that Brown did little or nothing to contribute to the oil discovery (it was his neighbors who first drilled the risky exploratory wells on their land) and that Brown did not buy the land but inherited it. This case seems exactly parallel to how social contingency and natural fortune bestow talents and abilities. If natural talents and abilities are considered by Rawls as collective assets, he logically should consider natural resources and land as collective assets also. Rights over income from natural resources and land also ought to vest collectively in the members of the community simply because they are members of the community. If a person's talents and abilities are a natural endowment which belong to everyone, it is difficult to see why land and resources which are nature's endowment should not also belong to everyone. Rawls could maintain consistency by abandoning the idea of natural talents as collective assets. However by giving up the idea he would give up much of what is distinctive in justice as fairness.

It is not possible to adequately evaluate Rawls' theory from the external point of view in this section. Far too much has been written in criticism of Rawls and in his defense to summarize here. There is no widespread agreement either that his theory is right or that it is wrong. What may be Rawls' most important contribution is his idea of a plurality of life plans which are rational and which are deserving of respect. Justice does involve the distribution of what is needed for each person to try to achieve the good life as he himself conceives of it. The last two chapters discuss what role ownership plays.

Conventionalists view ownership as a product of society, not as natural law. Moral principles may guide the selection of a form of ownership although the Conventionalists are not in agreement that there is one form right for all societies. And, while they disagree somewhat about the conditions which actually give rise to ownership, they are unanimous in rejecting the unrealistic assumption of abundance. Chapter V now discusses Marx and Owen who oppose private ownership.

CHAPTER V

Two Opponents

The focus of this chapter is upon the opposition to private ownership by Robert Owen and Karl Marx. Marx's opposition to private
ownership is frequently cited, but it is also frequently misunder-
stood. Owen's opposition is less widely known now, and so, therefore, are his remedies to the drawbacks of private ownership. Both
Owen and Marx agree in their opposition to private ownership of
land; they disagree however upon the rules for ownership of self
and labor. Owen shall be discussed first and then Marx.

It needs to be recalled at this juncture that Owen and Marx are
not the only opponents to private ownership. Plato opposes
private ownership and Rousseau believes private ownership
creates both poverty and the absence of ownables. Aquinas
defends a form of ownership which in some respects resembles
private ownership, but the form has other aspects which significantly differ. Although Aristotle claims he is defending private
ownership, his rules of land ownership are not private ownership
rules. Locke and Hume, who defend private ownership under
some conditions, also believe that civil governments may legitimately alter private ownership in order to promote the good of
the community. Finally, Rawls has argued against the idea of
private ownership of natural talents and abilities.

A. Robert Owen

Robert Owen is probably best known in connection with the co-
operative movement in England and the United States. His
training was neither philosophical nor academic, while his inspi-
ration arose from his practical business experiences. His ideals
grew out of the mills he operated or owned where Owen exper-

imented with differing forms of organization and reward. Later in his life, Owen devoted all of his time to proselytizing his ideas.

Owen shares a widely held outlook concerning the conditions of the working class in early nineteenth century England during the height of industrialized manufacturing and capitalism. Workers were poor, overworked, uneducated, and in a condition of moral decay. Owen's assessment of these evils focuses upon three main causes. The first is the absence of good education resulting in part from a misguided understanding of human nature. Second is the manufacturing system, which Owen believes depreciates both the value of human labor as well as the human himself. The third of the causes is private ownership of land and manufacturing which creates conflicts of interest, competition, and individualism. Owen's assessment of the causes needs to be explained more fully before his cure to the evils can be examined.

Owen criticizes the education of his time for failing to take into account the truth that "character is formed for and not by the individual."[1] In many ways Owen views this truth as the cornerstone of his theory. Owen believes that if education is not universal and if education does not provide both "practical and theoretical knowledge" as well as forming good moral habits of unity and charity, people will remain in a "period of ignorant selfishness."[2] Human character is molded by the environment and education thus; Owen's cure attempts to capitalize upon this by carefully controlling early education. Children are to live in dormitories separated from their parents. They will be collectively educated not only in practical skills needed for work and in theoretical knowledge needed for understanding, but also in what Owen calls principles of unity and universal charity.[3] Children's characters are formed for them by their education. Owen is well aware that education at the time he wrote was not universal and it failed to be directed towards the appropriate kinds of knowledge and character formation. The absence of education for the poor, Owen believes, perpetuates their devalued state. They do not have the skills to improve their condition so that they must compete among themselves for bad jobs. More importantly, they do not apply the principle of union which would enable them to co-operate with one another in order to improve their conditions.

The second of the causes, for Owen, is the use of machinery by industry. Machinery and industry:

. . . have created an aggregate of wealth, and placed it in the hands of a few, who by its aid, continue to absorb the wealth produced by the industry of the many. Thus the mass of the population are become mere slaves to the ignorance and caprice of the monopolists, and are far more truly helpless and wretched than they were before the names of Watt and Arkwright were known.[4]

Unlike Marx, Owen blames the introduction of machinery for devaluing labor rather than blaming the capitalist economic structure even where machinery is not introduced.[5] Owen believes that the greater productiveness of machinery simply makes labor less in demand and therefore less valuable. Owen has no theory of exploitation although he does recognize that private ownership of land and industry forces workers to be employed by others. Workers are not able to privately own sufficient quantities of land to be self-sufficient and self-employed.

To some extent, Owen anticipates one of Marx's criticisms of the division of labor. Owen attacks the division of labor because it dehumanizes workers by limiting their skills and abilities:

It has been a popular opinion to recommend a minute division of labor and a division of interests. It will presently appear, however, that this minute division of labor and division of interests are only other terms for poverty, ignorance, waste of every kind, universal opposition throughout society, crime, misery, and great bodily and mental imbecility.[6]

Division of labor restricts workers to low paying jobs which require little skill. They are not required to have great knowledge and skill and thus they receive none. Further, division of labor creates competition between workers, e.g., those who make spinning machines and those whom the machine replaces. Workers do not have the skills and abilities or the principle of union which Owen believes are necessary for any improvement of their condition. Not only are the workers in competition with one another, but Owen also believes that the interests of those who govern the system of manufacture and industry are opposed to the interests of the worker so that "while man remains individualized these evils must continue."[7]

The third of the causes, according to Owen, is private ownership of land and factories. Private ownership of land by the wealthy

118

cuts off the worker from sources of self-subsistence while private ownership of factories forces workers to find wage labor employment.

> But the lowest stage of humanity is experienced, when the individual must labor for a small pittance of wages from others – when he is not suffered to have land, from which, by his own labor, he may produce the meanest necessaries of life. . . .[8]

Workers who own neither land nor instruments of production must work for wages from others. Private ownership, therefore, permits the relatively small number of owners to enormously increase their wealth at the expense of the industrious classes who become, "poorer, more numerous, and more degraded."[9] Without access to land workers cannot become self-sufficient or improve their condition.

Owen further believes that private ownership fosters individual interests which place workers and owners in competition amongst themselves and with each other. Owners are in competition with one another to produce more and better products which are less expensive to purchase. Owners, therefore, introduce more and newer machinery to enhance production and lower costs. Increased use of machinery has the effect that workers are displaced by machines and are thrown into greater competition for fewer jobs. Wages are depressed even further. Owen believes that competition among the owners also stimulates competition among the workers. He also believes that there is competition between workers and owners. Raising the wages of the workers inevitably will reduce the owners' profits. Low wages, competition, and increased use of machinery, coupled with the absence of education for workers' children, makes any chance for the workers to improve their condition a remote possibility.

Owen's cure for these evils is the creation of a new kind of community for living and working. He uses a number of different names to refer to the new community. In some places he simply calls these communities "the cottage system."[10] In other places he refers to them as "villages of unity and mutual co-operation."[11] But what is probably the best known of the names he uses is "home colonies."[12] The home colonies are intended by Owen to be self-supporting, voluntary unions for mutual co-operation. These are communally owned, self-contained communities which provide for the needs of all their members and, if possible, their rational wants and desires.

Owen envisions home colonies to be composed of members who freely choose to live there and who collectively own all of the land, buildings, machinery, and other assets of the colony. Colonies originally will be founded by privately financed joint-stock companies with the private investors ultimately being bought out from the surplus produced by the colony.[13] Membership in the colony either will be generated from the children of its members or new members will be admitted from the outside by a vote of the members.

Owen believes that agriculture should be the mainstay of the colony's production.[14] Curiously, he advocates the use of hand cultivation rather than the mechanical plough. Hand cultivation puts more people to work, he believes, and he thinks hand culti-vation is more productive.[15] Owen also recommends that each colony be self-sufficient in manufacturing clothing and furniture for its own consumption.[16] Over and above producing the means of its own subsistence, a home colony is to provide decent living quarters, free education, medical care, baths, lecture rooms, art studios, dormitories for young persons, recreation gardens, parks, gymnasia, libraries, museums, classrooms, kitchens, and communal dining rooms.[17]

The dwelling houses have two kinds of living arrangements: apartments for adults and dormitories for children and young persons. The children of the colony live in dormitories, not with their parents, and the children are educated together by male and female members of the colony who work as teachers. Besides educating all of the children in practical and theoretical knowledge for jobs, they are also trained in principles of union and universal charity. All members of the colony eat together in common dining rooms with food that is prepared in common kitchens. The recreational and other educational facilities are available to all members.

The work of each colony is to be shared and rotated among the members.[18] While Owen is opposed to "minute division of labor," he believes in a division of labor based upon age and sex.[19] Women are to cook, wash, clean, and make garments. Men are employed on farms, buildings and manufacturing, gardens, and so on. Both sexes participate in the education of the children. Owen believes the work should be performed in healthful conditions and no one should work so long as to endanger mental or physical health. Under these working conditions, Owen predicts that the products will be far better made and with less labor.[20] More importantly for Owen, the home colonies shall unite all classes with good feelings to one another because working together and sharing in the products will destroy all contest and competition.[21] Individualism will be replaced by the principle of union.[22]

> There will be no occupation requisite to be performed by one, which will not be equally performed by all; and by all far more willingly than any of the general affairs of life are now performed by any class, from the sovereign to the pauper.[23]

Owen, however, is not consistent in his position about how members of home colonies are to be compensated for their work. Lodging, food, education for children, and recreational facilities are, of course, provided for all by the colony; but Owen gives three different answers to the question of how the remaining goods of the colony are to be distributed. At one place, he suggests that the members of the colony may freely take goods beyond mere necessities from a general store of the colony if a surplus exists.[24] Owen, elsewhere, utilizes the idea of labor notes for exchange so that goods which contain a certain quantity of labor may be obtained by a worker who presents a voucher acknowledging he has worked the requisite length of time.[25] In a third location, Owen suggests that members of the colony receive an equal yearly wage in addition to room, board, education, and so forth.[26]

These three different ways of distributing goods are very different from one another. They have different implications for the economic viability of home colonies and different implications as well for development and reward of the members. More shall be said about this shortly.

Owen's cure for the evils suffered by the workers is based upon abandoning private ownership of land, resources, the means of production, buildings, and the provision or supply of food within the home colonies. The criteria of title for this domain of ownables is simply that of being a member of the colony. The rights of title which vest in the members are the rights to use, to manage, and to a share in the income and benefits from the co-operative enterprise. Owen mentions nothing about the right to alienate the land, buildings, or resources although he does hold that surplus goods may be exchanged for goods a colony needs but cannot produce.

Private ownership of self and labor is also abandoned in Owen's cure. Members of a home colony collectively have the right to manage and direct the labor of each of the members; they have rights over the products of each member's labor as well as the right to control living arrangements, the food consumed, and the children's education. Each member of the colony, simply because he is a member of the colony, has a right to participate in decisions about how the labor of all is to be used and a right to a share of the product of the collective labor. As a result, members of the colony do not have the right to make individual decisions about the content or direction of their labor nor do they have the right to the product, or the fraction of the product, produced by their talents, abilities, and effort. Unless Owen believes that all members of the colony have equal talents and abilities as well as making an equal effort, those who have less will have a right to be subsidized by those who have more.

Owen would not believe these communal rights over the labor of the members of a colony to be a source of concern. He predicts that in the home colonies all classes will be united by good feelings and will be infused with a "spirit of universal charity."[27] Further, he believes union will benefit all members because co-operative production will create more and better goods with less labor than will competition. Members should therefore have no reason to complain about subsidizing others or feel any loss of autonomy and self-determination.

Owen's idea that members of the colony are collectively owned by the colony as a whole closely resembles Rawls' idea which is discussed in Chapter IV. Both Rawls and Owen agree that the members of a community as a whole have rights over the income from the labor of others. Owen goes further than Rawls insofar as he includes the right to direct the content and form of the labor itself. Owen permits less individual autonomy than does Rawls who limits the rights to income alone. What may save Owen from the charge that he justifies a totalitarian regime in which individuals become subordinate to the whole is that membership in home colonies may be voluntary. In theory, members are free to leave, perhaps preferring to live in a society which permits private ownership of self and labor. In contrast to Rawls who establishes his rules of ownership for all inclusive nation states,

Owen may consider his colonies to be voluntary associations which exist within a society otherwise operating a form of private owner-ship. (Owen is not clear on this, however.)

Home colonies are expected to cure the evils of private owner-ship based on capitalistic manufacture, competition, and individu-alism. Owen abandons private ownership for all domains of ownables in order to bring about union, co-operation, and charity which he believes are necessary to improve the condition of the workers. He frequently writes as if other attempts at a cure will be insufficient to bring about the desired goal. There are difficulties with Owen's conception of home colonies. They can best be discussed by arranging them into economic difficulties and moral difficulties.

For the purpose of presenting the economic problems of opera-ting home colonies, it is most fair to present them in the best economic light, i.e., by assuming the colonies function according to the rules Owen sets down. Thus problems such as providing efficient collective management or finding suitable land to support both agriculture and manufacture shall not be raised. The lack of standardization may also be a problem in finding parts for machinery, but it shall be assumed that this difficulty, also, can be surmounted. The first economic difficulty arises out of the relation of the colonies to the rest of society. Owen is not clear about whether the home colonies are intended to exist within a society which is elsewhere dominated by capitalist production and private ownership or whether they are intended to supplant private ownership capitalism as the dominant societal economic form. Both options have economic difficulties.

Consider the first option: that home colonies co-exist within a system of private ownership capitalism. There are problems about how the colonies can survive in an economy that is dominated by competitive and profit oriented capitalism. Owen might try to downplay the difficulty because he believes that the colonies should be as self-supporting as possible. Still, competitive private ownership capitalism will encroach upon the colonies. Purchasing the land which a colony ultimately will own by borrowing capital may become more expensive as there is increased competition for funds or capital that can be used to produce greater returns on the investment than a colony could provide. Colonies might be able to borrow money only if the colonies worked as hard or were as efficiently productive as their capitalist competitors. Also, colonies which need to purchase goods they themselves do not produce would be faced with the option of supporting capitalist competitors by buying from them or perhaps paying more by buying from other home colonies that are not as efficiently productive. Owen believes these problems would not arise because home colonies would produce better goods for less cost as a result of the better training of the workers and their enthusiastic attitude toward their work. Owen's belief is not without credibility; training and attitude are significant factors in efficient production. As Aristotle argues, people take more care with what they themselves own.[28] But the increased effort and training, which Owen believes the colonies will stimulate, may not be sufficient to balance the technological advances private ownership capitalism fosters to lower costs or to balance the lower costs of the capitalists due to the minimum wages which are paid to the workers. The difficulty of inefficient production leads to the economic drawbacks which would arise even if home colonies were to be the dominant societal economic form and not have to compete with private ownership capitalism.

Home colonies might have difficulty in providing incentives to their members for innovation and initiative because of the methods Owen recommends for rewarding labor. It might be thought that Owen's labor note voucher system might provide an incentive. Workers could be rewarded for work by using the labor notes to receive goods from the colony store. Owen's labor notes only reflect the length of time a member works; the notes do not reflect either the energy or skill the worker applies to his work. Innovation or initiative are not reflected except, at best, if there were to be some correlation between them and the quantity of time actually worked. Owen's second method of distribution, which permits members to simply take what they want of any surplus, obviously provides no incentives. Similarly, Owen's third way of distributing, where the members share equally in the goods produced by their colony, creates little incentive for members to make an extra effort necessary to invent new products or processes. Their share of what is produced is not increased; so unless they received other forms of reward, their extra effort would gain them nothing.

The principles of union and universal charity which Owen repeatedly predicts will replace individual selfishness as the primary motivating principle of human nature might conceivably produce the necessary incentives. Hume has maintained that increased benevolence would eliminate the need for private ownership and it might also eliminate the need for private reward.[29] Whether human nature can be so changed is a factual issue not yet settled and whether the methods required to bring about the change are morally permissible is also an issue far from being settled. Even if Owen were right and human nature could be altered in a morally permissible way, he fails to discuss anything in the arrangement or organization of home colonies which would institutionalize and finance innovation or research. It may not be impossible to organize the needed institutional framework with non-monetary rewards. Many modern businesses are well organized in this way.[30] Home colonies must, at the very least, devise a procedure for stimulating innovation which is compatible with the principles of union and universal charity rather than with a principle of individual benefit.

The second difficulty facing home colonies where they are the dominant form of economic organization within society is that of amassing sufficient capital for economies of scale and for specialized training or education of its members. Owen, writing in the nineteenth century, cannot be faulted for failing to see the need for large quantities of capital, but the home colonies cure for the degraded condition of the workers would stultify economic and technological progress. Owen's small self-contained home colonies could not individually create sufficient quantities of venture capital needed by many advanced industries nor could they afford the expensive education which is required for specialists in technologically advanced societies, even if the members of a colony worked many more hours than Owen believes is necessary. A home colony could not afford the huge expense in building, equipment, and specialized teachers which, e.g., is required by modern medical or engineering education. Even greater expense would have to be incurred if members of the colony rotated jobs and thus everyone, or almost everyone, would need specialized education. Colonies could not afford to build their own advanced factories, airports, or complicated energy generating facilities. Too much capital is needed for investment for small colonies to amass. Besides, were colonies somehow able to finance such products, social resources might not be efficiently allocated because too many factories, for example, might be constructed by colonies acting independently from one another.

These economic difficulties are clearly liabilities to be faced by self-sufficient home colonies. Even if home colonies could form federations with one another, as Owen suggests, to produce the advantages of large cities, raising capital may require long hard work.[31] The leisure time for improvement, the rotation of jobs, as well as the spirit of co-operation would be endangered by the economic requirements of progress and development.

An economy dominated by home colonies would therefore differ greatly from capitalism or even from a centrally planned economy. Many modern conveniences, not to mention many modern technological achievements, might not exist. Consumers would have far fewer products to choose among. Life might be simpler but, perhaps, far less comfortable. The economic drawbacks now begin to have serious moral implications.

Because of the form of ownership of self and labor practiced by home colonies, members do not have the same freedoms to choose employment, to choose living styles, to raise families, or even to choose meal times and foods as would members of societies based on market socialism, regulated captialism or, as shall be seen, on autonomous ownership. So long as home colony membership is voluntary and as long as adults have the freedom to leave and live under less restrictive forms of social organization, there is no unjustified restraint upon the rights of those who choose to surrender them to the colony. The voluntary trade off of autonomy in return for the security and well-being of membership is certainly an option adults have a right to exercise. Were all of society organized according to the principles of home colonies so that they were the only available form of social organization, significant moral issues would arise about legitimate freedom and autonomy.

Each member of a colony is owned by the colony as a whole. The labor, the income, and most of the living conditions of each member would be controlled by a collective decision made by members as a whole. In home colonies, the rules of ownership for one's self and one's labor would be identical to the ownership rules for things such as land, resources, and buildings. (It might be said that the identity of the rules implies that home colonies treat persons as things just as the identity of the rules of private ownership implies that things are treated as persons.) The form of ownership for one's self and one's labor which Owen prescribes for home colonies ignores individual autonomy by locating ultimate control over the individual in the colony as a whole. Each member of the colony has about as much authority over his own life as he has over the communal land he hand-cultivates. If no other form of social organization is available, members' rights may be unjustifiably limited.

Owen sees these limitations on individual autonomy as a necessary condition for improving the lives of the workers. Private ownership of both land and resources as well as self and labor must be abandoned in Owen's plan. While it may be true that workers' poverty already limited their freedom as much or more than would home colonies, the condition of the workers in nineteenth century England may not be the most appropriate benchmark for comparison. That the workers would be better off and perhaps more free in home colonies is not a sufficient justification. Other forms of social and economic organization might be better still. Chapters VI and VII defend a form of ownership which is justified by a principle of autonomy and which abandons only private ownership of land and resources.

There is a second moral issue raised by Owen's home colonies that needs brief comment. Owen desires to remake human nature by means of education. He believes education is a primary device for replacing what he calls the principle of individualism by the principles of union and universal charity. Owen's goal may be laudatory depending how the replacement principles are construed; increased benevolence or increased concern with the well-being of others may indeed be an improvement over narrow selfishness. Owen's method for achieving this goal may, however, be morally suspect. There is no single place where Owen describes his form of education in enough detail to pinpoint any objection. The overall impression he creates is that of manipulation to bring about the change he desires. There is a justified concern that the education Owen has in mind violates the autonomy of the educated. Owen seems willing to inculcate his ideas in the children of the colonies rather than permitting an environment of inquiry and experiment. The impression Owen gives is that he has discovered the truth and the truth is to be indoctrinated.

It is difficult to imagine such a thoroughgoing alteration of human nature without indoctrination. Were Owen to argue that merely living in a home colony without the individualistic influences of private ownership, people would change and their true nature manifest itself since the corrupting influences of private ownership were removed, he might avoid relying so heavily upon education. Owen does not argue in this way. Education creates character for man; man does not create his own character by education.

Owen believes workers will be better off living in home colonies than they were living under private ownership capitalism in the nineteenth century. There is still the question whether the lack of autonomy is necessary in order to improve the condition of the workers and whether the trade off between well-being and autonomy is worth it. Today, in technologically advanced countries, workers are far better off than in Owen's time, although it might be wondered if home colonies could have produced the advantages. It is not obvious, therefore, that so drastic a change with its limits upon autonomy are now necessary to improve the conditions of those not well off. Nor is it obvious that an erosion of autonomy can be morally justified by gains in well-being. People may have moral rights to direct their lives.

Individual autonomy is incompatible with Owen's cure for the evils of private ownership capitalism. Marx, writing after Owen, shares many of Owen's views about the symptoms, e.g., the poverty of the workers and their unhealthy, unpleasant work. Marx diagnoses a different cause of the symptoms. Marx places less emphasis upon factors such as education and industrialization. For Marx, the cause lies primarily in private ownership, division of labor, and the particular way in which capitalism exploits the workers.

B. Marx

Karl Marx may be the best known opponent of private ownership which he believes to be the cause of the evils of capitalism. His attacks upon private ownership are so numerous and so vehement that it is sometimes mistakenly thought that Marx is opposed to all property relations as such.[32] Marx's own conception of ownership, however, implies that some form or another of ownership must exist in all productive societies, i.e., a productive society without any form of ownership whatsoever is an impossibility. Moreover, Marx's criticism of private ownership capitalism, far from requiring the abolition of all private ownership, actually implies that the rights of title and the criteria of title over such ownables as one's labor and personal possessions closely resemble the rights of title and criteria of title of private ownership.

Marx gives three definitions of ownership which are equivalent. The apparent differences are explainable given the context in which each appears. The earliest definition comes from the *1844 Manuscripts* where ownership is defined as embracing both relations: "the relation of the worker to work and to the product of his labor and to the non-worker, and the relation of the non-worker to the worker and the product of his labor."[33] Later, in *The German Ideology*, Marx gives the following definition: "ownership is the relations of individuals to one another with reference to the material, instrument and product of labor."[34] Lastly, in the *Grundrisse*, he says, "we reduce this property to the conditions of production."[35] These three definitions are consistent with Marx's position in *Capital* where he argues that the objective appearance of ownership as a relation between things only belies the underlying reality of its existence as a social relation between producers.[36]

While Marx considers private ownership of the means of production as the cause of the social evils of capitalism, he also recognizes that all productive societies must have some form or another of ownership. Marx acknowledges that there are "general ideas" or "abstract concepts" which are applicable to all productive societies even though these societies may differ from one another in their economic organization and social structure. The general ideas or abstract concepts have what Marx calls "specific forms" which are applicable to only one society or possibly a few societies. Ownership is one of these general ideas, i.e., relations of individuals to one another with reference to the materials, instruments, and product of labor exist in all productive societies. There may be no single specific form which is shared by all societies; as Marx says, "it is one thing to say that some form of property is a condition of all appropriation; it is something quite different to deduce from this the necessity of private property (a form of appropriation) as the necessary condition of all appropriation."[37] Marx's attacks upon private ownership cannot therefore be construed as applying to all forms of ownership. Marx himself almost always refers to specific forms of ownership with such qualified terms as 'feudal property,' 'private property,' 'communal property,' and 'tribal property.' The term 'property' without qualification almost never is used to refer to specific forms; instead it is used either to refer to ownership in general or to refer collectively to all possible specific forms of ownership. Thus if Marx intends to abolish private ownership, some other specific form of ownership will have to be found to replace it. The remainder of this section discusses Marx's criticism of private ownership and then considers what possible form of ownership could replace private ownership and avoid Marx's criticisms.

Marx's criticism of capitalist private ownership relations is well known. His attack upon private ownership is usually understood to be grounded upon the contradiction in capitalism that simultaneously creates great wealth and many ownables for the few capitalists and little wealth with few or no ownables for the multitude of workers. This contradiction finds expression in Marx's concepts of alienation and exploitation. Alienation consists of three modes: alienation from the object of one's labor, alienation from one's activity of labor, and alienation from oneself, from one's species being, and from one's fellow man.[38]

Exploitation, as Marx expresses it in *Capital*, is the appropriation by the capitalist of the surplus value (unpaid labor time) produced by wage laborers who must sell their labor power in order to survive. Surplus value can be appropriated by the capitalist because the exchange value of labor power, i.e., what the workers receive in wages, is less than the use value of labor power, i.e., the value added to the raw material by labor power, since the exchange value of any commodity, including labor power, is the socially necessary labor time it takes to produce it; the exchange value of labor power for a week is the time it takes to produce the food and so on needed to sustain labor power for a week. Marx believes that in advanced industrialized countries it only requires a small fraction of a week to produce the goods needed to sustain the week's worth of labor. The wages workers receive will be less than the value their labor adds to the raw materials during the week. Were workers capable of self-employment they could receive the entire value added by their labor. Marx argues that self-employment is not a viable option for most workers because private ownership of land, resources, and the means of production by the capitalists cuts the workers off from access to what they would need to be self-employed.[39]

On a much deeper level, Marx's attack is best understood as grounded upon freedom and autonomy. He explains both alienation and exploitation as resulting from impediments to autonomy and from unequal freedom.

The three modes of alienation are explainable as a loss of individual autonomy. Marx believes that private ownership of land and the means of production, which is stimulated by division of labor, requires forms of production in which producers cannot exercise autonomous control. The first mode of alienation in which the workers are alienated from their labor, i.e., the activity of laboring, can be understood as the workers's loss of autonomous control over his labor. Control of the worker's labor is not a function of his own decision but is a function of economic and production requirements. An extreme example is assembly line labor where every aspect of the worker's labor on the job is dictated by his station on the assembly line complex. Marx believes that in these circumstances workers become slaves to the machines. Even outside assembly line jobs, workers are not free to labor as they, themselves, might choose; rather they must constantly strive to perfect those abilities and only those abilities which make them most economically competitive. A self-employed cabinet maker, for example, must relentlessly strive to perfect his ability and efficiency in order to remain competitive with other cabinet makers and with those who sell mass produced cabinets. Marx believes he must labor in this way because if he is not sufficiently competitive jobs will be lured away from him and he will lose the means of earning a livelihood. The self-employed cabinet maker, as all other workers, is not able to control the pace or form of his own labor. He has little choice but to fulfill the requirements imposed upon him by the economic system. Thus, according to Marx, the economic forces produced by private ownership capitalism remove the workers' autonomy over their laboring activity.

The second mode of alienation, alienation from the object of one's labor, also can be understood as loss of autonomy brought about by private ownership capitalism. According to Marx, before division of labor and private ownership created capitalism, the objects produced by labor were designed and produced to directly satisfy the needs and desires of the producer. Things were produced in order to be consumed by the producer and not in order to be exchanged or sold. There was no separation of producer and consumer so that each producer made goods to specifications which fulfilled his own needs and desires. Capitalist production which requires exchange and sale of commodities creates a separation of producer and consumer. Because commodities are produced for sale or for exchange, they must be designed and created to fulfill the needs and desires of consumers who are other than the producer. Even the self-employed cabinet maker must design and produce the kinds of cabinets which consumers desire. Thus the producer is not free to design and create the kind of goods he would choose; instead the producer must make the kind of goods needed or desired by the consumer if he is to succeed in selling or exchanging his goods. The object of the producer's labor is no longer his own. He is alienated from the object of his own labor because the economic requirements of sale and exchange reduce or eliminate his freedom to control what he produces. Forces outside of himself determine what he must produce.

It needs to be noted here that even though Marx correctly estimates the loss of freedom for the producer, he does not emphasize the freedom of the consumer who gains a wide range of options. Were producers more free to produce as they might prefer, consumers might have less control over what they purchase. Possible resolutions of this conflict shall be discussed shortly.

The third mode of alienation, alienation from oneself, one's species being, and one's fellow man, is for Marx a consequence of the first two modes. A person is alienated from himself because he is in autonomous control of neither his own labor nor the goods produced by his own labor. Insofar as a person defines himself through his activities and through what he produces, he is alienated from himself because economic forces outside of himself are in control. Alienation from one's species being or from human nature is also a result of the first two modes. Marx believes that humans are by nature multifaceted, i.e., capable of pursuing and enjoying a wide variety of activities, interests, and avocations. Capitalist economic pressures limit individuals' freedom to pursue this wide variety. They must only concentrate upon activities which help make them economically competitive. Individuals are not free to engage in such activities as writing poetry unless those activities are related to their job because, if they spend too much time writing poetry instead of developing their job required skills, they will not have the narrow range of skills which employers demand. Even the self-employed cabinet maker cannot afford to pursue other interests at the expense of his skills as a cabinet maker. Economic forces control what individuals can make of themselves rather than they, themselves, being in control. Finally, alienation from one's fellow man is also characterized by Marx as a loss of autonomy. Economic forces control how individuals must regard one another. Rather than view one another mutually as a co-operator, friend, or beloved, individuals are forced to regard each other as competitors. Even within the family which is supposed to be bound by ties of love, the potential employment of wives and children create competition with the husbands for scarce jobs. Even if individuals try to regard others as friends, Marx believes that the economic realities make them competitors.

Exploitation, the second prong of Marx's criticism of capitalism, is best explained as an inequality of freedom brought about by private ownership of land, resources and the means of production. One of the conditions Marx believes necessary for widespread capitalist production is that large numbers of people have no other means of earning a livelihood than by selling their labor power. No individual, who has a choice, would sell his labor power and be exploited by another if he could receive the full value of his labor by being self-employed. It is private ownership of land, resources, and the means of production which Marx believes forces the workers to sell their labor power. Individuals who privately own no land, resources, or means of production (and freed serfs who are thrown off their land) are forced to sell their labor power if they are to survive. They have no other means of earning a living. The private owners of land, resources, and the means of production therefore have power over the workers by which the owners are able to appropriate the surplus value produced by the workers. Private owners become rich, powerful and free, while the workers become poor, weak, and enslaved. Marx might say that the slavery of the worker is the condition for the freedom of the private owner capitalist.

Marx's criticism of capitalism has, at least historically, convinced many. But Marx is, himself, guilty of the kind of unrealistic utopian thinking he so often criticizes if he believes that all aspects of alienation can ever be entirely eliminated. It is unrealistic to suppose that alienation as Marx defines it, namely the lack of autonomous control of one's labor, of the object of one's labor and so on, can ever vanish. It is unrealistic to suppose that members of a society can ever make decisions about their labor and its object free from economic concerns encumbering their decisions. Economic imperatives will always impinge upon producers' decisions about what and how to produce. Even the self-employed cabinet maker will have to endure some loss of control if he is to earn a living by making cabinets. Perhaps alienation can be minimized but it can never entirely vanish. Marx is also mistaken if he believes that every sale of labor power to others by which they profit is exploitative. There are many situations in which both employer and employee can mutually benefit. There is little reason to believe, for example, that workers are exploited in instances where they freely choose their employment from several genuine options including the option of self-employment. If both sides freely agree to the bargain, it is hard to see exploitation. Of course if both sides are not free to refuse as Marx maintains is the case for the workers, then, possibly, the weaker side is exploited.

Even though there are some problems with Marx's concepts of alienation and exploitation, there is a principle which Marx mentions in *The Communist Manifesto* which captures what is of value in the two concepts and which can be used to explore possible forms of ownership which would be consistent with his thinking. Marx proposes that the communist society be based upon the principle that "the free development of each is the condition for the free development of all."[40] The principle by itself is difficult to interpret because of its sloganistic character. However, the analysis just given of alienation and exploitation can be used to make the principle more precise. Marx's free development principle (as it shall be named for brevity) would be violated by slavery or by laws which perpetuate exploitation, such as anti-union laws, because the freedom of the slave owner or the exploiter depends upon the absence of freedom for the slave or exploited worker. The owner gains time free from work because he is supported by the work done by others.

Marx believes that private ownership of land, resources, and the means of production also violates his free development principle. Private owners receive benefits from what they own. Private owners of land receive rent, private owners of resources and the means of production receive surplus value. These benefits provide the condition for their free development. Private owners can afford to pursue many interests, vocations, and activities. Such is not the case for workers. Marx believes that in capitalism the workers must be deprived of the conditions for their free development in order for the private owners to enjoy theirs. It is only because the workers are exploited that private owners can receive rents and profits. The workers therefore, Marx believes, are denied the material conditions for their free development, i.e., they are worked so hard and kept so poor that they cannot pursue the interests, activities, and avocations they desire. Private owner-ship of land, resources, and the means of production is seen by Marx as a violation of the free development principle and Marx calls for its abolition.

Marx says practically nothing about the specific forms of owner-ship he believes will eventually replace (or ought to replace) private ownership. Most of his comments are negative criticisms of other socialist thinkers of which his remarks in the *Critique of the Gotha Programme* are typical.[41] There are several possible explanations why Marx never offers a detailed account of owner-ship in a communist society, e.g., he believes that the conditions of production and the specific direction of technological progress cannot be predicted in advance. Because Marx believes that the form of ownership in any society depends upon its material conditions of production and its technology, the specific form of ownership for a communist society cannot be predicted if its conditions of production and technology cannot. This is an example of Marx's scientific or economic realism. It is a standard by which Marx criticizes other socialist thinkers.

While Marx clearly is opposed to private ownership of land, resources, and technologically advanced large factories, he does not appear to believe that all private appropriation needs to be abolished. Self-acquired and self-earned property, private possessions, can be retained.[42] It is not clear what criteria of title and rights of title Marx would include in a private possession form of ownership. "To each according to his need" cannot by itself function as a criterion of title for private possessions because a need criterion can be inconsistent, indeterminate, and incomplete. A criterion of title is imaginable by which each would privately possess what is allocated to him by a possession control board;[43] but there is no evidence that Marx entertained the idea. Besides such a possession control board would most likely violate Marx's economic realism because of its probable economic inefficiency. What the rights of title are over these private possessions is also unclear, e.g., can they be sold or exchanged? Marx does not think they can be bequeathed.[44] But if private possessions can be given away during one's life, (e.g., giving a present to one's daughter) any prohibition against bequest may be without force. It is not possible to know with any precision what rights of title or criteria of title Marx might have in mind for private possessions merely from his few and scattered remarks on the topic. Still, it is possible to speculate about what they might be by considering a form of ownership of oneself and one's labor which is consistent with Marx's free development principle.

Keeping in mind that Marx does not use the concepts of rights of title and criteria of title, it is nevertheless possible to construct a form of ownership for oneself and one's labor that is both economically realistic and consistent with his principle of free development. Once this form of ownership for self and labor is explained, it should be possible to formulate the rules which constitute the private possession form for other ownables.

A specific form of ownership which has as its object the labor of individuals can be constituted by criteria of title which are either status or performative. A status criterion would not depend upon the actions of others or of oneself, but upon a characteristic or set of characteristics which individuals might possess. One status criterion might be the criterion of being oneself, i.e., each person might exercise the rights of title over his own labor because it is the labor of his own person. Another status criterion might be one that John Rawls uses of being a member of a community where the community collectively exercises the rights of title over one's labor simply because each person is a member of the community. Performative criteria of title are based upon actions which individuals perform such as manumission or laboring to produce children. A performative criterion of title over one's labor seems to presuppose some status criterion. For example, the criterion of laboring to produce children can only avoid an infinite regress by postulating the existence of a first parent who is unparented and owns himself. The performative criterion of manumission likewise presupposes an owner who, because of his status, e.g., as a noble, needs no manumission.

Marx's principle that the free development of each is a condition for the free development of all requires a status criterion of title that each individual has the rights of title over his own labor simply because of his status as his own person. If others, because of their status, e.g., as members of the community, have rights over the labor of some person, he is to that extent under their control and not free to develop as he himself might choose. A criterion of title by which the community as a whole could exercise rights of title over individuals' labor would be incompatible with the free development principle. Individuals would not be free to develop in circumstances where their labor is directed by a vote of other members. Marx's free development principle therefore requires that the criterion of title over one's labor be the status criterion of being oneself. Performative criteria of title are excluded because they either involve an infinite regress or they must presuppose a status criterion. The only status criterion compatible with the free development principle is the status of being oneself.

The rights of title over one's labor also must not violate the free development principle. Obviously the rights to possess, control, use, and manage one's labor must be included in the rights because they are the conditions for the free development of any individual. Individuals who lacked these rights could not develop as free, autonomous moral agents. The right to bequeath one's labor is impossible given the nature of labor. What remains to consider are the rights of gift, exchange, and income. Marx sometimes seems opposed to any exchange of labor for wages or even for a proportional share of commonly produced goods.[45] But his opposition to exchange of labor is not an implication of his own principle and, further, it is economically unrealistic. The free exchange of labor for the wages a kind of labor can attract in a free and open labor market is one very efficient way of estimating the value of labor even if the valuation may not be the "morally correct" value, e.g., it is a way to estimate the value of a basketball player compared to a french horn player.

Similarly free market driven wage differentials do provide an efficient, non-coercive mechanism for allocating labor to tasks which need to be performed. A shortage of labor in an area would raise wages and attract more individuals to that area. Where there are many different employers seeking employees or where employers are not exclusively motivated by profit maximization, there is little reason to think that workers will be exploited. The right to exchange one's labor for wages historically did encourage the rise of capitalism. There are other possible economic systems, e.g., market socialism and forms of controlled or regulated capitalism, in which the right to exchange one's labor for wages need not be exploitative. Workers need not be required to work longer or be paid less than is required for efficient production. Efficiency in production is not equivalent to maximizing owners' profits at the expense of the workers. It is difficult to see how a market

137

socialism is exploitative if it does not create surpluses from the workers beyond what is necessary for incentives and capital investment. The mere fact that people must work in order to survive does not imply that work is exploitative. Marx himself recognizes "as a first premise of history" that human beings must labor to produce the means of their own subsistence.[46]

The rights of title over one's labor in a form of ownership which is consistent with Marx's free development principle include the right to exchange one's labor for wages or income as well as the right to possess, control, use, and manage one's labor. The right to give one's labor, as a one sided exchange, also is part of the rights of title. This form of ownership of one's labor differs from private ownership in that there is no right to permanently alienate one's right over one's labor. Private ownership does permit sale and permanent alienation, e.g., of houses, clothes, and cars, so that the two forms differ in at least that respect, as well as in criteria of title.

The rights of title over the ownables Marx calls private possessions can now be understood.[47] They derive from the right to income from one's labor. Such income, typically wages, takes the form of money payment. Money, however, is in itself only a surrogate for the goods which money can buy. The right to income must extend to rights over the goods which constitute income if the right to income is to have any value. Income or wages must be exchanged for things and the value of the things received in exchange partly depends upon the rights individuals can exercise over them. The rights of possession, use, and management surely constitute part of the value of what is received and the rights of gift, bequest, and exchange add to its value. Without these rights, income or wages would have little value. Marx's free development principle requires these rights over things since it is difficult to understand how an individual could be free to develop who could not exercise these rights over what he purchased with his income. A person who, for example, desires to go trout fishing or for whom trout fishing fulfills a recreational need must be able to acquire trout fishing equipment either by purchase or rental if he can afford it. Similarly people must be free to acquire books, records, art supplies, cameras, and so on. There is no reason to believe that the conditions which permit individuals to acquire goods as one of the means of development are incompatible with others' free development. (There are, of course, other sources of development such as love and friendship which may require no material conditions.) The rights to possess goods and to control them can therefore be included in the rights of title if the goods are sufficiently abundant.

Assumptions must be made about the economic and social structures of society if private possession rights of title are to permit the free development of each and all. Land and resources cannot, Marx believes, be privately owned. Also, while it is not the case that all of the means of production need to be communally owned as Marx seems to think, there must be a significant fraction of the means of production which is under public and not private control. Free development additionally presupposes quality education being available for all as well as a fair opportunity for employment. In a society where these assumptions are actualized, private possession rights of title should cause neither exploitation nor too much alienation.

The main difference between rights of title for private possession and for private ownership lies in commercial rights. A person who privately possesses woodworking tools is free to use the tools to mold toys for his children. Marx's free development principle also permits the right to give these toys to friends' children. There is also no reason why such a toymaker could not make these toys to be sold. Marx would draw the line at this point (the sale of the homemade toys), but his free development principle permits greater freedom. Marx's free development principle does not appear to exclude the toymaker from employing others to use his tools and work with him making toys for sale. As long as his workers choose to work for him and have other job opportunities, there seems to be no incompatibility between the toymaker's free development and his workers' free development. Were the owner or his workers prevented from freely choosing to earn their livelihood by making toys, others in the society would be exercising rights over the toymakers' labor and to that extent the toymakers would not be free. Marx's opposition to private employment and to wage labor is not implied by his own free development principle. The control of an individual's labor by the community can be both exploiting and alienating. Still, Marx's idea of private possession does differ from private ownership because of the limits upon exploitation caused by the narrow range of the domain of private ownables. Land and resources are not possible objects of Marx's private possession form. That land and resources must be communally owned places further limits upon the toymaker.

Because Marx, himself, says so little about ownership in a communist society, even this discussion of private possession may stretch his intentions. There is scant guidance for further speculation. His free development principle may be capable of interpretations which would have different implications for ownership. It is not possible to discover with greater conviction what Marx really has in mind.

This concludes the historical survey. Private ownership of land and resources has not been convincingly justified and several arguments have been raised against private ownership of self and labor. On another level, the methodology of state of nature arguments has been shown to be useless in attempting to justify a form of ownership. Progress toward a successful justification has been made by explaining the necessary logical structure of all forms of ownership which is an essential component in understanding how moral principles can be applied in justification. Finally, the task of justification has been simplified by the knowledge that some form of ownership or other must exist in all productive societies. Attempts at justification can therefore be directed towards specific forms of ownership while ignoring the question, why have any form of ownership at all? Chapters VI and VII present a justification of a specific form, autonomous ownership, which resembles private ownership for self and labor and resembles communal ownership for land and resources.

CHAPTER VI

Schema of Justification

A conclusive moral justification of any specific form of ownership must be composed of three factors: the necessary logical structure of ownership, a true or rationally defensible moral principle, and a description of the social and material conditions of the community in which the form of ownership is to apply.

The necessary logical structure of ownership is an essential component because proposed forms of ownership which fail to meet its requirements will not fulfill the function of ownership rules which is to assign to individuals rights over things and to provide a mechanism for the acquisition, transference, and alienation of these rights. The necessary logical structure is insufficient, by itself, to provide a moral justification. While it is true that the necessary logical structure does exclude some proposed forms, there are still many forms of ownership which are consistent with the necessary logical structure but which are not morally justifiable.

A true or rationally defensible moral principle is therefore required in order to select from among the logically possible forms. A moral justification of a form of ownership can only be as sound as the principle upon which it is grounded. The third factor, the material and social conditions of the community, is relevant because different conditions might require different forms of ownership. Which material and social conditions are relevant to the justification is in part a function of the moral principle and the necessary logical structure of ownership.

There is a problem at present in trying to offer a conclusive moral justification for a specific form of ownership. No universal agreement exists either among philosophers or among rational persons generally about which moral principle is true or rationally defensible. Rational persons differ about such issues as the primacy of certain rights, the strength of the duty to help others, and the moral relevance of personal and social well-being. Rational persons and philosophers also disagree about the methods to use in defending first moral principles. Some use a hypothetical original position, some use a dialectically necessary method, and others use an analysis of moral concepts.[1] Since there is no one moral principle which is acceptable to all rational persons upon which to ground a conclusive moral justification of a specific form of ownership, there is little chance that any present justification of a form of ownership will be acceptable to all rational persons.

Because justifications of forms of ownership must at present be inconclusive does not imply that nothing of moral interest can be said about the topic. It is possible to construct a schema of a justification.[2] A schema is the formal conditions of justification to which the employment of a moral principle is restricted. Unlike a conclusive justification, a schema raises no questions about the truth or rational defensibility of the moral principle, or about the truth or falsity of the conditions in which the moral principle is assumed to apply. A schema of a justification would be a conclusive justification if the moral principle were known to be true or if it were acceptable to all rational persons and if the social and material conditions were known to be true. A schema, however, need not be an unrealistic fiction like so many state of nature arguments. Material and social conditions can be assumed which closely approximate the condition of modern communities in which the question of the moral justification of ownership now arises. Similarly, the justificatory moral principle can be one which has a widespread plausibility. The moral principle obviously will not coincide with all beliefs of rational persons but it may, nevertheless, closely match a great many of them.[3] A schema so constructed is as powerful and as conclusive a justification as is at present possible.

What follows in this and in the final chapter is only a schema of justification. Autonomous ownership shall be shown to logically derive from a moral principle in a set of social and material conditions which are presupposed by the schema. Autonomous ownership is only, therefore, as plausible as the plausibility of the schema. The next three sections defend the plausibility of the moral principle as well as the social and material conditions. They are not intended to conclusively establish the truth of the presumptions beyond any doubt, but they are intended to demonstrate a very high degree of plausibility.

A.   The principle

In the important book *The Theory of Morality*, Alan Donagan explains and defends what he believes to be the first principle of Hebrew-Christian morality. Donagan contends there are two ways of formulating the first principle. He attributes one to Aquinas and the other to Kant. On Donagan's view the primary and common principle of the Thomist natural law may be formulated as: "Act so that the fundamental human goods, whether in your own person or in that of another, are promoted as may be possible, and under no circumstances violated."[4] Donagan glosses fundamental human goods as goods which are fundamental to human flourishing and to a full life as a rational being. Such goods are life itself, communicable knowledge, and friendship.[5] Kant's principle is more familiar: "Act always so that you respect every human being, yourself or another, as being a rational creature."[6] Donagan goes on to explain that respecting a being as a rational creature is respecting him as autonomous, i.e., "as having the right, subject to the moral law, to decide for himself what his own good is, and how to pursue it."[7] The two principles are similar although Donagan believes that Kant's version may be more defensible.[8]

It is possible, from the two principles which Donagan believes are fundamental to all Hebrew-Christian morality, to construct a moral principle that should have wide plausibility. The principle, which for ease of reference can be called the autonomy principle, is that every one ought to act so as to respect each person's equal right to decide for himself what his own good is, how to pursue it, and to promote where possible but never violate each person's fundamental well-being. Stated more simply, the principle implies that each person has an equal right to decide upon his own good and how to pursue it while respecting others' autonomy, and a right to the necessary means of acting autonomously while never violating that right in others.

The connection between autonomy and well-being must be stressed. The right to decide upon one's own good and how to pursue it has little value at all and may be an empty hollow right without the ability to make decisions and to act upon them. Basic needs, such as food, clothing, shelter, and so on must be fulfilled in order that a person be alive and make decisions. Without the satisfaction of basic needs autonomy is impossible.[9] Basic needs are the most minimal set of conditions required for human life. While autonomy is impossible without the satisfaction of basic needs, their satisfaction alone may not be the only necessary conditions for human autonomy as a rational being. Donagan mentions communicable knowledge as an additional condition for deciding upon one's own good and how to pursue it.[10] Communicable knowledge presupposes language and some form of instruction. There may be other conditions as well. The concept of fundamental goods can be used to refer to those conditions of well-being in addition to basic needs which must be fulfilled if autonomy is to be possible. The autonomy principle must therefore include the right to both basic needs and fundamental goods.

The autonomy principle can be used in a realistic schema for the justification of a form of ownership because it should seem plausible to a wide range of rational beings. On the one hand, philosophers who criticize forms of utilitarianism because they do not take seriously the inviolability and uniqueness of persons can subscribe to the autonomy principle. The autonomy principle proscribes using persons either by violating their right to determine their own good or by disregarding their well-being in order to promote social well-being. One person's well-being may not be violated to promote the well-being of others (although there is a duty to help others). Also each person, subject to the restraint of respecting others' autonomy, has the right not only to decide upon his own good but also how he shall pursue his good. An individual's conception of his good life is not, therefore, to be sacrificed in some overall social plan. On the other hand, philosophers who criticize deontological moral theories as heartless insofar as they fail to consider everyone's well-being or because they are based upon rigid rights which ignore the consequences of actions, can also subscribe to the autonomy principle. The autonomy principle morally requires a person to promote the well-being of others inasmuch as he can (do) without proportional inconvenience to himself.[11] The autonomy principle may be viewed as bridging the gap between utilitarianism and right based theories. Individuals have rights to well-being, specifically the rights to basic needs and fundamental goods. These are rights which others may have a duty to recognize and respect. Similarly the consequences of actions are relevant to their rightness or wrongness insofar as they affect the rights or the well-being of others.

The autonomy principle prohibits coercing or deceiving people except for self-defense or legitimate punishment. Coercion is prohibited because it violates the equal right to decide upon one's own good, and how to pursue it. A person who is coerced is forced to act not according to his own conception of his good or how to pursue it but to act according to the desires of the person who is coercing. The person who does the coercing violates the right of the person he coerces because he does not give him an equal opportunity to decide upon his own good and how to pursue it, but the coercer tries to get his way at the expense of the person he coerces. Deception, in effect, attempts the same kind of control over others as does coercion but without force. A person who deceives another violates the autonomy principle because he uses deception to get what he wants but could not get if the deceived person knew the truth. The deceived person, who presumably is pursuing his own good as he, himself, perceives it, would act differently were he to know the truth. For example, someone who signs a contract to purchase a plot of land which he has been deceived into thinking habitable would presumably not sign the contract were he to know the land is an uninhabitable swamp. He would not sign because the land would not be a means of pursuing his own good of purchasing land upon which to build a house. Thus those who deceive others are not respecting the equal right of others to decide upon their good and how to pursue it. Coercion and deception both fail to recognize the equal right to decide.

The autonomy principle requires that individuals help others who are in genuine need. The principle that every human being, yourself or another, ought to be respected as a rational being implies a certain fundamental equality among human beings. It might be thought that such fundamental equality requires that no one rationally prefer the satisfaction of his own wants and desires to the satisfaction of another's wants and desires simply because his wants and desires are his own rather than someone else's. Why should one's own wants and desires have an automatic priority simply because they are one's own, if indeed all human beings are to be respected equally as rational creatures? If another person needs and desires help, is it rational to ignore his need and desire simply because his needs are not one's own? If carried to an extreme, such a conception of fundamental equality would result in a denial of selfhood and autonomy. Whenever there are any conflicts between the wants and desires of two individuals, equality might require a stalemate which could only be arbitrarily decided. Suppose Green wants to go fishing and Black wants Green to drive him to the supermarket. If the wants of Green and Black are to be considered equally, the only resolution of the conflict might be arbitrary. Black and Green cannot be under an obligation to each other. Nor can Green and Black ignore each other. Even in conflict, the wants and desires of others, if those others are one's equal, must be considered in one's own deliberation.

There is a way of understanding fundamental equality which can show when the wants and desires of others might take precedence over one's own and thus when others ought to be helped. It is possible to rationally construct a hierarchy of wants and desires that ranks wants and desires according to their value or importance. Basic needs, which must be satisfied if any life at all is to be possible, are the most primary or valuable for anyone who wants to live. Secondary in value or importance are the fundamental goods over and above basic needs, which are not necessary for life but are necessary for minimal human flourishing. The want or desire for basic needs or fundamental goods has a greater value or importance than the want or desire for such things as a color television or a new fly fishing outfit, which can be called fanciful goods. Fanciful goods may fulfill rational wants and desires, but they have a lesser value, immediacy, or importance than basic needs or fundamental goods. This hierarchy lays down a necessary but not a sufficient condition for determining when there is an obligation to help another. In situations where a rational creature needs help in satisfying a more valuable or important want or desire than the want or desire of the person who is in a position to help, then there may be an obligation to help, i.e., there is a good reason for preferring the satisfaction of another's desire to the satisfaction of one's own. In instances where one's own wants and desires are more important or valuable, they ought to be satisfied, e.g., no one is under an obligation to forgo the satisfaction of his own basic needs in order to help another obtain such fanciful goods as a new fly fishing outfit. Only where the wants and desires are of equal value or importance, e.g., the desires of two persons for fanciful goods, does it seem that a sufficiently good reason for preferring the satisfaction of one's wants and desires is that they are one's own.

Two brief comments need to be made about the hierarchy. First, it seems likely that additional distinctions between categories of wants and desires can be arrived at through a more thorough study than can be supplied here. Second, the hierarchy for prioritizing wants and desires is not based upon external criteria imposed upon rational persons. It is rather the case that each person, insofar as he is rational, should himself recognize that the satisfaction of wants and desires for basic needs and fundamental goods is more valuable and more important than other desires because they are causally necessary for the satisfaction of all his other wants and desires. Thus each rational person ought to be able to understand and accept the rationality underlying the hierarchy.

A hierarchy of wants and needs is not by itself sufficient to decide when help is morally required. Merely because another rational being needs help in fulfilling a more primary want or need it may not be morally required that help be given. First, the cost to the person who helps must be less than the benefit of assistance. Second, the person assisting must be reasonably sure that he can successfully offer the assistance, i.e., no one is morally required to try to assist others unless there is a reasonable likelihood that he can succeed. Third, neither the person assisting nor the person in need of help is bound by special or contractual obligations that would require a third party to offer the help. And, finally, help is morally required only where the person needing help did not intentionally choose to be in such a condition. The well-worn but nevertheless perspicuous example of a non-swimmer who slips off a pier and falls into the water can serve as an illustration. If a person standing on the pier can easily extend a rope or plank of wood to the drowning man the cost of so doing is negligible compared to benefit of saving a life. Of course, if the drowning man were far away and the person on the pier were only a marginally competent swimmer, then the cost might be higher especially if there were an appreciable risk that the rescuer might drown. The second·condition is fulfilled if the drowning man is within easy reach of the pier so that the rope or plank can most likely save him. Where the drowning man is far away, the likelihood is less. If there is a lifeguard on duty, it is obviously his duty to attempt the rescue and not the duty of bystanders. Finally, the drowning man did not intend to slip or fall into the water. He did assume some risk by walking out on to the pier, but unless some special assumptions are added to the example, his action is not unreasonably risky. In this situation, a bystander has a moral duty to assist or help the drowning man and he is also morally culpable or blameworthy if he fails to do so.

The idea that persons are morally culpable for their failure to help others where it is morally required makes perfectly good sense. If a person chooses not to act to assist someone where he has a duty to do so, he can be blamed in proportion to the evil or harm he does not prevent, and the degree of his responsibility. The greater the evil he could have (easily) prevented, and the greater his responsibility in failing to prevent it, the more blameworthy he is. It is conceivable that sufficiently blameworthy acts of refusing to help those in need might be punishable. Laws which punish the failure to help might be difficult to enforce because of the difficulty in discovering the degree of responsibility of persons who choose not to act to help. Still, in principle, they might be justifiable.

There are other implications of the autonomy principle, e.g., that each human being ought to promote what will enable him to use his autonomy wisely, but, for the purposes of the justification of a specific form of ownership, the most salient implications are the moral prohibitions against coercion and deception and the moral duty to help others. The right of all rational beings to decide for themselves their own good and how to pursue it is incompatible with coercion or deception, but it does, however, create a duty to help others.

A moral duty to help others requires that each individual may from time to time owe assistance to others in the form of his labor or in the form of the products of his labor. Much depends upon the conditions in which people live and the ability to actually help those who fall into need. In modern affluent societies those who cannot find work of any sort, not merely well paying or pleasant work, deserve to be helped while those who choose not to work when work is available do not.[12] Help owed to persons who live far away or in other countries depends upon the likelihood that the attempt at assistance will be successful and the actual benefit received will be greater than the cost to the donor. How this duty to help others translates into ownership rules will be discussed following an examination of the social and material conditions. At the very least, a duty to help others implies that persons do not have an absolute right over their labor or over the products of their labor which excludes any rights of others. Others may have rights over one's labor in circumstances which give rise to a moral duty to help.

Another implication is that the autonomy principle requires, in practice, procedures for resolving conflicts between persons whose autonomously adopted plans conflict with one another. Persons may adopt plans that are within the limits of the respect for the autonomy of others which nevertheless conflict and cannot both be satisfied. Not all of these conflicts can be resolved by the hierarchy of wants. Brown and Black may both plan to fish the same part of a trout stream, but if the stream is too narrow both may be unable to do so without scaring away all of the fish. The most obvious procedure for conflict resolution is to permit the two who are involved to decide which plan is to be carried out and which plan must be altered or abandoned. The two fishermen may decide to flip a coin to decide who may fish, or they may decide upon other procedures such as a priority rule which would award the first fishing privilege to the one who had least recently fished there, or they could choose to allow an agreed upon arbitrator to decide.[13]

Where the number of persons whose plans may conflict becomes greater, multilateral bargaining becomes too costly so standardized or conventional procedures may need to be established. Some procedures may simply evolve and become accepted, such as a procedure which would give preference to the fisherman who first arrived on the stream. Other conflict resolution devices may themselves have to be adopted by a decision procedure. There are several procedures available to do this, consistent with the requirements of the autonomy principle. They range from simple majority decision making rule, through various qualified majority rules, to a unanimity decision rule.[14] A simple majority rule can resolve conflicts between plans consistently with each person's right to decide for himself what his own good is, and how to pursue that good while respecting the same right in others. A simple majority rule would be invoked only in situations where the conflicting plans are morally permissible. Plans which involve the deception of others or coercion except for legitimate punishment are morally impermissible plans and should be excluded from consideration by the majority rule.[15] Similarly decisions reached by a majority rule procedure must not violate requirements of autonomy, e.g., a decision reached by a majority rule procedure to enslave a minority would be void because of its disrespect for the minority's autonomy or well-being. The use of the majority rule also presupposes such rights as free speech, the right to participate in politics, and the right of opposition.[16] Therefore, the domain of decisions reached by the majority rule is quite circumscribed. The autonomy of individuals who are subject to decisions reached by the use of a majority rule, within this area where permissible plans may conflict, is not disrespected even if the decision goes against them. The equal right to decide for one's self what one's good is and how to pursue it is not a right to always have one's own way. The plans of others must also be considered and weighed on a par with one's own plan giving appropriate weight to basic needs, fundamental goods and so on. Merely the fact that the plan of another is chosen is therefore not a sufficient condition that one's autonomy is violated. If, as in a majority rule decision procedure, each person's plan is given equal weight and each person is permitted to campaign for his own point of view, then, within the circumscribed domain in which the majority rule procedure ranges, autonomy is not disrespected even if one's plan is defeated. Simple majority rule is therefore consistent with the autonomy principle.

If the simple majority rule is consistent with the autonomy principle, so also are qualified majority rules which require more than a mere fifty plus percentage. Two-thirds or three-fourths majority rules are also consistent. A unanimity rule is consistent with the principle if bargaining and compromise are possible and not too costly in time and effort. The rule which a particular community should adopt depends upon its size, the cost in time and effort of more inclusive rules, and the preference of its members, and so on.

The full relevance of the majority rule procedure will not be evident until the new form of ownership is fully explained. But at least this much is now clear. In joint or common ownership where there are many individuals in whom title vests, a majority rule procedure for resolving conflicting plans about the exercise of their rights of title is consistent with the autonomy of each. Private ownership is therefore not the only form of ownership which is consistent with the autonomy of owners. Joint and common owners, both collectively and individually, can exercise autonomous control over what they own so long as appropriate decision procedures are followed.

The assignment of ownership rights by a specific form of ownership is a third procedure for resolving conflicts between autonomously chosen plans. If one of the two fishermen privately owns or has leased the land surrounding the trout stream, he has the right to decide who may enter upon the land. The conflict is resolved because the form of ownership vests in one of the fisherman the right to decide who may fish. However, ownership rules as a procedure for resolving conflicting plans must themselves be consistent with the autonomy principle. Not all forms of ownership are. One form which is obviously not consistent is a form which permits slavery, i.e., the private ownership of one person by another. A specific form of ownership must itself be justifiable by the autonomy principle in order to justifiably resolve conflicts between plans. The first step is to determine which form or forms of ownership over which domain of ownables is required by the autonomy principle. This will justify the ranges of rights which individuals may legitimately exercise over ownables and therefore constitute an additional morally correct procedure for resolving conflicts.

B. *The necessary logical structure and justification*

The necessary logical structure of all forms of ownership determines how moral principles apply to the justification of specific forms of ownership. Both rights of title and criteria of title of a specific form must meet the justificatory requirements of the principle for each relevant range of ownables. The utilitarian principle can serve as a brief illustration. A specific form of ownership would be morally justifiable only if it produced the best consequences for the community in which it exists. In other words, the utilitarian principle requires each community to adopt that form of ownership which for it has the best possible consequences. This implies that the rights of title and criteria of title must be optimific for each domain of ownables. The consequences of particular rights of title and criteria of title depend upon the kind of ownables involved, e.g., the consequences from ownership of rivers, of automobiles, of clothing, and of land may not have the same value for a particular set of rights of title and criteria of title. Where there are relevant differences in kinds of ownables, there will have to be differences in the rights of title and criteria of title of these ownables in order to produce the best possible consequences.

The necessary logical structure of ownership controls how the autonomy principle applies to the justification of a specific form. Both the rights of title and the criteria of title must be consistent with each person's right, subject to the same right of others, to decide for himself what his own good is, how to pursue it, and the well-being necessary for autonomy. Still, there is no reason to assume that identical rights of title and criteria of title are required by the autonomy principle for all kinds of ownables.

Consider the rights of title and criteria of title for such different ownables as oneself and a plot of land. The autonomy principle requires rights of title over oneself which closely approximate the rights of private ownership. Each person has the right to use himself as he chooses just so long as he respects the autonomy of others. Included in this right to use oneself as one chooses is the right to possess, to manage, the right to income from one's labor, and the right to exchange some of one's labor, or give some of it to others. The autonomy principle is, therefore, inconsistent with forms of ownership of oneself, such as Robert Owen's or John Rawls', which give others rights over one's natural talents and abilities. Insofar as others have these rights each person is not free to decide for himself what his own good is and how to pursue it. Similarly, forms of dictatorial communism which control individuals' choices of occupation are incompatible with the autonomy principle. The criterion of title over oneself required by the autonomy principle must be the status criterion of being oneself. Other criteria of title, such as performative criteria of gift and exchange which depend upon the actions of others, or criteria of title which vest in the community rights over the individual, violate the autonomy principle's requirement that each person have the right to decide for himself. To this extent the criteria of title for oneself differs from private ownership which depend upon the actions of others and gift and exchange as valid criteria of title.

The autonomy principle has different implications for land ownership. The rights of title and criteria of title for land ownership differ markedly from private ownership. The autonomy principle requires that each person has a right to participate in decisions about how land is used and a right to income from the land. The arguments for this are complex and will be discussed fully in the next chapter, but a sketch of the argument can be given here. The argument has two parts: one negative, the other positive. The negative argument deals with the implausibility of original appropriation claims which must be presupposed by private ownership. The private ownership criteria of title – gift, bequest, and exchange – presuppose that what is given, bequeathed, or exchanged is already privately owned. Thus there must be an additional and independent criterion of title to make the set of criteria complete. John Locke, for example, uses labor upon what is unowned as the additional criterion. But, as has been shown, all such arguments for original private appropriation are either question begging or based upon unrealistic or incoherent assumptions.

The positive argument about the form of land ownership concerns how private ownership of land affects the autonomy of non-owners where non-owners is to be understood both in the sense of those who own no land at all and in the sense of those who do not own a particular parcel of land. Private ownership rights of title over land are incompatible with the autonomy of non-owners. It shall be demonstrated that private ownership of land violates each person's right to decide for himself what his own good is and how to pursue it as well as placing in jeopardy the right to the well-being required for autonomy. Thus where there are relevant differences between kinds of ownables the autonomy principle requires different rights of title and criteria of title.

Even though the autonomy principle requires different rights of title and criteria of title for different kinds of ownables, it still makes sense to speak of the autonomy principle requiring one specific form of ownership. It is possible to speak of one specific form in this instance because the rules by which it is constituted derive from the autonomy principle. The case is analogous to the specific form of ownership in the English common law. In English common law there are different rights of title and different criteria of title for different kinds of ownables, but because the rules which constitute the form are all derivable from the decisions of common law judges, it makes sense to speak of it as one form. The same is true for the United States and modern Great Britain where the unity is supplied by rules derivable from legislative enactments as well as judicial decisions. The phrase 'specific form of ownership' therefore has a certain ambiguity. On the one hand, it means a form where all ownables are governed by the same set of rights of title and criteria of title, e.g., private ownership of all ownables without distinction. On the other hand, the term may mean a form in which all the rules are derivable from one principle even though different sets of rights of title and criteria apply to different ownables. No confusion should arise if the context makes clear which sense is being used.

Finally, it is worth reiterating here that the necessary logical structure of ownership requires that criteria of title be consistent, determinate, and complete.

C. *The conditions*

A moral justification of a specific form of ownership requires not only a true moral principle to apply through the necessary logical structure of ownership but also a set of social and material conditions in which the specific form is to function. The conditions will affect what happens as a result of the functioning of the specific form of ownership within a particular society, e.g., communal ownership might inhibit capital formation in a poor society or private ownership might promote concentration of wealth in a few persons within a society which is rapidly industrializing. What makes a particular set of conditions relevant to the justification of a particular specific form of ownership is the justificatory requirements of the grounding moral principle. Rawls' principle of justice would, for example, focus upon the ways in which specific forms of ownership affect the well-being of those who are worst off while some utilitarians would be concerned about the maximization of average utility. Both Rawls' principle and forms of utilitarianism might prescribe radically different forms of ownership in societies with different social and material conditions, but this is not true of all moral principles. Some moral principles might prescribe forms of ownership which are basically similar to one another for societies with social and material conditions that differ significantly. Nozick's entitlement theory, based upon what are called Lockean rights, is an example of a principle which would require basically similar forms of ownership in societies with different sets of conditions. As shall be seen in Chapter VII, the autonomy principle resembles more closely those principles which prescribe similar forms for societies with different conditions although for at least one domain of ownables the social and material conditions will significantly affect the content of the ownership rules for those ownables.

State of nature conditions, such as those envisioned by John Locke, have no place in a moral justification of a form of ownership. His two ideas, that there is abundance of land and resources and that there is little or no patterned social organization, are unrealistic and perhaps incoherent. Further, the process of grounding ownership upon first appropriation of what is unowned by labor or some other act of appropriation is a question begging presumption in favor of private ownership. State of nature conditions were originally conceived as demonstrating the priority of morality over legal or conventional social rules. If moral rules applied to all persons in conditions before there were any governments or any informal social conventions, then it was assumed that moral rules applied to governments also. It is now understood that temporal priority does not imply prescriptive priority or overridingness. The priority of moral prescriptions over other action-guides is a matter of logic or reason rather than a priority of time. Thus there is no reason to resort to state of nature arguments in order to prove that a morally justifiable form of ownership is one that societies or governments ought to adopt. Finally, state of nature conditions which base ownership upon original acquisition are irrelevant to the justification of a form of ownership by the autonomy principle because the right to determine one's own good, how to pursue it, and the well-being necessary for autonomy is not extinguished or overridden simply because someone else is first upon the scene. "It's mine because I got it first" is not a compelling argument which respects each person's autonomy.

In order to make this schema of justification plausible, it is best to choose conditions which are as close as possible to actually existing social and material conditions. Although Hume wrote some time ago, his appraisal of social and material conditions is still germane. First of all, and in many ways most important, there is scarcity of land, resources, goods, labor and effort. There are, of course, many degrees of scarcity. At the very least, scarcity implies that minimal effort or labor is required in order to acquire or produce something, and effort and labor must themselves be scarce. A being who has infinite labor or energy could appropriate or produce whatever he chose even if the raw material were otherwise scarce. So at one extreme scarcity can be interpreted as requiring some effort, however slight, to make or to appropriate. At the other extreme, scarcity can be interpreted as a shortfall so pronounced that even a disproportionately large investment of effort and labor is insufficient to satisfy even the smallest demand. Ownership rules are most likely unnecessary at the first extreme of scarcity and at the second extreme it is unlikely they would be possible because community would be impossible. The scarcity to be assumed by the schema must fall within the range in which ownership rules for the relevant domain of ownables are both necessary and possible. The material conditions for most ownables in most countries today fall within the range where ownership rules are both necessary and possible although there are exceptions in some countries where food scarcity brought about by drought (or mismanagement) falls below the range. In modern technically advanced countries scarcity is inevitably within the required range. For the purposes of the schema, it is best to assume material conditions which closely approximate those which now exist in almost all countries. Unlike Marx's belief that the ideal communist society has the best chance if it comes about in already heavily capitalized and industrialized countries, this assumption is not made here because modern technologically advanced countries create fewer problems for a justifiable form of ownership; rather, the scarcity assumption is made solely because it makes the schema more realistic and relevant.

The second part of Hume's appraisal, that people have only limited benevolence towards others, is also an essential part of the conditions for the schema of justification. Benevolence admits of degrees as does scarcity. At one extreme is what might be called unlimited benevolence towards others. While it is difficult to imagine just what unlimited benevolence might be, some saints or persons who frequently perform supererogatory acts might serve as close approximations. The other extreme, where there is little or no concern for the well-being of others, can be illustrated by Hobbes' diffident egoist. Actual human nature lies somewhere between these two extremes. In modern, technologically advanced countries, benevolence perhaps extends only to the immediate family and a small circle of friends. Less advanced societies have sometimes exhibited a greater range of benevolence perhaps because of emotional ties to extended families or clans. While the possibility of a greater range of benevolence might exist in industrialized countries, basing a schema upon that assumption runs a risk of being too unrealistic.

Both limited benevolence and scarcity are needed assumptions for a realistic schema. But it is the assumption of scarcity which is really essential. Persons who care about the well-being of others, even a fairly large number of others, would still require ownership rules. It would still be necessary to know who owns what if for no other purpose than to know who may be in need and what may be given to them. In addition, even if people cared about others and were generous with their labor, ownership rules would be required to know what productive resources belong to whom. People would need to know what resources they could work and develop even if they intended to give to others what is produced. Well intended persons who desire only what is their share nevertheless need to know what their share is. The scarcity assumption is also essential because even greedy egoists could get along quite well without ownership rules if there were no scarcity at all.

Both scarcity and limited benevolence will be included in the schema in order to keep the schema realistic. The proof that autonomous ownership is morally justifiable will not depend upon any assumption of abundance or of unlimited concern for others.

Additional elements of the social and material conditions which are assumed by the schema of justification include social institutions such as a legal system which provides police protection, enforces contracts, settles civil disputes through law courts, and makes laws where necessary through a legislative body. Banks and financial institutions are assumed to be in place as well as schools, institutions of higher learning, hospitals, industry, roads and so on. The form by which they are owned is explained in the next chapter, but the form must be one which is required by the autonomy principle.

The conditions of scarcity and limited benevolence in a modern technologically advanced society are sufficient for defining the material and social conditions in which the issue of moral justification arises with respect to forms of ownership. The autonomy principle, however, requires two further social conditions be added to the schema. The first is that governance of the community, society, or country must be democratic. Non-democratic forms of governance, by monarchs, by presidents for life, by aristocrats, or by committees which are not formed by some measure of democratic participation, are incompatible with the principle of autonomy. Each person's equal right to decide for himself what his own good is, how to pursue it, and the well-being required for autonomy cannot be respected except by governance which is democratic. Constitutional democracies with representatives are here considered democratic governance. Thus included in the schema are only communities which are democratic. The second additional social condition required by the autonomy principle is that there must exist a free labor market. There are two ways of regarding this requirement. The first is that a labor market which is controlled by an individual, or group, who has the authority to decide how others are to work violates their individual autonomy. The other way of regarding it is that it violates each person's individual ownership of himself. The next chapter shows that the two ways are equivalent. Communities without free labor markets are also excluded from the schema.

D. Private ownership and the economy

Forms of ownership have different effects upon society's economic organization. Economic organization should be understood as encompassing a society's productive, commercial, and financial activities, i.e., how society materially produces and sustains itself. A form of ownership determines or greatly influences how society's wealth is produced and distributed. This is obvious once ownership is understood as a right constituted relationship between persons with respect to things, and it is the things in life which constitute wealth. Since different specific forms of ownership prescribe different sets of rights over what is owned as well as having different domains of possible ownables, there are different economic effects upon how well or efficiently what is owned can be used to produce wealth and how justly or equitably wealth is distributed. Some forms of ownership may stimulate economic growth more than others, some may have tendencies toward greater equality of wealth, some may encourage individual effort, some may foster a more rational allocation of the factors of production, and some forms may simplify or reduce the cost of economic decision making and planning.

The purpose of this section is to examine private ownership and to dispel some of the misconceptions about private ownership' effects upon the economy. Many of the results of this section find application in the justification of autonomous ownership.

The private ownership form is claimed to be economically optimific, i.e., as having the best economic consequences. Private ownership is said to give owners rights which permit the economic system to efficiently allocate factors of production including labor, to keep supply and demand near equilibrium, to create sufficient motivation for entrepreneurial activity which is needed to keep economic growth rates near an optimum level, to minimize decision making or administrative costs, and to provide an efficient distribution of income on the basis of market valued marginal productivity. Other forms of ownership such as communal ownership are supposed to have less economically optimific effects. Inefficiencies in production, market disequilibrium, lack of incentives for growth, incomes which are divorced from marginal productivity, and high administrative decision making costs are said to plague non-private forms of ownership. From the economic perspective, private ownership is thought to affect society in the best way possible.

Before discussing to what extent the private ownership form is optimific, it is important to remember that specific forms of ownership are to be evaluated from the moral as well as from the economic perspective. The moral perspective takes precedence and shall be discussed in great detail later, especially in the next chapter. But neither should it be assumed that economic criteria are wholly irrelevant to a moral justification of a specific form of ownership. Economic inefficiencies can imply a wasteful utilization of resources or labor which from a moral perspective might be unjustified because people might be forced to labor without any productive or beneficial outcome. In a similar way, high administrative costs might consume wealth which morally might be put to better use. Thus an examination of the allegedly economic optimific effects of private ownership is indeed relevant to the overall moral justification of autonomous ownership as an alternative form of ownership.

One typical argument for the economic superiority of private ownership is made by Harold Demsetz in the *American Economic Review*.[17] He argues that private ownership of land and resources facilitates a more rational use of land and resources, specifically by preventing a too rapid depletion, and that private ownership reduces the costs of internalizing externalities. Demsetz contrasts private ownership with communal ownership. He defines communal ownership as "a right which can be exercised by all members of the community;" walking a city sidewalk is an example, and "private ownership implies the community recognizes the right of the owner to exclude others from exercising the owner's private rights."[18] Demsetz also defines state ownership which he views as implying "that the state may exclude anyone from the use of a right as long as the state follows accepted political procedures for determining who may not use state-owned property;"[19] but, for some unmentioned reason, state ownership does not enter into his argument. Demsetz argues that if land and resources are communally owned, i.e., each member having the unlimited right to appropriate for himself, then resources will be depleted too quickly. Each person who tries to maximize the value of his own right will be able to pass some of the costs on to others. In this situation, the richness of the land and resources will be depleted too quickly to maximize economic return. Communal owners could undertake negotiated agreements to slow depletion, but, as Demsetz argues, the costs of negotiation will be high.

Private ownership of land can prevent too quick depletion according to Demsetz's argument:

> If a single person owns land, he will attempt to maximize its
> present value by taking into account alternative future
> streams of benefits and costs and selecting that one which he
> believes will maximize the present value of his privately-owned
> land rights. We all know that this means he will take into
> account the supply and demand conditions that he thinks will
> exist after his death. It is very difficult to see how communal
> owners can reach an agreement that takes account of these
> costs.[20]

It is not at all clear that this argument proves what it is supposed to prove. That an owner needs to consider the conditions which may occur after his death insofar as they affect the present value of this land makes sense only if the owner intends to sell his land or if he intends to bequeath a valuable piece of land to his heirs. But if the private land owner is only concerned about his own income from the land without any concern about selling it or what he may be able to bequeath, then the private owner might well exploit his land at a rate calculated to maximize his income over his life expectancy. If the owner could know with some precision the date of his death, then, given the assumed values, he rationally should adopt an income maximizing exploitation policy which would have the land depleted at, or just after, the time of his death.

Demsetz's argument is plausible only on the assumption that private owners are also motivated by a concern for the value they can bequeath to their heirs, i.e., they are not exclusively concerned with maximizing their own income from the land but they care about what value the land has for subsequent generations. It should be noted at this point that corporations of one sort or another and extended families can perform the function of considering future value and income if it is assumed that corporations or extended families continue beyond the death of any of their individual members. If members are added to the corporation to replace those who leave, then the corporate management must then consider future income. But unless some assumption is made about care for future generations, there is no superiority in land utilization of private ownership except for possible gain of land value which may last a whole generation instead of only a partial one. Further, if the assumption about motivation which is needed to make Demsetz's private ownership argument plausible is applied in the communal ownership setting, it is not at all obvious that communal owners, who care about what subsequent generations might inherit, would too quickly deplete the land and resources.

The decision making costs involved in internalizing externalities also depend upon the motivational assumption. Demsetz argues that the decision making costs for communal owners will be high because of the profitability for the holdout who may extract exorbitant terms.[21] If a concern for the value left to future generations functions as a motive for the holdout also, then it is not clear how high the decision making costs will be. At this point Demsetz's neglect of state ownership becomes relevant to the argument about decision making costs since state ownership as an alternative to private ownership is one way of reducing the decision making costs of communal ownership. A comparison of decision making costs in private ownership and in state ownership would be the more interesting comparison especially because of the similarities between state ownership and autonomous ownership. Joseph Schumpeter points out, in *Capitalism, Socialism and Democracy*, that private owners may have high decision making costs if they are ignorant of what other private owners are doing, i.e., the information cost component of decision making costs may be higher in a private ownership competitive economy than in a state ownership economy.[22] Lack of information may also lead to bad decisions which have costs also. To be fair to Demsetz, he seems to be more concerned with presenting a plausible economic rationale for the evolution of the modern manager-administered limited liability joint stock company than exploring state ownership and similar alternatives. His argument about the superiority of private ownership in land and resource use is nevertheless flawed, and it does not establish the superiority of private ownership over other plausible forms of ownership.

The second of the supposed economically optimific consequences of private ownership is its role in an economic system which motivates individuals to engage in productive work by the lure of amassing great wealth. Private ownership of labor, land, resources, and the means of production in a free market economy enables some individuals to become wealthy by efficiently producing saleable commodities, on their own or by employing others, thereby strongly motivating individuals who desire wealth to work hard.[23] It is assumed that only the desire for wealth is a powerful enough motive to induce sufficient numbers of individuals to work sufficiently hard so that society as a whole will prosper. It is thought that other forms of ownership in other economic systems either do not provide sufficient motivation for productive work or they must rely upon kinds of motivation which violate the moral requirements of individual autonomy and non-coercion.

The assumption that the desire for wealth is the strongest or primary motive to work has been questioned.[24] While the assumption can be held in extreme forms which are undoubtedly false, a more moderate version of the assumption is surely reasonable, namely, that the desire to be materially well off and secure is a significant motive for engaging in productive work. Some individuals may be motivated by love or benevolence but there is no inconsistency in also believing that the desire for secure material well-being is a strong motive too.

There are forms of ownership which are incompatible with the more moderate assumption about motivation. Specific forms of ownership in which the distribution of wealth or goods is made equally or based upon some principle of need will create disincentives to hard productive work which will vary directly with the strength of the desire for wealth. Forms of communal ownership, in which not only are land and resources communally owned but in which each person's talents and abilities are likewise considered communally owned assets, also may fail to induce sufficient numbers of individuals to work sufficiently hard. If individuals must share their income with others or receive less income than they could in an uncontrolled market for labor because their talents and abilities are considered communally owned assets, then from their perspective they may have disincentives to work since they regard themselves as underpaid. The strength of the disincentive will depend upon the difference between the actual income and the perceived market value of the labor and upon how strong the desire for wealth is in the individuals, i.e., where the desire for wealth is weak the disincentive will be weak and where the desire is strong the disincentive will be strong. It might be possible to find other work incentives than the desire for wealth, well-being or security, such as honor, reputation, or the desire to contribute to the common good. How strong these motives are is a question not yet satisfactorily answered. Other strong motives, such as the desire not to be shot, are both economically and morally undesirable.

Private ownership over the domain of land, resources, the means of production and labor may not be the only form of ownership which is compatible with the assumption about motivation. The salient feature of any economic system which is compatible with the assumption about motivation is a free labor market. In a free labor market each individual has the right to seek the kind of employment he prefers. Any individual has the right to try to become a tax attorney, for example, although market forces and professional standards may restrict the number of individuals so employed to a select few. The root concept behind a free labor market is that each individual has the right to decide how his labor is to be used and that no other members of society, either individually or collectively, may decide for him so long as what he does lies within the bounds of respect for everyone's autonomy. In order, therefore, to attract individuals to labor, jobs must be made sufficiently attractive and, if the assumption about motivation is correct, most of what makes jobs sufficiently attractive are the material rewards which are offered. Potential employers will compete for workers and the purchasers of services will compete for services by offering material incentives. The greater the demand for a kind of labor given its supply or the smaller its supply given the demand, the larger the material rewards will be which are needed to attract sufficient number of individuals to labor. The converse also is true, i.e., less demand or greater supply will lower the size of the needed incentive. Rational wealth seeking individuals will try to choose the kind of employment which maximizes the expected economic return upon their talents, skills, and training. Other non-material non-economic factors such as status or safety might also have a role in guiding choices of employment, but to the extent these factors do have a role the assumption that wealth and security is the primary motive is also weakened.

Private ownership of one's labor is an economic requirement for stimulating hard productive work and for allocating labor to market demand. Private ownership of land, resources, and the means of production is another issue entirely. There appears to be no logical reason why land, resources, and certain factors of the means of production must also be privately owned in order to provide the kinds of incentives required by the motivation assumption. What is essential is that the rewards for labor approximate market valued marginal productivity, but there is no logical impossibility of achieving this even if land, resources, and some of the means of production are not privately owned. For example, economic forces which require managers of communally or collectively owned firms to compete for labor with each other and with self-employment options for workers would create the same free labor market forces as would private owners in similar circumstances.[25] Forms of ownership which do not permit private ownership of land, resources, and all of the means of production are not logically incompatible with the motivation assumption if something resembling private ownership of labor in a free market is part of the economic system. Autonomous ownership in which everyone may participate in decisions concerning land use therefore requires a free labor market because of the right to direct one's own labor. The practical compatibility of a free labor market with autonomous ownership of land, resources and means of production ownership will be discussed later, but it is worth noting here that the practical question seems to center around enterpreneurship and growth rates rather than around the price or rewards for labor.

The last of the alleged economically optimific consequences of private ownership to be discussed is its role in economic growth and technological progress. Technological progress is usually considered a concomitant of economic growth. It is frequently argued that only an economic system based upon private ownership of labor, land, resources, and the means of production will supply sufficient incentives through financial rewards for firms to expand and entrepreneurs to take risks. If neither the manager of the firm nor the entrepreneur is able to share in the profits of expansion or of new technology, then there will be insufficient incentive for adequate growth.

This argument is a corollary of the argument about hard work, centering upon one kind of hard work: that which leads to economic growth as a result of creating new products, new processes, and new services. It is further assumed that the creative initiative required for the discovery and production of new products, processes, and services is inherently individual and cannot be a consequence of bureaucratic administration or a product of special managerial organization. Therefore, specific forms of ownership other than private ownership (i.e., forms of ownership which separate the rights of management and control from the rights to income and equity or which distribute income from the firm and rights to shares in its equity throughout society) will inhibit economic and technical growth because individuals will have insufficient economic reasons for undertaking economically risky activities. Growth rates will therefore be economically inadequate.

The claim that economic and technological growth is inhibited by non-private forms of ownership is not easy to prove empirically since there are so many other variables involved, e.g., the degree of technological and economic development or the scarcity of resources and capital; the data is subject to a variety of plausible alternative interpretations. Not all actual planned or socialist economies have inadequate growth rates in all areas of the economy, nor do all private ownership capitalist economies show adequate growth in all industries and services, e.g., in the United States' steel and automobile production. Since much data is inconclusive, and if the people are motivated as assumed earlier, there appears to be no reason why a society which adopts some form of non-private ownership of land, resources, and some of the means of production could not have adequate economic and technological growth. Clauses could be written into managerial contracts with pay incentives to managers who create new goods and services or who expand production and, conversely, extract penalties from managers of firms that decline. Such contracts are already common in private ownership for managers of large firms owned by many shareholders. From the perspective of the manager, there would seem to be little difference whether the stockholders, who ultimately are the source of his incentive contract, are society as a whole or some large sub-set of society. The manager would have the same incentive to expand existing output if needed or to produce new goods. How large or small the manager's incentive would need to be would have to be discovered by trial and error.

In small firms where "ownership" and management are not separate, e.g., heating and plumbing companies where the "owner" is actively involved in managing the firm and perhaps involved in the actual labor or production, non-private forms of ownership may inhibit growth because of lack of economic incentives. Small firms which consume much of the private owner's labor could not be socially owned without loss of growth potential. These small firms which primarily provide services, i.e., specific kinds of labor, cannot separate the rights of management from the rights to income in a free labor market and still expect adequate incentives. Owner-managers of these small service firms would not then be receiving the market value of their marginal productivity. More will be said on this issue in Chapter VII.

So far it has been tacitly assumed that economic growth is desirable and that the optimum rate of growth is easily calculated. There is, however, no general consensus about what an optimum growth rate should be. Rawls' difficulty in *A Theory of Justice*, in specifying an optimum savings rate, is merely an isomorphism of the growth rate difficulty: how much goods and services ought to be consumed or labor and capital ought to be invested in order to supply future generations with what level of goods, services, and the potential for still further growth. Present sacrifice for future growth may temporarily cause increased unemployment; in fact, Marx believed that economic expansion is profitable only on the condition that an "army of unemployed" is maintained to keep wages low during the growth-expansion quadrant of the business cycle. How much suffering is justifiable? It is difficult to know with any precision, or with any generality, what an optimum growth rate should be.

The absence of any clear general specification of the growth rate undercuts the objection against planned economies that collective decision procedures will result in too little capital being set aside for future growth. This objection assumes that self-interested individuals will prefer their own present consumption to future consumption by others. Consequently, members of society who are given a voice through collective decision procedures will choose production levels which favor themselves at the expense of future members. Future generations would then inherit capital equipment which is too obsolete and too worn out to adequately satisfy their needs. Thus it is believed only private ownership in which investment decisions are made privately would provide sufficient safeguards for future growth. But this is again Demsetz's argument that private owners concern themselves with economic conditions which go beyond their own life span. It is of course true that some private corporations have such concerns but this may be due to the fact that private corporations are expected to survive their present members. Yet it might be asked why present members of private corporations do not prefer their own present consumption (income from the corporation) to the consumption of future stockholders. Two answers seem to make sense. First, (antihypothesi), they do care about the income future stockholders will receive even if it is only their own descendants who inherit the shares of stock. Second, because generations are not discrete, either in society or in the private corporations, stockholders and younger members of society influence the older ones into taking a more long range perspective. In either case, private corporations and planned economies based upon socialist ownership could perform in similar ways.

To summarize briefly this section on the relation of the forms of ownership to economic systems, it is clear that different specific forms of ownership have different effects upon economic systems which need to be explored in any attempt at moral justification for a specific form of ownership such as autonomous ownership. Private ownership may have better economic consequences than some other forms, but private ownership is not uniquely optimific since there are other forms of ownership with equally good economic consequences.

Before undertaking the justification of autonomous ownership by the autonomy principle it is important to understand that the justification ignores the fact that actually existing communities already have specific forms of ownership. The justification provides a fresh beginning which makes no concessions to forms of ownership actually in place. It is vital first to demonstrate that autonomous ownership is morally justifiable within the schema of justification. Unless this is known, the practical question how to adopt autonomous ownership need not be answered. As important as the practical question is, "How to get from here to there," it cannot be answered until it is known where "there" is.

CHAPTER VII

Autonomous Ownership

It is now possible to derive the new theory of ownership based upon the autonomy principle in the conditions outlined in the schema of justification. The specific form of ownership required by the autonomy principle is named 'autonomous ownership.' Not all of the ownership rules which constitute autonomous ownership are new. Many of these rules have appeared before in philosophical discussions or in actual practice. What is new about the theory is, first, that all the rules of autonomous ownership follow from the single moral principle of autonomy. Even though some of the rules are familiar, their arrangement together into one specific form of ownership by the autonomy principle is new. Second, autonomous ownership is part of a new theory of ownership because it is the first specific form of ownership consciously designed to fulfill the necessary logical structure of all forms of ownership. Autonomous ownership is therefore grounded upon a solid logical foundation as well as upon a plausible, if not demonstrably true, moral principle.

The two most important features of autonomous ownership are the rules for the domains of self and labor, and for land and resources. The ownership rules for these two domains define the rights of title and criteria of title for all other possible ownables. The combinations of ownership rules for these two domains constitute a form of ownership which is incompatible with most existing forms of ownership. The ownership rules for the first domain of self and labor are incompatible with any form of social or collective ownership which considers the self and labor on par with collectively or socially owned value producing resources such as land or machinery. It is in this domain that private ownership finds its vindication. The rules of autonomous ownership for the second domain of land and resources are incompatible with forms of ownership in which land and resources are privately owned or in which everyone cannot participate in decisions about how land and resources are used. Thus the autonomy principle can be shown to require a form of ownership which excludes both private ownership of land or resources and social ownership of self or labor.

While the proof of this form of ownership follows in the next section, it is important to understand beforehand what is at stake. The autonomy principle, or principles which closely resemble the autonomy principle, is frequently used to justify private ownership of land and resources.[1] Locke, Nozick, and Donagan use the autonomy principle, or at least the individual freedom implicit in the autonomy principle, in order to justify private ownership of land and resources. While each of the three imposes limits upon the conditions in which private ownership of land and resources is morally justifiable, none of them reach the conclusion that autonomy is fundamentally inconsistent with private ownership of land and resources. They fail to see the fundamental incompatibility between individual autonomy and private ownership of land and resources. The autonomy principle, or again the individual freedom implicit in the principle, is also used to justify forms of ownership in which the self and labor are socially or collectively owned. Some readings of Marx carry this implication as would a reading of Rawls in which the difference principle follows from the conditions of freedom inherent in the original position. The autonomy principle, however, can be demonstrated to be incompatible with any social or collective ownership of self or labor. To the degree that the autonomy principle is a plausible first principle of morality and to the extent that other moral principles resemble aspects of the autonomy principle, it must be concluded that neither private ownership of land and resources nor collective ownership of self and labor is morally justified.

The next section supplies the schema of proof for autonomous ownership rules for the two domains. In section B, the ownership rules for the remaining domain of ownables are discussed. Finally, Section C, under the heading of "Ownership and justice," highlights aspects of the social order which can be based upon autonomous ownership.

A.   *The two domains*

The rights of title in autonomous ownership for the domain of self and labor must be consistent with the equal right of each person to decide upon his own good, how to pursue it, and the right to possess the requisite well-being for autonomy. The rights of title must therefore have an extensive range. The rights of title must include the rights to use and manage one's labor, the right to whatever income can be earned by one's labor, and the right to give or to exchange portions of one's labor with others. Permanent alienation of one's self or labor to others is not included in the rights of title because such a right is incompatible with autonomy.[2] The autonomy principle limits the right to use one's own labor to coerce or deceive others because there is no right to use one's labor in a morally impermissible way. The right to use one's labor or the income from it as one chooses is also limited by the duty to help others. In situations where others ought to be helped, they have a legitimate claim to a portion of one's labor and income.

The criterion of title for self and labor must be the status criterion of being oneself. Other criteria of title would be inconsistent with the autonomy principle. Performative criteria of title which make vestiture of the rights of title dependent upon the actions of others are clearly inconsistent with autonomy. Similarly criteria of title which vest rights over one's labor in a community are also inconsistent because others would share in the rights over one's labor without needing one's consent.

That autonomous ownership is incompatible with the idea that self and labor are communally owned assets does not imply that all collective decisions democratically reached about self and labor are incompatible with autonomy. Democratic collective decisions in many cases are the only way to resolve conflicts which arise between autonomous individuals. The need for such procedures was discussed in Chapter VI. The incompatibility addressed here is the exclusion of democratic collective decisions ranging over individuals' choice of occupation and leisure time vocations. The autonomy principle prohibits only this form of collective interference. The respect for the autonomy of others and living up to the duty to help those in need may at times permit or require democratically reached collective decisions.

Autonomous ownership of self and labor very closely approxi-

171

mates private ownership. The most significant difference is that private ownership permits the right to permanently alienate what is owned while autonomous ownership of self and labor does not. In addition to the rights of title, the criteria of title also differ for the two forms. While both forms recognize gift and exchange for vestiture of rights on a temporary basis and both forms presuppose an additional criterion of title for completeness, the two forms differ in kinds of criteria which complete the set. Private ownership requires a performative criterion of title which vests rights over so-called unowned objects in persons because of some action they perform. Autonomous ownership of self and labor completes the set of criteria of title with a status criterion. Rights over oneself and one's labor vest in each person simply because of his status as a person. In other respects autonomous ownership for the domain of self and labor is the same as private ownership.

Autonomous ownership restricts social techniques available for allocating labor within a community. Autonomous ownership of self and labor implies that only a free labor market is compatible with the moral requirements of the autonomy principle. Authoritative and coercive allocations of persons' labor is not morally permissible. Individuals have the right to manage how their labor is used, i.e., they have the right to give their labor to whom they please or to exchange their labor with those who are willing to pay for it. Thus, autonomous ownership adds moral support to economic arguments for a free labor market. While a free labor market may be necessary for economic efficiency, autonomous ownership proves that there are also moral reasons which support a free labor market, namely, each person's autonomous ownership of himself and his labor.

That a free labor market is a moral requirement does not, however, exclude all forms of socialism. Socially owned enterprise can be compatible with autonomous ownership of self and labor if socially owned firms compete for workers who are free to choose from among possible employers or who are free to seek self-employment. The salient requirement of autonomous ownership of self and labor is that individuals have the right to choose between possible kinds of employment. That some of the choices involve employment by socially owned firms is not a morally relevant limitation so long as a range of choices is possible. Any economic system compatible with autonomous ownership must include competition for employees and managers by offering employment incentives including competitive salaries, fringe benefits, profit sharing, etc., to entice people to work. The only forms of socialism excluded by autonomous ownership are those which authoritatively assign people to jobs.

It is important to understand that not all forms of social ownership are incompatible with autonomous ownership of self and labor. As it turns out, the autonomy principle requires rules for the ownership of land and resources which require social, and not individual, control of land and resource use.

The ownership rules for the domain of land and resources required by the autonomy principle differ markedly from the ownership rules for self and labor. Land and resources are here to be understood as those things which exist independently of any human labor. Autonomous ownership rules for land and resources more closely resemble social ownership than they do private ownership. The autonomy principle morally requires that rights over land and resources ultimately vest in all members of the community.[3] Specifically, each member of the community has the right to participate in decisions concerning how land and resources are to be used. The argument to establish this implication of the autonomy principle for ownership of land and resources has two phases. The first is negative and shows that arguments for original private appropriation are question begging and incoherent. The second phase shows that autonomy is violated unless all individuals have the right to participate in decisions concerning land and resource use.

All First Appropriationist arguments which attempt to justify private ownership are question begging. This is true of Locke and Nozick and it is explicitly admitted by Kant.[4] These arguments presuppose that land and resources are unowned in the sense of not being privately owned by anyone. Without this assumption that land and resources are unowned, acts of appropriation could not be considered as a valid mechanism for vesting title. But assuming that unowned means not privately owned by anyone within a system of private ownership, which recognizes first appropriation as a legitimate criterion of title, presupposes the form of private ownership which first appropriation allegedly justifies. The sense of 'unowned' in which unowned means not owned according to form x, where x is left unspecified, leaves open the question whether first appropriation does vest title. If, for example, land were viewed as being communally owned by everyone, then either their direct consent would be required for private appropriation or the appropriation would be illegitimate. Thus, only by ignoring other forms of ownership through the assumption that private ownership is permitted can first appropriation conceivably function to establish private title over land and resources. Only if private ownership is presupposed can the possible rights of others over land and resources be ignored.[5]

The commonly made assumption that land is sufficiently abundant so that private appropriation does not harm others or does not violate their rights is incoherent. It is based upon an idea of abundance which makes no sense at all. If labor or effort is required for appropriation, that requirement by itself is sufficient to show that land is not abundant. Others clearly are affected by such appropriation since they may have to labor harder in order to make similar appropriations. Besides, unless it is already presumed that first appropriation vests private title, then even with abundant land, the fact that a greater portion is unoccupied does not imply that private appropriation violates no one's rights. The notion that it never would be missed is not a good reason for assuming that no rights are violated by private appropriation.

These two considerations prove that private ownership cannot be justified by first appropriation. People cannot acquire rights over land and resources merely by being the first to use them. Additional moral considerations would be required, e.g., that private ownership maximizes utility or that private ownership is consistent with autonomy. Private ownership as a whole must be shown to be morally justified; it cannot creep in step by step through individual acts of appropriation. People are not justified in claiming private ownership rights unless the private form of ownership is as a whole justified.

The autonomy principle requires ownership rules for the domain of land and resources which respects each person's right to decide upon his own good, how to pursue it and to possess the well-being needed for autonomy. Both criteria of title and rights of title must respect the right. It follows that forms of ownership which do not permit each person to participate in decisions about how land and resources are to be used are incompatible with the autonomy principle.

Consider a specific form of ownership such as private ownership in which rights over land use vest only in some but not all of the members of the community. Suppose there are individuals who own no land or resources at all. They would need the permission of land owners to move about from place to place, to find a place to live, or even find a spot upon which to rest their feet.[6] Individuals without any land at all in a private ownership system would be at the mercy of the land owners. The right of non-owners to decide upon their own good, how to pursue it, and to possess the well-being necessary for autonomy would not be at all equal to the rights of landowners. Those who privately own land would be at a considerable advantage. Land owners would have the right to dictate under what conditions non-owners could pursue their own good.

It is no defense of private ownership of land and resources that those who own no land still privately own themselves and their labor which they have the right to exchange for money or subsistence. Even if the labor or talents of non-owners is well rewarded by the free market, they still must exchange, purchase, or lease rights over land. Non-owners may lack sufficient capital to do this. Land owners are not forced to make such exchanges; they have the right to use their privately owned land as they wish without anyone else's permission and without any exchanges. The same right, namely to decide how the land is used without another's permission, does not vest in non-owners of land. They do not have the same rights as do the private land owners.

Not only are the rights to decide upon and how to pursue one's own good unequal between private land owners and those who own none, but the rights to the well-being necessary in order to be autonomous may well be unequal. Even if exchange for labor is possible, those who do not privately own land can be at a disadvantage in the bargaining process. They may lack the bare necessities for life. Those without especially desirable skills may have little leverage in the bargaining process, and thus they may be unable to secure a level of well-being necessary for autonomy. Furthermore, if Marx is right in his contention that, in a capitalist market where there is private ownership of land and resources, wealth will tend to concentrate in fewer and fewer persons while greater numbers of persons will live in or near poverty, then the numbers of persons who have insufficient levels of well-being for autonomy will also grow larger. Even if Marx is only partially right, private ownership rules vest in private landowners the right to ignore the well-being of non-land owners. Private ownership rules permit land owners the right to use and manage their land without any obligation to consider the well-being of others except as it affects themselves. That private owners may use their land and resources as they see fit even if such usage adversely affects the well-being of non-owners demonstrates that there is not an equal right to the well-being necessary for autonomy.

The autonomy principle is therefore incompatible with any form of ownership such as private ownership in which ownership rules do not permit each member of the community to participate in decisions about how land and resources are to be used. Neither the right to decide upon one's own good and how to pursue it nor the right to the well-being necessary for autonomy would have to be respected according to such forms.

Although it has been assumed that there are those who own no land or resources, this conclusion about what kind of ownership rules the autonomy principle requires does not depend upon there being members of society who own neither land nor resources. The inequality of rights is most easily seen in the instance of the landless; but the inequality of rights nevertheless also must exist in communities with private ownership of land and resources where everyone privately owns some land and resources.

Before imagining the most unlikely situation where everyone privately owns land and resources, it is necessary to note how much has already been established. The autonomy principle is incompatible with forms of private ownership of land and resources in which not everyone owns land and resources. Nowhere, today, where private ownership of land and resources is practiced, do all members of the community privately own some land or some resources. Thus there does not now exist any form of private ownership which is compatible with the principle of autonomy. Imaginary societies in which everyone owns some land and resources, or an equal share of land and resources, shall be examined, partly for the sake of completeness and partly to further illuminate the underlying conflict with autonomy. But it needs to be stressed that these are highly implausible conditions, and, for all practical purposes, the principle of autonomy has been shown to be incompatible with private ownership of land and resources.

Consider a community in which everyone privately owns some land and resources. Individual holdings may be equal or unequal. If they are unequal then the same inequalities of respect for well-being and of the right to decide upon one's good would arise which exist in communities where not everyone privately owns land and resources. Those with larger holdings might be able to dominate those with lesser holdings. Those individuals who privately own land which contains large quantities of scarce valuable resources, e.g., crude oil reserves, might have an unjustifiable advantage because they would have the right to control essential resources while others lacked the same right. Other private owners would have no right to participate in decisions about how those resources are to be used. Suppose, now, that the holdings are equal, i.e., that each private land owner's holdings have the same market value or have the same (homogeneous) mixture of minerals, fertility, water, and so on. Although it is possible to imagine equal initial holdings, it may not be possible to imagine them staying equal. As Hume is well aware, differences in care and industry, not to mention luck, will quickly upset equal holdings.

Even if all private holdings are equal, the autonomy principle is incompatible with private ownership or any other form of ownership which does not permit everyone in the community to participate in decisions about how all of the land and resources are used. This supposition of equal holdings is implausible; but if private ownership is incompatible with autonomy in a situation where land and resources are so equal, then private ownership is clearly incompatible with autonomy in every situation. Private owner Green has the right to use his land or resources as he chooses. Green has the right even if his exercising his right makes it impossible for his neighbor, White, to decide upon his own good and how to pursue it. Green, for example, might decide to cut the timber upon his land and plant sunflowers in its place. The private ownership form gives Green this right and he need not consult White, or anyone else, about his decision. Green, but no one else, has the right to participate in the decision about how this plot of land is used. Even though White has the right to decide about how his plot is used, and though the value of his own plot is equal to that of Green's, White's autonomy is not respected. White has no right to participate in the decision about how Green's plot is used. The fact that the holdings have an equal value or content is irrelevant to Green's or White's autonomy. Autonomy is the right to decide upon one's own good, how to pursue it, and the necessary well-being. Autonomy is not merely the right to control holdings similar to or as valuable as anyone else's. Green's decision to plant sunflowers may not affect the value of White's land. Green's sunflowers may even increase the value of White's land. The value of White's land is not the issue here. White's autonomy is not respected because private ownership rules give Green the right to decide how the land is used without any consideration for White. That White may likewise decide without consulting Green does not avoid the disrespect. The autonomy principle is not satisfied by the mutual, equal disregard for others' rights.

Private ownership places Green and White in a position of conflict where each has no right to any say in what the other does with his land. Neither has a right to participate in decisions about how the other's land is used even if his autonomy is affected. Private ownership arbitrarily "resolves" the conflict between Green's and White's autonomy by vesting in each the right to ignore the other. But ignoring the autonomy of others is not respecting their equal right; autonomy requires a way of really resolving the conflict by allowing both to participate in such decisions.

Green and White could explicitly agree together that each may do with his own land as he sees fit. But not all land and resource use decisions are bilateral as in the Green and White example. Green's private decision actually excludes all others from participation, not only White. Everyone has a right to be consulted. The autonomy principle does not imply that it is permissible to disregard a third party's rights by means of a bilateral agreement. Violations of anyone's autonomy are impermissible.

The autonomy principle therefore requires ownership rules for land and resources which permit everyone to participate in decisions about how the land and resources are used. Land and resources are unique in this respect since they exist independently of human labor. Products of labor have different ownership rules because of the rights which individuals exercise over their own labor. Everyone does not have the right to participate in decisions about how products of labor are used.

Autonomous ownership rules for the domain of land and resources must include a status criterion of title which vests the rights of title in all members of the community simply because they are members of the community. Because the right to participate in decisions about how land and resources are used is essential to autonomy (even if a person might choose not to exercise the right on occasion), rights of title are not permanently alienable. Gift, bequest, and exchange cannot be valid criteria of title for permanent alienation in the domain of land and resources in autonomous ownership although leasing arrangements are possible where rights are reserved and remaindered by the community. The status criterion of title for the domain of land and resources is consistent, determinate, and complete. Land and resources cannot both be owned and not owned by the same person at the same time and in the same way; and it is not possible for land resources to be owned without a rule by which they can be owned.

The rights of title for autonomous ownership of land and resources obviously include the right to participate in decisions about how they are used – which includes the right to manage. Also included in the rights of title which vest in all members of the community is the right to income from land and resource development and utilization. The right to income derives from the clause in the autonomy principle which grants an equal right to the well-being needed for autonomy. The right to alienate land, permanently, is not included in the rights of title since such alienation would be an abandonment of autonomy. The autonomy principle also seems to require a duty to preserve the usefulness of the land for succeeding generations. While the precise nature of this duty is difficult to ascertain, it is reasonable to suppose that future generations or the youth of the present generation have some right that land and resources shall be available for them in sufficient quantities for their own autonomy.

Autonomous ownership of land and resources requires democratic procedures for deciding how they are to be used. While direct non-representative democracy is one way of satisfying these moral requirements, it is apt to be time consuming and costly in any large nation state community. A legislative body of elected representatives could decide how land and resources are to be developed and used. This body could be charged with deciding about land and resource use as well as being charged with making other laws, or the body could perform only one of the tasks. While both arrangements are consistent with autonomous ownership, economic concerns might dictate the single task option especially if the workload of the legislative body is a heavy one. Economic concerns might also require that the body which decides about land and resource use be protected from too frequent oscillations in public opinion that might deter valuable development projects which require long term investments. A decision making body which is appointed by the legislature or a decision making body of members who are elected for relatively long terms (some of them standing for election each year) might provide a measure of economic stability while still preserving democratic participation. Of course democratic control of day-to-day decisions will be less if the decision making body is appointed or elected for long terms. Each community would therefore have to choose between greater economic stability and efficiency on the one hand and greater direct democratic control on the other. Autonomous ownership is consistent with a variety of options so long as they are genuinely democratic and respect each person's right to participate. Each community would have to decide for itself which option best fulfills the requirements of autonomous ownership.

Autonomous ownership of land and resources enables the community to internalize externalities. The problem of too rapid depletions of resources, which Demsetz attributes to uncontrolled communal ownership of land and resources, can be resolved through the rights of title in autonomous ownership. Members of the community, or their representatives, can establish rates for resource development and depletion. They might also permit market pressures similar to those in private ownership to operate in establishing resource utilization rates. How this can be accomplished is explained in the section on mixed ownables. Pollution of air and water can also be controlled through autonomous ownership. Since these resources are autonomously owned, the members of the community can set standards for air and water quality. The costs of this would be a deduction from the income produced by land and resource utilization which would be borne equally by all the members.

There are several ways in which a community can choose to develop its autonomously owned land and resources. The two most feasible are direct development and a leasing system. Direct development involves governmental operation of land and resources. The democratic government would operate firms which farmed, mined, and manufactured goods which are resource intensive. These firms might be independent of one another, compete for land resources through competitive bidding for resources and capital, and compete for labor with both governmentally and individually owned firms. The reasons for independence and competition between governmental firms are not merely ones of economic efficiency. Autonomous ownership of self and labor morally requires that governmental firms freely compete for workers at all levels from top managers down. Because of each individual's right to use and manage his own labor, governmental firms must depend upon incentives to attract workers. Such incentives would include not only competitive wages but also working conditions, length of vacations, and benefits such as medical insurance, profit sharing, a voice in the management and the like. In addition, even if the community decides upon direct governmental development of land and resources, autonomous ownership of self and labor guarantees individual rights to self-employment in areas which are labor intensive. Doctors, lawyers, teachers, plumbers, cabinet makers, bartenders, secretaries, accountants, and so on, all have a moral right to start their own firm and compete with any governmental firm. Thus governmental firms not only must compete for a supply of labor but they also may have to compete with individual firms in providing services and products. This shall be more evident in the next section on mixed ownables.

The other option for land and resource development is to lease autonomously owned land for development by individual firms. The length of the lease and its price could be set by free market competition between individual firms. For some industries where there is large capital investment in plant and machinery, leases will have to be relatively long in order to be economically feasible. The community could permit market factors to wholly control land and resource use through competition for leases. But, also, the community could decide to reserve some land as public recreation areas or wildlife preserves and decide to place environmental protection clauses in the leases to individual firms. The community could also choose to subsidize certain kinds of production such as food. While the community might suffer a reduction of money income from a decision to so limit land and resource development, the community might still decide that the limitations are necessary to preserve other important values. Communities may opt for a combination of direct development and leasing. Some forms of development, such as strip mining of coal, pose significant dangers to the environment so that the community might directly develop strip mines in order to closely supervise the operations while permitting a leasing arrangement for other kinds of mining. Similar mixtures might be permitted in other areas. In farming, large scale grain production might be directly developed while farming of table vegetables might be leased to individuals if it is proven to be more efficient. The choice between direct development and leasing thus admits of many degrees.

The income from land and resource use belongs to the community as a whole. Each member has a right to an equal share. The community could choose to use the income for such expenditures as defense, police, and fire protection (which in this instance may not involve any income transfer). Or the community could decide to distribute the income in money rather than in services. Both alternatives are consistent with the autonomy principle as would be a distribution that is a mixture of money and services. It is impossible, here, to estimate how large the income from autonomously owned land and resources would be. Much depends upon the community's resources and level of technological development. Autonomous ownership of land and resources cannot be assumed to guarantee a high standard of living for everyone as utopian thinkers hoped. Only empirical study can give even rough estimates about the size of the income. The moral justifiability of autonomous ownership does not, in any case, depend upon the size of the income as it would if the justification were utilitarian. Autonomous ownership is morally justified because it is an implication of the equal right to decide upon one's own good, how to pursue it, and the well-being necessary for autonomy. It is not justified by its utility.

B. The domain of mixed ownables

Mixed ownables are the product of labor upon land and resources. Calling them 'mixed ownables' follows Locke's metaphor of mixing one's labor with the fruits of the earth. The category of mixed ownables is the broadest of the three domains of autonomous ownership since it includes everything made by labor out of resources. Unlike the rules for the domains of self and labor or of land and resources, the rules of autonomous ownership for the domain of mixed ownables are not uniform but vary within the domain according to three variables. The first variable is the labor-resource variable. The more labor intensive a product in the domain of mixed ownables is then the closer the rights of title and criteria of title will approximate autonomous ownership rules for self and labor; while the more resource intensive a product is the more its criteria of title and rights of title will approximate autonomous ownership rules for land and resources. The proportion of labor to land and resources in the production of a mixed ownable roughly determines the degree of individual control or of community control.

The second variable in determining ownership rules for the domain of mixed ownables is the purpose to which the produced object is ultimately put. A product such as dry breakfast cereal may contain a low proportion of labor compared to land and resources because farming and production may be heavily mechanized or automated. But, because the cereal is produced for individual consumption, the most appropriate ownership rules would be those which closely resemble those for the domain of self and labor. Similarly, capital goods used in manufacturing may be regulated by rules resembling land and resource rules even if the goods are somewhat labor intensive. Individual autonomy requires a wide range of rights of title over goods produced for direct personal consumption. Community control over consumer goods, either in the form of what goods are produced or control in the form of what uses consumer products may be put to, would violate autonomy. While the dry breakfast cereal illustration is, by itself, trivial, the principle behind it applied to other mixed ownables is not at all trivial. The idea that autonomy requires a wide range of rights of title over consumer goods implies that so-called consumer sovereignty is a moral as well as the economic requirement to maintain the value of income and to achieve or measure efficiency. That consumers legitimately exercise a wide range of rights of title over goods for personal consumption applies not only to what they actually purchase but to what is available for their purchase. Not only should individuals be able to exercise a broad range of rights of title over their living quarters, for example, but they should also have a wide range of options about the kinds of living quarters made available. Even if there is direct social development of living quarters by governmental firms, a variety of kinds ought to be available, e.g., apartments, row houses, single family homes, and so on, depending upon consumer demand. Governmental interference with consumer demand for mixed ownables is incompatible with autonomy. Only if demand for a certain kind of mixed ownable were incompatible with previous democratic decisions concerning land and resource development would the government be justified in interfering with the consumer market. Or, the elected government might, in some instances, re-evaluate its policy.

There is another way that the purpose of production is a variable in determining ownership rules for mixed ownables. Producers of goods such as automobiles or computers could produce them either for sale or for lease. The criteria of title and the rights of title would then depend upon the leasing agreement or the terms of sale.

The third variable in determining autonomous ownership rules for mixed ownables is the community's decision whether to employ direct governmental development or a leasing system for resource intensive industry. If direct governmental development is chosen, then factories which manufacture capital production goods such as steel, heavy machinery, transportation equipment, as well as mining and other extractive industries would be governmentally operated. Development by leasing would permit groups of individuals to form firms and to compete for development and production rights. Individual firms would acquire the rights of title by paying rent to the community. Whichever option the community decides upon, direct development or individual leases, autonomous ownership of self and labor morally requires a free labor market in which firms compete for labor and in which individuals are morally free to seek employment or to try to establish their own firm in a labor intensive field. There are two important economic implications of this moral requirement. One, which has been discussed already, is that all firms including governmental firms must compete for workers at all levels. The second implication is that individuals must have the right to compete with government firms for finances, resources, and sales. Even if the community decides upon direct governmental development of land and resources, individual labor intensive firms must have the right to compete for resources and finances. Individuals would have the right to raise capital from either governmental or individual sources. Government banks would be required to base their decision upon the economic feasibility of the project and not upon whether the developer is a governmental or individual firm. This could be accomplished if government banks were independent and charged to operate according to principles of sound financial management. Individuals could also be a source of capital either through loans or through the purchase of shares of control.

Further, there is no reason why individuals could not lend money to governmentally developed firms.

Autonomous ownership further implies that individual firms have the right to sell their products to other individuals or to government firms. The right to individual self-employment thus creates an obligation upon government firms to purchase from individual suppliers if the product supplied is economically competitive. If necessary, social rules must be established to guarantee that governmental firms respect the moral rights of individual producers.

Economic competition in a system of autonomous ownership has a moral underpinning; it is not merely a practical addition to stimulate efficiency. Autonomous ownership of self and labor limits the options which are available to the community in developing autonomously owned land and resources by requiring a range of individual freedom and initiative. That economic competition as a factor in autonomous ownership is likely to stimulate economically efficient production may be a good additional reason for subscribing to autonomous ownership. Nevertheless, the moral justification of autonomous ownership depends exclusively upon its respect for autonomy, not upon its possible economic efficiency.

The three variables: labor-resource, purpose of production, and decision by the community, permit many different sets of rights of title and criteria of title within the domain of mixed ownables. Each community is permitted a great deal of leeway over mixed ownables within the limits determined by the other two domains. Thus it is not possible to discuss all the kinds of rules communities might adopt for mixed ownables. It is possible, however, to illustrate a range of plausible options which a hypothetical community, here called Autmos, might adopt for four typical kinds of mixed ownables.

It is to be assumed that Autmos is a democratic community which fulfills the social and material conditions outlined in the schema of justification. In Autmos, there is autonomous ownership for the domains of self and labor, and of land and resources. The four kinds of mixed ownables in Autmos to be considered are: (1) a resource intensive steel factory, (2) dwellings for commercial or residential purposes, (3) a labor intensive retail furniture outlet, and (4) personal possessions such as clothes. While it is not possible to illustrate all of the options from which the citizens of Autmos may morally choose, the more viable ones are discussed. It is important in discussing the options for mixed ownables to separate moral considerations from those of economic efficiency or aesthetics. Many of the choices the citizens of Autmos make will be based upon economic considerations. They are free to use economic considerations but only where it is morally permissible to do so. It will be assumed that citizens of Autmos recognize their duty to respect everyone's equal right to decide for himself what his own good is, how to pursue it, and the right to well-being necessary for autonomy takes precedence over merely economic concerns. In many cases morality and economic efficiency coincide, but where they do not moral considerations override economic ones.

The citizens of Autmos must decide how to develop their land and resources before they can be of any use to them. Since the land and resources which all the citizens of Autmos have rights over must be developed by their labor which is under each individual's control, any development falls into the domain of mixed ownables. In the case of resource intensive development, represented by the steel factory, the citizens of Autmos may choose between the options of direct governmental development or development through a leasing arrangement with individual firms. In direct government development the managers of the steel factory would be responsible to the citizens of Autmos or their elected representatives. Income from the operation of the factory would belong to all the citizens. Because a free labor market is a moral requirement of the autonomy principle, the steel factory must compete in the labor market with other firms by offering such incentives as high pay, vacations, medical benefits, and perhaps efficiency rewards or participation in the management. The government developed steel factory would have to compete for workers and managers, not only with other governmentally developed firms but also with individually owned firms in the labor intensive sector. Competition for workers and managers, however, is not the only area in which the government steel factory would have to compete. Since the citizens of Autmos have the right to seek self-employment or to form individual firms (either co-operative or hierarchical), there is a moral obligation to permit them to compete with government firms for resources, for capital, and for customers. Individual firms may compete with the steel factory for resources. Suppose that both the steel factory and an individual firm need gasoline for their vehicles. Both would have to bid (or buy) from the gas producer or distributor. Because the individual firm has a right to compete, the gas distributor would be obliged to sell gas to both, or if gas were scarce, sell to the higher bidder. Similar competition would arise in the financial market. Lenders, either individual or governmental, would lend to those borrowers who offered the highest secure return. Besides the competition which the government steel factory is morally obliged to engage in, the citizens of Autmos might decide to require the government steel factory to compete with other government firms for profits as a means of stimulating economic efficiency. Their decision would make good economic sense, but it is not morally required by the autonomy principle.

The primary advantage for Autmos' citizens of direct government development would be their greater control over the steel factory and possibly a larger share of the income. By direct development, Autmos' citizens could control such "externalities" as air and water pollution, noise, and the aesthetics of the factory. A second advantage is that income from steel production would not have to be shared with individual developers. The disadvantage of direct development would be the complexity of controlling the management of numerous governmental firms. Centralized planning might be hopelessly inefficient, but it is not clear how inefficient the government firms of Autmos would be with decentralized management and economic competition between government firms in which managers and workers were financially rewarded for efficient production. To simplify its governance, Autmos might choose a leasing system for the development of land and resources.

A leasing system would permit citizens of Autmos to form firms for the manufacture of steel. As individuals, or groups of individuals, they could acquire rights over lands and resources from the community as a whole. Individual steel developers could lease iron bearing land and land upon which to build their steel factory. They could purchase equipment and materials from other developers, either individual or governmental, in order to manufacture steel. The terms of the negotiated lease would be partially determined by preferences of the citizens over such concerns as air and water pollution, location of the factory, and so on, and partially by the economics of steel production. Individual developers would be obligated to obey the same moral requirements for the free labor market as are governmental developers. The leases would run for a specific number of years, contain provisions for rent, and whatever other restrictions the citizens of Autmos choose to impose. The developers would gain rights of title over the land in exchange for rent for the duration of the lease. Within this range the developers alone would be entitled to exercise rights of title. Because the leases would have to be economically viable, in situations where development involves large capital investment, the leases would have to run for a long duration. Also included in the lease would be provisions stipulating what rights the developer and what rights the citizens would exercise over any improvements at the termination of the lease. It might, for example, be required that the developer reforest any land stripped for mining purposes, or that the developer be able to sell any structures he has erected. Further, leases might, for economic reasons, give the developer first right of renewal, the right to sublease, or the right to request periodic renegotiation of certain aspects of the lease.

For the second kind of mixes ownable, i.e., dwellings for commercial and residential purposes, the options available to Autmos are basically the same as for the steel factory. Dwellings can either be directly developed by the government or developed through a leasing arrangement or both. In any case, the citizens' preferences would place limits upon development, e.g., the citizens of Autmos might choose to designate some areas for residential development, some for commercial, some for agricultural, and some for industrial development. Government developers could be instructed to provide a variety of kinds of dwellings for residential purposes – single family homes, row houses, apartments – guided as would be individual developers by market demand. Dwellings for all purposes could be rented or "sold outright." A dwelling which is "sold" would vest in the title holder rights of alienation by gift, bequest, or exchange. The community as a whole would still exercise its rights over the land by collecting income, by exercising rights over the environment, or zoning the purposes to which the dwelling may be put. But unlike rented dwellings there is no term on the duration of the lease although there would be provisions for default (e.g., non-payment of rent).

Autmos may exercise these options as it chooses. It may also choose a mixture of them depending upon its democratically arrived at decisions. The options are all consistent with each citizen's equal right to autonomy. There may be additional economic reasons for preferring one option over another or other reasons not having to do with the equal right implied by the autonomy principle but they cannot be discussed here. While this seems like a lot of decisions for the citizens of Autmos to make, many of the decisions need to be made only infrequently and other decisions can be made by the elected representatives.[7]

There is one salient difference between the autonomous ownership rules for dwellings and for resource intensive manufacture. The autonomy principle implies a duty to help those who are in need. If individuals in Autmos cannot afford living quarters because, through no fault of their own, market forces have priced dwellings beyond their means, then there is a duty upon the other citizens of Autmos to help them secure living quarters. Even though all members of Autmos share in the income from land and resource development, there is no guarantee that the income will be sufficiently large for those who cannot find work to afford living quarters as well as the other basic needs or fundamental goods. Autmos will have a duty to help in some way, e.g., by supplying low cost or rent subsidized housing or by income supplements. All members of Autmos have a right to this help if they are genuinely in need.

The rules for dwellings as mixed ownables in autonomous ownership closely resemble ownership rules which are thought to be private ownership. In the United States as in other western countries, so-called privately owned dwellings are subject to taxation, zoning ordinances, building codes and environmental protection standards. It is possible to interpret these present restrictions on the rights of so-called private owners as an exercise of the rights of autonomous ownership. Real estate taxes could be interpreted as the rent owed to all members of the community for the use of land while zoning ordinances, building codes, and environmental protection standards could be interpreted as the terms of the lease.

On a deeper level, a community's right to regulate by zoning ordinances, building codes, environmental protection laws and a community's right of eminent domain all presuppose rights which are identical to the rights of autonomous ownership of land and resources. It is not possible to understand why it is morally permissible for members of a community to enact zoning ordinances which restrict the uses which so-called private owners may make of their land unless it is assumed that the members of such

189

a community have the right to participate in decisions about how land and resources are used. The same assumption must underlie the right to enact building codes or environmental protection laws. While the idea that pollution affects others might be used as a rationale to support the right to participate in such decisions because autonomy is involved, the right to participate in environmental decisions through democratic procedures clearly presupposes the right of autonomous ownership of land and resources. The presupposition is most obvious in the example of eminent domain. A community has the right to appropriate for its own use land and resources which are supposedly privately owned by one of its members (if fair compensation is paid). The only way to justify eminent domain is to assume that the members of a community (for that reason) ultimately have the right to control the land and resources of their community.

Autonomous ownership is not, therefore, a radical departure from practices already considered morally permissible in the United States and elsewhere. The point of this comparison is not merely a reminder that private ownership in its pure form is not actually practiced, but to also demonstrate that parts of autonomous ownership are already presupposed by contemporary laws. This interpretation is not, however, intended to show that autonomous ownership is consciously practiced in the United States. Clearly its citizens do not consider themselves practicing autonomous ownership in the sense they explicitly recognize in themselves the right to participate in decisions about how all land and resources are to be used.[8] Nevertheless, some of the rights they do exercise presuppose autonomous ownership.

The third kind of mixed ownable is a labor intensive furniture retail outlet. Because a retail business such as the furniture outlet demands a high proportion of labor in selling the merchandise, in selecting the stock, in ordering and so forth, the mixed ownership rules in this instance must closely resemble the rules for autonomous ownership of self and labor. There is little room for choice by the citizens of Autmos. Autonomous ownership of self and labor vests in each individual the rights to exchange portions of his labor, and to the income such exchanges can bring. The citizens of Autmos must respect these rights by permitting individual initiative and employment in labor intensive enterprises.

The retail furniture outlet is run by Black in whom vests the rights of use, management and income, along with the rights to alienate by gift, bequest, or exchange. Black founded the furniture outlet when he discovered that no stores in his town stocked the kind of desk he wanted to purchase for one of his daughters. Black found a government developed manufacturer who made the kind of desk he wanted, and in the process of ordering the desk from the manufacturer, the idea arose that Black open a retail outlet which would carry the manufacturer's line of furniture. In order to finance his venture Black borrowed money from his wife's parents and from the furniture manufacturer. The manufacturer included in the terms of Black's loan that he must stock their complete line of furniture for at least fifteen years and for the first ten years Black could stock no other desks but their line. The manufacturer also agreed that for the term of the loan Black's furniture would be their sole outlet in Black's town.

Black found storespace in a shopping mall which happened to be individually developed upon leased land. The mall might have been one directly developed by the government. The mall developers gave Black a twenty year lease which specified not only a monthly rental fee but also required Black to pay them one percent of his gross receipts. In return, the mall owners would provide Black with security, heat, air conditioning, and an option to renew at the end of twenty years.

Black set up his store in the mall by ordering furniture not only from the governmental firm which loaned him the money but also from other firms whose furniture Black admired. Some of the other firms were individually owned and some were co-operatives. Black also found a local cabinet-maker who agreed to sell unique dining room tables on consignment. Black would receive one-third of the price for each sale. The local cabinet-maker purchased the wood he used to make the tables directly from the government operated forest products company.

As Black's furniture became successful, he hired several people to work in his store as salespersons. He also registered the store's name and logo so that others could not pretend to be Black's furniture. Black is presently thinking about retiring and giving the store to his daughters. They are planning to open a second store in a nearby town.

The story of Black's furniture illustrates how autonomous ownership rules would apply to a labor intensive firm. The rights which Black exercises over the business vest in him by several criteria of title. His rights over the store vest because of the leasing agreement with the shopping mall. The rights over the furniture, except for the dining room tables which are on consignment, vest in Black because he purchases them from the manufacturers. Black's right over the consignment tables is limited to one third of the price if they are sold. Black's right to exclusively use the name and logo vest in him alone because he created them, and anyone else's use of them without his permission would violate Black's right over his labor. Some of the rights of title which Black may exercise depend upon the agreements he has made, e.g., he does not have the right to sell any desks but those of the government firm for the first ten years; other rights, such as employing salespeople, derive from the autonomous ownership rules for self and labor.

While Black's furniture may be typical of labor intensive business, there is a kind of labor intensive employment which deserves special attention. The professions such as doctor, attorney, teacher, musician, writer, sculptor, etc., employ highly skilled and highly trained labor. These professionals, whose product is almost wholly their labor, might be thought to have the right to whatever income their labor can bring; this is true, but there are some limitations upon their right. If their education or training were financially subsidized by the citizens of Autmos, e.g., through publicly supported colleges, then the professionals would owe a debt to the community which they would have to repay either through monetary payments or through services. Of course, if their training were in no way subsidized by Autmos there would be no debt to repay. The second restriction upon professionals' rights over their labor derives from the duty to help others. Insofar as the professionals' labor affects basic needs or fundamental goods, then if citizens of Autmos are in need professionals have a special moral duty to help. The skills which many professionals voluntarily acquire place them in a position where they, uniquely, can offer help. Their special duty is not an unfair burden even though it may not be shared by the non-professional citizens of Autmos. Those who freely enter such professions should realize that their special training and skills also create special obligations. Moreover the duty to help may not be unfair because the duty seems to vary directly with the income which professionals can receive in a free labor market. If the number of persons who need help is assumed to be constant, then the smaller the number of professionals there are the greater will be each professional's duty to help, but his income will also be greater because of the limited supply. If the number of professionals were greater their income would be smaller but so would their share of the duty to help, assuming that those who are in need remain constant. Other than these limitations, the professionals have the rights of use, management, and income from their labor. It would be a violation of their rights for the citizens of Autmos to require professionals to work only for governmental firms. This is not to say that Autmos could not establish governmental firms which compete with individual employment options. Such governmental firms are morally permissible so long as they do not coercively interfere with the free labor market.

The final kind of mixed ownable is what can be called personal possessions or, perhaps, consumer goods. They are what is purchased by individuals other than dwellings and which are not used for creating income. Food, clothing, books, furniture, theater tickets, and hotel rooms are some of many obvious examples. The criteria of title for these ownables are gift, bequest, and exchange unless they are created by the consumer himself. Rights of title include all innocent uses although rights over leased rather than purchased goods, e.g., hotel rooms, may be limited by the lease agreement. Autmos ought not limit the rights of title over these goods beyond innocent use because any such limitation would involve disrespect for autonomy. Autmos also ought not limit the production of such goods (by either individual or governmental firms) if there is sufficient consumer demand for the goods to be economically produced within the democratically adopted policy for land and resource development. Consumer goods are for many people essential to the definition of their good and their pursuit of their good.

This discussion of four kinds of mixed ownables in Autmos is intended only to illustrate autonomous ownership rules for mixed ownables. It is not intended to present all of the possible options. Many options are tied to the material conditions in which communities find themselves. The choice between direct governmental or individual development in agriculture, for example, depends upon such variables as the fertility of the soil, rainfall, and length of growing season, not to mention the level of technology available for agriculture. Similarly, variables such as available capital or raw materials affect the options available for the development of industry. These differences in material conditions can affect autonomy. Agricultural failures can affect the well-being needed for autonomy. Ownership rules for mixed ownables in developing nations which might inhibit the production of consumer goods or which might limit employment opportunities also would be violations of autonomy. Thus, the autonomous ownership rules for the domain of mixed ownables must be appropriate to the particular conditions of the community. The domain of mixed ownables is therefore unlike the domains of self and labor or land and resources in which the rules are fixed and unchangeable for all communities. The criteria of title for the domain of mixed ownables must be determinate, complete, and consistent. This does not imply that the criteria of title are constant throughout the domain. As in the case of Autmos, the criteria may vary within the domain of mixed ownables where there are relevant differences between kinds of mixed ownables.

What is required is that the criteria within any of the sub-sets of the domain be determinate, complete, and consistent. There might be inconsistencies between the sub-sets but there is no difficulty if the sub-sets are relevantly different. Insofar as simplicity is desirable for ownership rules, the number of sub-sets should be kept at a minimum and the rules be as similar as possible in each of the sub-sets. The rules for the domain of mixed ownables actually discussed for Autmos are determinate, complete and consistent. And, while a wide range of options are presented, it may be possible to construct a set of rules which further reduces the differences between sub-sets and still meets the requirements of the autonomy principle.

C. *Ownership and justice*

The thrust of this chapter has so far been to explain ownership rules which are implied by the autonomy principle. To the extent that the autonomy principle is rationally defensible, the rules for autonomous ownership also ought to be rationally defensible. The logic of moral justification for a social institution such as ownership requires derivation from a true or rationally defensible principle. While the procedure is in itself sufficient to establish the moral justifiability of a form of ownership, it may not by itself be wholly persuasive. It may be wondered what a society based upon autonomous ownership would look like, i.e., how it compares to visions of a just society which have captured the imagination of other philosophers.

Autonomous ownership does not fit neatly into any political or economic categories currently in use. For one thing autonomous ownership is neither capitalist nor socialist. Land and resources are owned by all members of the community in the sense that they all have a right to participate in decisions about how land and resources are used as well as a right to share the income. To this extent autonomous ownership resembles socialism. Autonomous ownership also permits individual development of land and resources as one option, and it requires that individuals be free from society's interference to be self-employed or employed by individually developed firms in labor intensive enterprise. To this extent autonomous ownership resembles capitalism. The economy in a society with autonomous ownership therefore must be a mixture of government and individual firms in free competition with one another. To this extent, autonomous ownership appears to be the direction towards which some so-called communist countries are moving. The competition with individual firms might stimulate government firms to greater efficiency by using incentives to boost efficiency just as it does in individual firms. Managers as well as workers might have contracts which tie the salaries to profits. The mixed economy also ought to provide a great many different kinds of opportunities for workers. As in capitalism, there would be a number of different employers as well as the opportunity to start a business oneself. Yet, as in socialism, autonomous ownership of land and resources might reduce exploitation of land and resources because of community control.

Autonomous ownership should also reduce the possibility of exploiting workers because land and resources cannot be privately owned by a relatively small number of individuals. There cannot be a inequality of power because land and resources are controlled by only some but not all members of the community. There will be no members of the community who are disadvantaged because they own no land or resources. Everyone will be equal in this respect.

Autonomous ownership would not create a society of equality of income. Free market forces would reward jobs according to supply and demand. Income could also be generated through investment in individually developed firms. Yet each person in a society practicing autonomous ownership would receive an equal share of the income from land and resource development. The income would be generated from leases and from the profits of governmentally developed firms. It is impossible to predict how large this income would be because, among other reasons, it is impossible to predict how much direct government development a community would choose. The income share might not be equivalent to the level of income received by Rawls' least well off, or even large enough to supply each individual with all of the basic needs or fundamental goods. But autonomous ownership does nevertheless guarantee an equal share. That land and resources are autonomously owned, while not guaranteeing the elimination of poverty, might reduce the size of the differential between the highest and lowest incomes compared to economic systems in which individuals can privately own large quantities of land and resources. Those who are poor because of factors not under their control can expect to receive various forms of assistance because the autonomy principle implies a duty to help others.

Autonomous ownership reflects the idea that people are equal as human beings and also that people are unequal in morally relevant ways. Human equality is expressed through autonomous ownership of land and resources. Each person is equal in his rights to participate in decisions about how land and resources are to be used and to a share in the income from land and resource utilitization. Legitimate inequality derives from autonomous ownership of self and labor. Each person has the right to direct his own labor and has a right to the income and products of his labor. Insofar as there are differences between people, their skills, abilities, and efforts, there will be legitimate differences in their rewards.

Autonomous ownership can also promote individual initiative and opportunity. Unlike forms of socialism in which all employment is by the government, autonomous ownership requires individual employment in the labor intensive sector. Individuals have a right to be economically rewarded for their own initiative. Even within governmental firms, rewarded individual initiative would be a desirable stimulant to economic efficiency. Individual opportunity should be greater than in some forms of socialism and more nearly equal than in some forms of capitalism.

Autonomous ownership does permit bequest of wealth as one of the rights over self and labor. To this extent some individuals may have a greater initial opportunity than others. Of course unequal opportunity would exist in any system in which individuals with greater income could spend it during their lifetime on advantages for their children. But because private ownership of land or resources is incompatible with autonomy, that source of inheritable wealth is excluded from the system. Autonomous ownership presumes a background of fair equality of opportunity. Children who are disadvantaged with genetic or social handicaps should be able to receive the help they need. All individuals would also have their share of land and resource income which might give them a better start than many of the poor in some private ownership forms. The poor would have some incentive to produce large families in order to increase their family income. However, unless the income share were sufficiently large, the costs of a larger family would still outweigh the value of the increased income. Even so, the right to a share in the income cannot be judged upon its utility but the right must be judged by its respect for autonomy.

Autonomous ownership thus lies between private ownership capitalism and state ownership socialism. Autonomous ownership is not intended to be a compromise between the two nor is it intended to be an optimific amalgam of the best elements in each. The rules of autonomous ownership follow logically from the principle of autonomy. That it contains elements from both socialism and capitalism may only demonstrate that those two systems, whether they were consciously designed or evolved incrementally as a result of numerous individual decisions, have benefited from accumulated wisdom and are therefore, unsurprisingly, not wholly immoral.

In the schema of justification, it is argued that autonomous ownership presupposes democratic political institutions. Autonomous ownership also should perpetuate and strengthen democracy. Milton Friedman's argument, in *Freedom and Capitalism*, that capitalism is a necessary condition of democracy centers on his belief that there must be a non-elected independent check upon democratic government.[9] Even though Friedman's argument is questionable, autonomous ownership should provide the kind of check upon government Friedman demands since it both permits and requires a non-government economic sector. Individuals can seek non-governmental employment as well as accumulate sufficient wealth to finance an opposition party. Further, autonomous ownership might strengthen democracy by removing some of the conflicts between the interests of its citizens. In democracies where only some of the citizens control and profit from land and resource development, their interests might well conflict with the interests of the other citizens. Such conflicts of interest might destabilize a democracy or any form of government for that matter. In autonomous ownership that source of conflict would not arise because all have an equal stake in land and resource development. While there might be additional strains upon democracy because of the wider range of decisions which would have to be made by the citizens in order to decide upon land and resource development, it cannot be said with certainty how great such strains would be. Development by a leasing arrangement would certainly create fewer strains than would direct development. But it is not at all clear that even the strains of direct development decisions, especially if they are delegated, would be significantly more severe than the strains which presently face some democracies in dealing with privately owned land and private resource development. Only empirical trial and error could begin to supply data sufficient to decide the issue.

Autonomous ownership is derived from a principle which requires respect for individuality and differences. Individuals ought not be forced into conformity with narrow social norms. The right to define one's good and how it is to be pursued implies that a society in which autonomous ownership is an institution must be a society which takes rights and individuals seriously.[10] Neither individuals nor their rights ought to be sacrificed merely to promote some social policy. Individuals should be free to pursue their own good as they perceive it within the limits of the autonomy principle. Few impediments should be placed in the way of self-fulfillment. In a society based upon autonomous ownership, each individual should have the greatest possible range of control over his life and over the conditions for his fulfillment which are compatible with the autonomy of others. A society which practices the autonomy principle is not however a society of isolated individuals who have no responsibility for their neighbors. The autonomy principle implies a duty to help those who are in need; therefore, autonomous owners have a moral duty to give of their income and labor to the needy.

Finally, although this has not been discussed, autonomous ownership does seem to imply that all of the world's lands and resources are autonomously owned by all of its inhabitants. Just as original appropriation of land and resources does not justify private ownership by individuals, original habitation by a nation state also seems insufficient to justify private ownership by nations. While there may be severe practical problems with democratic world government by billions of individuals, it nevertheless seems that all persons wherever they happen to live have an equal right to participate in decisions concerning how any of the world's lands or resources are used.

At present, the status of fundamental justification in ethical theory unfortunately does not permit any greater certainty than presented in this book about which specific form of ownership is morally justifiable. Whether or not autonomous ownership is judged an essential part of a just society depends, of course, upon the conception of justice by which it is judged. If the autonomy principle is deemed justified or rationally defended, then no question should arise about the justifiability of autonomous ownership provided that its derivation has been adequate. If other standards of justice are applied to autonomous ownership, then, at the very least, autonomous ownership has been shown to be in part compatible with several of those standards.

Notes

Chapter I   The Concept of Ownership

1 See Bruce Ackerman, *Private Property and the Constitution*, Yale University Press (New Haven: 1977), p. 26.
2 For Hobbes's conception of ownership, see *Leviathan*, Chapter XV of Book I.
3 Karl Marx and Frederick Engels, *Collected Works*, International Publishers (New York: 1975), vol. 5, p. 32.
4 John Locke, *The Second Treatise on Government*, Peter Laslett, ed., 2nd edn, Cambridge University Press (Cambridge: 1967), sec. 138.
5 H. L. A. Hart, *The Concept of Law*, Oxford University Press (Oxford: 1961), pp. 77ff.
6 Leopold Kohr, "Property and Freedom," in *Property in a Humane Economy*, S. L. Blumenfeld, ed., Open Court (La Salle, Ill.: 1974), p. 49.
7 I am following A. M. Honoré here. See A. M. Honoré, "Ownership," *Oxford Essays in Jurisprudence*, Oxford University Press (Oxford: 1961).
8 The concept of legitimate use will be explained later.
9 The question of intersystem legitimacy will be discussed later.
10 A. Alchian and H. Demsetz make a similar point more formally in their article "Production, Information Costs and Economic Organization," in E. Furubotn and S. Pejovich, eds, *The Economics of Property Rights*, Ballinger (Cambridge, Mass.: 1974), p. 306:

> Team production of Z involves at least two inputs, X_i and X_j, with $d^2z/dx_i dx_j \neq 0$. The productive function is not separable into two functions each involving only inputs of two separable functions to treat as the Z of the team production. . . . There exist production techniques in which the Z obtained is greater than if the X_i and X_j had produced separable Z. . . . Team production, to repeat, is production in which (a) several types of resources are used and (b) the product is not a sum of separable outputs of each cooperating resource. An additional factor creates a team organization problem – (c) not all resources used in team production belong to one person.

11 Joseph Raz, *The Concept of a Legal System*, 2nd edn, Oxford University Press (Oxford: 1960) p. 176.
12 Raz, p. 176.
13 Raz, p. 177.
14 For a more complete discussion see my "Property Rules Property Rights," *Pacific Philosophical Quarterly*, October 1980.
15 In trusts the owner, or his legal guardian, designates the trustee.
16 A. M. Honoré, "Ownership," p. 112.
17 Lawrence Becker, "The Moral Basis of Property Rights," in J. Roland Pennock and John W. Chapman, eds, *Property, NOMOS XXII*, New York University Press (New York: 1980), p. 187.
18 R. M. Hare, *Freedom and Reason*, Oxford University Press (Oxford: 1963), ch. 3.

Chapter II   The Natural Perfectionists

1 Plato, *The Collected Works*, Edith Hamilton and Huntington Cairns, eds, Pantheon Books (New York: 1961) Stephanus, 416. All citations will be made by the Stephanus page number.
2 Plato, 551.
3 Plato, cf., 421.
4 Plato, 416.
5 Plato, 421.
6 Plato, 422.
7 Plato, 465.
8 Plato, 462.
9 Plato, 464.
10 Plato, 423.
11 Plato, 551.
12 Plato, 423.
13 Plato, 739.
14 Plato, 740.
15 Plato, 831.
16 Plato, 676.
17 Plato, 913.
18 Plato, 740.
19 Aristotle, *Collected Works*, Richard McKeon, ed., Random House (New York: 1941), 1330[a].
20 Plato, 743.
21 Plato, 742.
22 Plato, 847.
23 Plato, 919.
24 Plato, 920.
25 Plato, 916.
26 Plato, 954.
27 Aristotle, 1263[b].
28 Aristotle, 1180[b] 7.

29 Aristotle, 1261ᵇ 34.
30 Aristotle, 1263ᵃ 25.
31 Aristotle, 1339ᵃ 18.
32 Aristotle, 1263ᵃ 25.
33 Aristotle, 1270ᵃ 15.
34 Aristotle, 1323ᵃ 36.
35 Aristotle, 1257ᵃ 33.
36 Aristotle, 1257ᵃ 6.
37 Aristotle, 1267ᵃ 37.
38 Aristotle, 1266ᵇ 24.
39 Aristotle, 1267ᵃ 9.
40 St. Thomas Aquinas, *Summa Theologiae*, vol. 38, Marcus Léfebure, O.P., trans., Blackfriars/McGraw Hill (New York: 1975), 2a 2ae, 66, 7.
41 Aquinas, 2a 2ae, 66, 2.
42 Aquinas, 2a 2ae, 66, 2.
43 Aquinas, 2a 2ae, 66, 7.
44 Aquinas, 2a 2ae, 66, 7.
45 Aquinas, 2a 2ae, 66, 7.
46 Jacques Maritain, *The Social and Political Philosophy of Jacques Maritain*, J. W. Evans and L. R. Ward, eds, Image Books (New York: 1965), p. 56ff.
47 St. Thomas Aquinas, *Summa Theologiae*, vol. 29, David Bourke and Arthur Littledale, trans., Blackfriars/McGraw-Hill (New York: 1969), 1a 2ae, 105, 2.
48 Aquinas, 2a 2ae, 66, 5.
49 Aquinas, 2a 2ae, 66, 2.

Chapter III   The First Appropriationists

1 Locke, sec. 27.
2 Locke, sec. 138.
3 I have borrowed most of this list from A. M. Honoré. Honoré uses his list for purposes other than explicating Locke's theory.
4 J. P. Day, "Locke on Property," in Gordon Schochet, ed., *Life, Liberty and Property*, Wadsworth (Belmont, Calif.: 1971), p. 109.
5 Locke, sec. 4.
6 The handicapped and the crippled can be ignored here, since Locke, himself, seems to ignore them.
7 Hastings Rashdall, "The Philosophical Theory of Property," in *Property*, Macmillan (London: 1915), p. 52.
8 Locke, sec. 26.
9 Locke, secs 40–46.
10 "Enough and as good" must be taken quite literally. Local scarcity, as with drained farmland or picturesque scenery, may create disutility from some appropriations. In that case, however, the enough and as good condition is not fulfilled. It may be that the proposition "where

there is enough and as good, appropriation causes no disutility" is analytic.

11 Alan Ryan, "Locke and the Dictatorship of the Bourgeoisie," in Schochet, p. 89.
12 Locke, sec. 31.
13 Locke, sec. 36.
14 See C. B. MacPherson, *Possessive Individualism*, Oxford University Press (Oxford: 1964) and Murry N. Rothbard, *For A New Liberty*, Macmillan (New York: 1978).
15 Locke, sec. 3.
16 For a more detailed discussion of this conflict see James O. Grunebaum, "What Ought the Representative Represent?", in N. Bowie, ed., *Ethical Issues in Government*, Temple University Press (Philadelphia: 1981), pp. 54ff.
17 Locke, sec. 87.
18 Locke, sec. 87.
19 See Chapters VI and VII in which this claim is made good.
20 Immanuel Kant, *The Metaphysical Elements of Justice*, Bobbs-Merrill (Indianapolis: 1965), p. 57.
21 Kant, p. 91.
22 Kant, p. 63.
23 Kant, p. 64.
24 Kant, p. 57.
25 Kant, p. 52.
26 Kant, p. 53.
27 Kant, p. 59.
28 Kant, p. 53.
29 Jean-Jacques Rousseau, *The Social Contract and Discourses*, G. D. H. Cole, trans., Everyman Library (London: 1947), p. 17.
30 See Chapter II, sec. C.
31 Rousseau, p. 55.
32 Rousseau, p. 17.
33 Rousseau, p. 15.
34 Rousseau, p. 6.
35 Rousseau, pp. 192ff.
36 Rousseau, p. 41.
37 See Chapter I, sec. B.
38 Rousseau, p. 12.
39 Rousseau, p. 18.
40 Rousseau, p. 202.
41 Rousseau, p. 205.
42 Robert Nozick, *Anarchy, State, and Utopia*, Basic Books (New York: 1974), p. 151.
43 Nozick, p. 156.
44 Nozick, p. 156.
45 Nozick, p. 174.
46 Nozick, p. 171.
47 Nozick, p. 171.

48 Cheyney C. Ryan, "Mine, Yours, and Ours: Property Rights and Individual Liberty," *Ethics*, vol. 87, no. 2 (Jan. 1977), p. 131.
49 Nozick, p. 175.
50 In Locke's state of nature argument that private ownership of oneself and labor is here presupposed. A temporary private usufruct form of ownership may be justified if one ignores the fact that Locke's enough and as good hypothesis undercuts any reason for ownership rules at all.
51 Nozick, p. 176.
52 Cf. Nozick, p. 39.
53 It is interesting in this respect to compare Nozick's arguments to Bentham's distinction between the primary and secondary consequences of a mischievous act in *The Principles of Morals and Legislation*, Chapter XII.

Chapter IV   The Conventionalists

1 See Hans Kelsen, *The Pure Theory of Law*, University of California Press (Berkeley: 1970).
2 Locke may interpret Hobbes this way.
3 Thomas Hobbes, *Leviathan*, Everyman Library (New York: 1950), p. 104.
4 Hobbes, p. 103.
5 Hobbes, p. 106.
6 Hobbes, p. 106.
7 See H. L. A. Hart, *The Concept of Law*, Oxford University Press (Oxford: 1961).
8 Hobbes, p. 143, italics omitted.
9 Hobbes, p. 148.
10 Hobbes, *Leviathan*, p. 149, and *De Cive*, Appleton-Century-Crofts (New York: 1949), pp. 80–81.
11 Hobbes, p. 209.
12 Hobbes, p. 210.
13 Hobbes, p. 211.
14 Hobbes, p. 213.
15 Hobbes, p. 213.
16 Hobbes, p. 213.
17 Hobbes, pp. 213–214.
18 Hobbes, p. 214.
19 Hobbes, p. 209.
20 David Hume, *A Treatise of Human Nature*, L. A. Selby-Bigge, ed., Oxford University Press (Oxford: 1964), and *Enquiries Concerning the Human Understanding and Concerning the Principles of Morals*, L. A. Selby-Bigge, ed., Oxford University Press (Oxford: 1963).
21 Jonathan Harrison, *Hume's Theory of Justice*, Oxford University Press (Oxford: 1981).
22 Hume, *Treatise*, p. 494.

23 Hume, *Treatise*, p. 487.
24 Hume, *Treatise*, p. 487.
25 Hume, *Enquiries*, p. 188.
26 See Nicholas Rescher, *Distributive Justice*, Bobbs-Merrill (Indianapolis: 1966), p. 95.
27 Hume, *Treatise*, p. 494.
28 Hume, *Enquiries*, p. 184.
29 Hume, *Enquiries*, p. 184.
30 Locke, *Second Treatise*, sec. 33.
31 See Chapter I, sec. D.
32 Cf. Hume, *Treatise*, p. 322.
33 Hume, *Treatise*, p. 494.
34 Hume, *Enquiries*, p. 183.
35 Cf. Aquinas in Chapter II, sec. C.
36 Hume, *Treatise*, p. 490.
37 Hume, *Treatise*, p. 491.
38 Hume, *Treatise*, p. 491.
39 Hume, *Treatise*, p. 491.
40 Hume, *Enquiries*, p. 196.
41 See Chapter I, sec. A.
42 Hume, *Treatise*, p. 489.
43 Hume, *Treatise*, p. 501.
44 Hume, *Treatise*, p. 502.
45 Hume, *Treatise*, p. 502.
46 Hume, *Treatise*, p. 502.
47 See Chapter III, sec. D.
48 Hume, *Enquiries*, p. 194.
49 Hume, *Enquiries*, p. 194.
50 Hume, *Enquiries*, p. 194.
51 Hume, *Enquiries*, p. 194.
52 Hume, *Enquiries*, p. 195.
53 Hume, *Treatise*, p. 490 and *Enquiries*, p. 195.
54 See Harrison, pp. 78–89.
55 See for example Hume's footnotes in the *Treatise*, pp. 506–510.
56 Hume, *Treatise*, p. 503.
57 Hume, *Treatise*, pp. 504 and 506.
58 Hume, *Treatise*, p. 503.
59 Hume, *Enquiries*, p. 194.
60 Hume, *Treatise*, pp. 504–9.
61 See Chapter III, sec. A.
62 Hume, *Treatise*, p. 508.
63 See William Blackstone, *Commentaries on the Laws of England*, University of Chicago Press (Chicago: 1979), vol. 2, p. 263.
64 See Chapter II, sec. A.
65 Hume, *Treatise*, p. 509.
66 Hume, *Treatise*, p. 509, note 2.
67 Hume, *Treatise*, p. 510.
68 Hume, *Treatise*, p. 510.
69 Hume, *Enquiries*, p. 196.

70 Hume, *Treatise*, p. 514.
71 Hume, *Enquiries*, p. 195.
72 Hume, *Treatise*, p. 529.
73 Hume, *Treatise*, p. 529.
74 John Rawls, *A Theory of Justice*, Harvard University Press (Cambridge, Mass.: 1971), p. 101.
75 Rawls, p. 179.
76 Rawls, p. 438.
77 Rawls, p. 60.
78 There are other factors involved such as supply and demand but they can be ignored for this argument.
79 Rawls, p. 73.

Chapter V   Two Opponents

1 Robert Owen, *A New View of Society and Other Writings*, G. D. H. Cole, ed., Everyman Library (London: 1963), p. 110. (All italics omitted from citations to this work.)
2 Robert Owen, *A Development of the Principles and Plans on Which to Establish Self-Supporting Home Colonies*, AMS Press (New York: 1975), p. 30. (All italics omitted from citations to this work.)
3 Owen, *Home Colonies*, p. 47.
4 Owen, *A New View*, p. 258.
5 Owen, *A New View*, p. 211.
6 Owen, *A New View*, p. 183.
7 Owen, *A New View*, p. 218.
8 Owen, *Home Colonies*, p. 6.
9 Owen, *Home Colonies*, p. 26.
10 Owen, *A New View*, p. 213.
11 Owen, *A New View*, p. 227.
12 Owen, *Home Colonies*, p. 37.
13 Owen, *Home Colonies*, p. 37.
14 Owen, *Home Colonies*, p. 61.
15 Owen, *A New View*, p. 254.
16 Owen, *Home Colonies*, p. 61.
17 Owen, *Home Colonies*, pp. 38–40.
18 Owen, *A New View*, p. 283.
19 Owen, *Home Colonies*, pp. 46–48.
20 Owen, *Home Colonies*, pp. 55–56.
21 Owen, *Home Colonies*, p. 57.
22 Owen, *Home Colonies*, p. 30.
23 Owen, *Home Colonies*, Appendix V, p. 32.
24 Owen, *A New View*, p. 289.
25 Owen, *A New View*, p. 262.
26 Owen, *Home Colonies*, Appendix IV, p. 28.
27 Owen, *Home Colonies*, pp. 57–58.
28 See Chapter II, sec. B.

29 See Chapter IV, sec. B.
30 See T. J. Peters and R. H. Waterman, *In Search of Excellence*, Harper & Row (New York: 1982), ch. 8.
31 Owen, *A New View*, p. 265. E. Furubotn discusses socialist workers' propensity to reinvest in their firms. see. "Bank Credit and the Labor-Managed Firm: The Yugoslav Case," E. Furubotn and S. Pejovich, eds, *The Economics of Property Rights*, Ballinger (Cambridge, Mass.: 1974), p. 257.
32 See Schlomo Avineri, *The Social and Political Thought of Karl Marx*, Cambridge University Press (Cambridge: 1970), p. 109.
33 Karl Marx and Frederick Engels, *Collected Works*, vol. 3, p. 281.
34 Karl Marx and Frederick Engels, *Collected Works*, vol. 5, p. 32.
35 Karl Marx, *Grundrisse*, Martin Nicholaus, trans., Random House (New York: 1973), p. 492.
36 Karl Marx, *Capital*, S. Moore and E. Aveling, trans., International Publishers (New York: 1967), vol. I, p. 72.
37 Karl Marx, *Grundrisse*, M. Nicholaus, trans., Random House (New York: 1973), p. 87.
38 Karl Marx and Frederick Engels, *Collected Works*, vol. 3, pp. 290ff.
39 Karl Marx, *Capital*, S. Moore and E. Aveling, trans., International Publishers (New York: 1967), vol. I, p. 71.
40 Karl Marx and Frederick Engels, *Collected Works*, vol. 6, p. 506.
41 Karl Marx, *Critique of the Gotha Programme*, C. P. Dutt, ed., International Publishers (New York: 1966).
42 Marx and Engels, *Collected Works*, vol. 6, p. 498.
43 See Chapter II, sec. C.
44 Marx and Engels, *Collected Works*, vol. 6, p. 505.
45 Marx and Engels, *Collected Works*, vol. 6, pp. 105ff.
46 Marx and Engels, *Collected Works*, vol. 5, p. 31.
47 Cf. Marx and Engels, *Collected Works*, vol. 6, p. 505.

Chapter VI Schema of Justification

1 For examples of these methods see John Rawls, *A Theory of Justice*, Harvard University Press (Cambridge, Mass.: 1971); Alan Donagan, *The Theory of Morality*, University of Chicago Press (Chicago: 1977); and Alan Gewirth, *Reason and Morality*, University of Chicago Press (Chicago: 1978).
2 Cf. Immanuel Kant, *Critique of Pure Reason*, Norman Kemp Smith, trans., Macmillan (London: 1963), p. 182.
3 I use the notion of belief rather than the notion of intuition in order to include not only pre-analytical or pre-theoretical ideas but also those ideas which result from a careful study of ethics.
4 Alan Donagan, *The Theory of Morality*, p. 61.
5 Donagan, p. 61.
6 Donagan, p. 65.
7 Donagan, p. 67.

8 Donagan, p. 65.
9 Donagan, p. 85.
10 For a more complete discussion of basic needs see my article "What Ought the Representative Represent?", in *Ethical Issues in Government*, N. Bowie, ed., Temple University Press (Philadelphia: 1981), p. 60.
11 Donagan, p. 61. Up to equality; but Donagan does not actually state this.
12 What is owed to the children of those who choose not to work is an important but difficult question which cannot be fully discussed here.
13 See Robert Paul Wolff, *In Defense of Anarchism*, Harper Torchbooks (New York: 1970).
14 One of the most accessible, and, I believe, still one of the best discussions of decision procedures is J. M. Buchanan and G. Tullock, *The Calculus of Consent*, Ann Arbor Paperback, University of Michigan Press (Ann Arbor: 1965).
15 The exclusion of morally impermissible plans violates two of Arrow's axioms: (1) The Condition of Unrestricted Domain and (2) The Independence of Irrelevant Alternatives. But because the axioms are violated no voter paradox may be generated. See Kenneth J. Arrow, *Social Choice and Individual Values*, John Wiley & Sons (New York: 1966), p. 23 and p. 26.
16 See Robert Dahl, *A Preface to Democratic Theory*, University of Chicago Press (Chicago: 1956). Also see Carl Cohen, *Democracy*, University of Georgia Press (Athens: 1972) or Alan Gewirth, "Political Justice," in R. Brandt, *Social Justice*, Prentice-Hall (Englewood Cliffs, N.J.: 1962).
17 Harold Demsetz, "Toward a Theory of Property Rights," *American Economic Review*, no. 75, 1967, p. 347.
18 Demsetz, p. 354.
19 Demsetz, p. 354.
20 Demsetz, p. 355.
21 Demsetz, p. 357.
22 Joseph Schumpeter, *Capitalism, Socialism, and Democracy*, Harper Torchbooks (New York: 1962), p. 134.
23 See Robert Nozick, *Anarchy, State, and Utopia*, Basic Books (New York: 1974), where playing basketball well is a saleable commodity.
24 For an important discussion, see C. B. MacPherson, *Democratic Theory: Essays in Retrieval*, Oxford University Press (Oxford: 1975).
25 See Abba Lerner, *Economics of Control*, Macmillan (New York: 1944).

Chapter VII Autonomous Ownership

1 The autonomy principle has been used to justify forms which closely resemble private ownership if not the precise form of private ownership explicated in Chapter I.

2 Unless autonomy includes the right not to decide for oneself what one's good is, how to pursue it, and the right to the necessary well-being. While persons may temporarily relinquish the right, the autonomy principle prohibits permanent alienation of the right.

3 The implication of the autonomy principle is actually much broader. Political boundaries are historically arbitrary accidents which may be morally irrelevant. It seems to me that a strict implication of the autonomy principle morally requires that rights over the world's lands and resources vest in everyone without any national distinction. For the purposes of exposition, however, it suffices to show that rights to land and resources vest in all members of a nation state.

4 Immanuel Kant, *The Metaphysical Elements of Justice*, John Ladd, trans., Bobbs-Merrill (Indianapolis: 1965).

5 See Chapter III for a more detailed discussion.

6 Herbert Spencer, *Social Statistics*, Robert Schalkenback Foundation (New York: 1970), p. 104.

7 Compare: Michael Polanyi, *The Logic of Liberty*, University of Chicago Press (Chicago: 1969), ch. 10, "Management of Social Tasks."

8 What I have in mind here resembles H. L. A. Hart's rule of recognition from the internal point of view. See *The Concept of Law*, Oxford University Press (Oxford: 1961).

9 Milton Friedman, *Freedom and Capitalism*, University of Chicago Press (Chicago: 1971), pp. 18ff.

10 See Ronald Dworkin, *Taking Rights Seriously*, Harvard University Press (Cambridge, Mass.: 1977).

Index

Accession, 104, 106, 107, 108, 109
Ackerman, Bruce, 200
Acts of private will, 71, 72, 74
Adverse possession, 34
Alchian, R., 200
Alienation, 130, 131, 132, 133, 134, 139
Aquinas, 2, 25, 26, 46–51, 75, 107, 116, 143
Aristotle, 2, 25, 26, 33, 35 – 46, 47, 48, 49, 54, 77, 96, 107, 116, 124
Arkwright, R., 118
Arrow, K., 208
Association of ideas, 103, 104, 107, 108
Autmos, 185, 186, 187, 188, 189, 190, 192, 193, 194
Autonomous ownership, 1, 2, 3, 140, 142, 159, 161, 164, 167, 168, 169, 170, 171, 173, 174, 175, 179, 180, 182, 183, 184, 185, 186, 188, 189, 190, 191, 192, 193, 194, 195, 196, 197, 198, 199
Autonomy, 2, 122, 126, 127, 128, 130, 131, 132, 133, 143, 144, 145, 146, 149, 150, 151, 152, 153, 158, 163, 169, 170, 171, 174, 175, 177, 178, 179, 181, 183, 185, 188, 189, 193, 194, 197
Autonomy principle, 3, 127, 143–5, 148, 150, 151, 152, 153, 155, 157, 167, 169, 170, 171, 172, 173, 174, 176, 177, 178,
179, 182, 186, 188, 189, 194, 197, 198, 199
Avineri, S., 207

Balboa, 71
Basic needs, 144, 146, 150, 196
Becker, L., 201
Bentham, J., 204
Bequests, 10, 16, 17, 23, 24, 30, 33, 39, 47, 51, 55, 58, 61, 62, 63, 66, 67, 79, 82, 90, 108, 109, 111, 137, 178, 193, 196
Blackstone, W., 205
Buchanan, J. M., 208

Capitalism, 128, 129, 131, 133, 134, 137, 195, 196, 197, 198
Capricious appropriation, 19, 20, 21
Cohen, C., 208
Common law, 1, 5, 10, 12, 34, 106, 108, 153
Communal ownership, 1, 5, 13, 14, 27, 28, 29, 31, 32, 35, 36, 39, 43, 46, 73, 74, 75, 81, 82, 83, 84, 94, 107, 111, 113, 114, 137, 150, 154, 159, 160, 163, 171, 180
Communism, 152, 195
Completeness, requirement of, 13, 14, 16, 17, 55, 100, 106, 107, 109, 112, 153, 172, 179, 194
Consistency, requirement of, 13, 14, 55, 64, 72, 77, 106, 109, 112, 179, 194
Corporate ownership, 1, 4, 8, 80

210